The Silver Manifesto

By

David Morgan

&

Christopher Marchese

David Morgan is a widely recognized analyst in the precious metals industry and consults for hedge funds, high net worth investors, mining companies, depositories, and bullion dealers. He is the publisher of *The Morgan Report* on precious metals, author of *Get the Skinny on Silver Investing*, and featured speaker at investment conferences in North America, Europe, and Asia. He has degrees in both engineering and finance. A longtime adherent to the Austrian School and Honesty Money, David has devoted most of his life to the study of money, economics, and precious metals.

Christopher Marchese is the equity and economic analyst for *The Morgan Report*. He has worked for Vishni Capital as a portfolio strategist and at Morgan Stanley as a research and equity analyst. His formal educational background includes a B.A. in Finance and M.A. in Accounting. It was The Mises Institute that provided him with a strong economic background, that of the Austrian School. Chris has published over 100 articles on economics, mining, and investing. He is the co-founder of America's Great Awakening at AmericasGreatAwakening.com.

SPECIAL DISCOUNT: RECEIVE 25% OFF ON ANY SUBSCRIPTION TO THE MORGAN REPORT BY USING THE FOLLOWING PROMO CODE: manifesto1913

*all lowercase, no spaces
** Offer not valid on Premium Memberships

To sign up go here: www.TheMorganReport.com

ISBN10: 1-634-43136-7
ISBN13: 978-1-63443-136-1

© By 2015 David Morgan and Christopher J. Marchese

Acknowledgements

It is impossible to acknowledge everyone who deserves to be recognized here, and I do regret any unintentional oversights in this regard. First, let me acknowledge in a general way, all of the radio and television interviewers who have requested me or one of our team from *The Morgan Report* to contribute to their particular program. How grateful we are for the many public and private investment conferences that have asked for our presence either on a solo or group basis.

I also appreciate the vast number of Web sites and other researchers and newsletter writers who have built very strong relationships with us over many years and contributed to my thinking in many different areas, particularly economics and the precious metals. It is important to state that two publications on the silver market—one from CPM Group and one from the Silver Institute—are valued as resources to our work.

Next and going to the beginning of our Internet presence, Jim Puplava of Financial Sense must be recognized as being one of the very first to listen to the silver story and feature me on a weekly basis for several months. Thank you, Jim and the entire staff at Financial Sense.

David Smith, who is a longtime friend and contributor to The Morgan Report, played a significant role in the book at many levels, having edited chapters and "tweaking" my work with a sense of purpose and accomplishment that only he could provide. Having met David Smith at the first Silver Summit in 2003, we became friends almost immediately; and a few years later he became a contributor to our reports, and this book could not have been completed without his help.

Julie Meredith of The Meredith Agency did the proofing of this book and has proofed/edited The Morgan Report for years. With Julie's help we have done our best to make this book as word perfect as possible, and it is important to recognize she followed us all the way with each tiny change we felt added to the book. Simply stated, her patience and perseverance were well beyond reasonable-- Thank you Julie!

A gracious thanks to Mr. Eric Sprott for writing the forward foreword to The Silver Manifesto. Also to Rick Rule and the entire Sprott staff, thank you for supporting my rather difficult and demanding questions on some of the more detailed aspects of the Sprott organization. John Embry must also be acknowledged as we have become even closer friends from the time we sat next to each other on the flight home from the GATA 21 event in the Yukon so many years ago.

I must mention Hugo Salinas Price as a true friend and thank him here for mentoring me on practical ways to introduce silver to the public at large. On a personal note, Laura Stein must be included, as she has never tired of the industry, seems to know almost everyone at all levels, continues with a high degree of energy, and has been a true source for making connections for us that probably could not have happened any other way.

Edward Fuller, a consultant to us for years, contributed throughout the book, notably putting together an extension of the study conducted by the late Adrian Douglas regarding intervention in the gold and silver markets. We would like to thank the Mises Institute and Austrian Economics in general, with specific thanks to Ludwig von Mises.

It is important to recognize our membership because many of them have been helpful in numerous ways—asking the right questions, attending our events, and suggesting ways to improve all aspects of our work.

No doubt, as stated in the beginning, there are probably some I have not remembered to mention here by name, and if so, I'm sorry. It wasn't until I began thinking about how our work has grown over the past 16 years and how that was possible that I was actually overwhelmed with emotion, as it has always been my dream to be of maximum service to others.

Finally, let me thank the many of you from so many different backgrounds and locations who have been so willing to help me in my mission "to teach and empower people to understand the benefits of an honest financial system."

–David Morgan

Foreword

Back in October 2010, when Sprott Asset Management LP was launching its silver trust (PSLV:NYSE), I had the occasion to visit many large U.S. financial institutions to discuss the outlook for silver. My favorite question before I began my presentations was to ask the attendees whether they had ever heard of three people—mainly, David Morgan, Ted Butler, and Jason Hommel. To my surprise invariably there was a universal ignorance of these people, whereupon I would suggest that the attendees obviously know nothing about the silver market, as these three individuals, at the time, were the most respected analysts following the silver market. I would point out that the analyst with the broadest coverage of silver was and still is David Morgan.

In managed markets that we participated in and most particularly the silver market in my opinion, it is important to listen to and appreciate the prognostication of the stalwart silver analyst that David Morgan is today.

The history of silver is a long one and its future will be very exciting. The battle will rage on between the pricing in paper markets and the real physical silver market of which Dave is an expert.

I have spent many hours reading Dave's analyses and have come to respect him as a true expert in this field. I am sure you will enjoy his analyses of the past, present, and future for silver.

-Eric Sprott

TABLE OF CONTENTS

INTRODUCTION ... -1-

CHAPTER 1: A MONETARY HISTORY OF SILVER – 3,400 B.C. - 1792 ... -4-
- THE ORIGIN OF MONEY ... -6-
- IS DEFLATION REALLY A BAD THING? ... -8-
- SILVER'S USE AS MONEY: A BRIEF HISTORY ... -10-
  - *The Lydian System* ... -11-
  - *The Medieval Period* ... -14-
- CHINA: THE BIRTHPLACE OF PAPER MONEY ... -15-
  - *The Song (S'ung) Dynasty* ... -16-
  - *The Chin Tartars* ... -17-
  - *The Yuan Dynasty* ... -18-
  - *The Ming Dynasty* ... -20-
  - *Silver Fever in Asia* ... -20-
- THE RENAISSANCE AND DISCOVERY OF THE AMERICAS ... -21-
- THE MISSISSIPPI BUBBLE—A LOOK AT EARLY EXPERIMENTS WITH PAPER MONEY IN THE WESTERN WORLD ... -24-

CHAPTER 2: A MONETARY HISTORY OF SILVER IN AMERICA ... -27-
- THE U.S. CONSTITUTION: NOTABLE SECTIONS AND ARTICLES ... -27-
- BIMETALLISM AND GRESHAM'S LAW ... -28-
- SILVER AND GOLD IN THE UNITED STATES (REVOLUTIONARY WAR-PRESENT DAY) ... -29-
- THE REVOLUTIONARY WAR: THE FIRST U.S. FIAT MONEY COLLAPSES IN THE CONTINENTAL ... -30-
- COINAGE ACT OF 1792 ... -31-
- THE FIRST BANK OF THE UNITED STATES: 1791-1811 ... -32-
- THE SECOND BANK OF THE UNITED STATES 1816-1836 ... -33-
- THE RISE OF THE JACKSONIAN MOVEMENT AND HARD MONEY IN THE U.S. ... -34-
- COINAGE ACT OF 1834 ... -34-
- THE COINAGE ACT OF 1837 ... -36-
  - *The Coinage Acts of 1853 and 1857* ... -36-
- FREE BANKING ERA ... -41-
- THE CONSTITUTIONALITY OF FIAT "PAPER MONEY" ... -42-
- CRIME OF 73' ... -43-
- SILVER PURCHASE ACT OF 1934 ... -45-
- COINAGE ACT OF 1965 ... -45-

CHAPTER 3: SILVER SUPPLY DYNAMICS ....- 48 -
The Changing Composition of Silver Production by Type of Mine ....- 48 -
Potential New Mines ....- 51 -
Largest Silver Producing Mines ....- 53 -
The True Cost of Mining ....- 56 -
Peak Silver ....- 58 -
Silver Production Growth Key Region – The America's ....- 61 -
North & Central America ....- 61 -
South America ....- 62 -

CHAPTER 4: SILVER DEMAND DYNAMICS ....- 65 -
Silver Studies ....- 67 -
The True Money Supply (TMS) ....- 73 -
Industrial Demand ....- 77 -
   Photovoltaic Demand ....- 79 -
   Ethylene-Oxide (EO) ....- 80 -
   Solid State Lighting, Flexible Display, Interposers ....- 81 -
   Batteries ....- 83 -
   Super-capacitors ....- 84 -
   Wood Preservatives ....- 84 -
   Automotive ....- 84 -
   Radio Frequency Identification (RFID) ....- 85 -
   Water Purification ....- 85 -
   Medical Uses ....- 86 -
   Food Packaging ....- 87 -
Looking Ahead—2015 and Beyond (Investment Demand) ....- 87 -

CHAPTER 5: MONEY & BANKING ....- 91 -
Loan Banking vs. Deposit Banking ....- 92 -
   Loan Banking ....- 92 -
   Deposit Banking ....- 93 -
Fractional-Reserve Banking (w/o a Central Bank) ....- 93 -
Fractional Reserve Banking in a Fiat Monetary System ....- 96 -
Maturity Mismatching ....- 96 -
The Federal Reserve System ....- 97 -
How the Supply of Money and Credit Expands and Contracts ....- 98 -
Phases of Inflation ....- 103 -
   Phase I ....- 104 -
   Phase II ....- 104 -
   Phase III -...- 104 -
Additional Considerations ....- 104 -

CHAPTER 6: INTERVENTION INDUCED PRICE SUPPRESSION IN SILVER AND GOLD — 106 -

- Fractional Reserve Bullion Banking ... - 110 -
- Precious Metal Leasing ... - 111 -
- The Gold Carry Trade ... - 113 -
- Futures Markets ... - 113 -
- Commitment of Traders Report ... - 114 -
- Forensic Studies ... - 115 -

CHAPTER 7: AUSTRIAN BUSINESS CYCLE THEORY — 121 -

- On Capitalism vs. Socialism ... - 121 -
- Origins of the Coming Currency Crisis ... - 122 -
- Time and Action ... - 125 -
- Interest and Economic Calculation ... - 126 -
- Capital formation and accumulation ... - 127 -
- Market Process ... - 129 -
  - Why Socialism (Central Banking) Can Never Work ... - 129 -
  - The Fed and a Long History of Failure ... - 130 -
- Economic Growth and Increased Credit Expansion Backed By an Increase in Voluntary Savings (Capitalism) ... - 131 -
  - The Natural Rate of Interest ... - 133 -
- The Central Bank Induced Business Cycle (Socialism) ... - 140 -
  - From Boom to Bust ... - 140 -
  - Maturity-Mismatching and Business Cycles ... - 144 -
- Examining the Central Bank Induced Business Cycle from a Capitalist's Point of View: Ranking Investment Projects ... - 145 -
  - Additional Considerations ... - 148 -

CHAPTER 8: MONETARY MALFEASANCE — 150 -

- "Tech Boom and Bust" ... - 151 -
- The 2008 Financial Crisis ... - 153 -
- Credit Default Swaps ... - 157 -
- Asset Price Inflation During the Housing Bubble ... - 159 -
- Papering Over the 2008 Financial Meltdown ... - 160 -
- Real Median Household Income ... - 164 -
- The True Money Supply and GDP Growth ... - 164 -
- A Look at Real GDP (Y/Y%) v. True Money Supply (Y/Y%) ... - 165 -
  - TMS Growth and Forecasting GDP growth: 1977-1991 ... - 166 -
  - TMS Growth and Forecasting GDP growth: 1991-2001 ... - 167 -
  - TMS Growth and Forecasting GDP growth: 2002-2001 ... - 167 -
  - What the Growth Rate in the TMS is telling us now ... - 168 -

CHAPTER 9: THE DEBT BOMB — 171 -

TOTAL DEBT OF MAJOR WORLD ECONOMICS	- 171 -
THE DERIVATIVES BOMB	- 173 -
FINANCIAL POSITION OF THE FEDERAL GOVERNMENT	- 177 -
CONGRESSIONAL BUDGET OFFICE (CBO) BASELINE PROJECTIONS OF REVENUE AND SPENDING	- 179 -
Debt-to-Revenue Sensitivity Analysis	- 179 -
Deficit Spending Sensitivity Analysis	- 180 -
CBO Scenario A Projections	- 180 -
CBO Scenario B Projections	- 181 -
CBO Scenario C Projections	- 181 -
Interest-to-Revenue Ratio w/ 4 Alternative Scenarios	- 182 -
Baseline Interest-to-Revenue Ratio	- 182 -
Alternatives 1 and 2 Interest-to-Revenue Ratio	- 183 -
Alternatives 3 and 4 Interest-to-Revenue Ratio	- 183 -
CONCLUSION	- 185 -

CHAPTER 10: BUILDING A PRECIOUS METALS PORTFOLIO .... - 190 -

HOW TO BUY PHYSICAL PRECIOUS METALS	- 190 -
PRECIOUS METALS OPTIMIZE EVERY PORTFOLIO:	- 191 -
ROYALTIES	- 194 -
NET SMELTER RETURN (NSR)	- 194 -
NET PROFIT INTEREST (NPI)	- 195 -
NET ROYALTY INTEREST (NRI)	- 195 -
STREAMING	- 195 -
A PASSING LOOK AT ETPS (EXCHANGE-TRADED PRODUCTS)	- 203 -
OPTIONS	- 205 -
FUTURES CONTRACTS	- 209 -
WARRANTS	- 211 -
DEBT INSTRUMENTS	- 213 -

CHAPTER 11 : MINING STOCK APPRAISAL .... - 215 -

QUALATATIVE ANALYSIS	- 216 -
The MAG Test	- 217 -
FINANCIAL POSITION REQUIREMENTS:	- 218 -
Current Ratio & Acid Test	- 218 -
Interest Coverage	- 219 -
Debt/Equity	- 219 -
Total Assets/Total Liabilities	- 220 -
QUANTITATIVE ANALYSIS	- 225 -
NET ASSET VALUE CALCULATION	- 227 -

CHAPTER 12: BEYOND SILVER .... - 233 -

RESOURCES .... - 239 -

Introduction

Let us start at the beginning—why the name Silver Manifesto?

As defined by the dictionary and as derived from the Italian word *manifesto*, which itself is derived from the Latin root of *manifestum*, a manifesto is a published verbal declaration of the intentions, motives, or views of the issuer, whether it an individual, group, political party, or government. A manifesto usually accepts a previously published opinion or public consensus and/or promotes a new idea with prescriptive notions for carrying out changes the author believes should be made. The latter should be emphasized because the market money, or people's money, has always been silver and gold. It is not, as many say, because of tradition, but rather the unique characteristics held by both metals.

It is far from public consensus that silver could or even should be in the monetary system, although in times past it was the fundamental element used in commerce throughout the ages. So, let us address some of the motives, views, and specifically the intent that we wish to be of service to you, the reader. We hope to help you to understand the monetary, economic, and political systems with a much deeper understanding, using this book and many other forms of information to set you on a path of critical thinking and questioning.

Academia no longer teaches or mentions that the United States was founded on a silver standard or that Article 1, Section 10 of the U.S. Constitution (which has not been amended) declares nothing but gold and silver coin are to be used as a medium of exchange! The monetary system was corrupted and could have fallen apart in the 19th century; however, at that time, some political will was strong enough to keep the U.S. on constitutional money. The defense of sound money allowed the dollar to double in purchasing power in 1895 relative to 1890 and it could be argued it was the primary reason there developed a large middle class. As we discuss, monetary inflation is the cause of increasing consumer prices but is primarily a redistribution of wealth. It is the banking corporations and political elites that receive the new money first, which benefits them the most.

Indeed our purpose is to provide the reader information about the silver market from several different perspectives. After absorbing much of the manifesto the reader could be inclined to see the merits of investing in this precious metal. Certainly, the authors and many of the contributors to this work are firm believers that the biggest move in the precious metals markets are ahead of us, perhaps in the 2016-2017 timeframes. Other associates of ours insist that the top of the silver market is not due until 2020 or 2022. Frankly, no one knows for certain. What we do know is that the current monetary system is based primarily on the U.S. dollar and in just over 100 years this "money" has lost about 95% of its purchasing power. This would be a huge wake-up call to anyone using dollars, yet it is largely ignored by the general public, as few know or understand what is happening to the monetary system. This is not a new story it is something that has occurred time and time again. Highly regarded philosopher Voltaire stated that paper money always returns to its intrinsic value, zero.

To fully appreciate the importance of the precious metals at this pivotal point in world history, we provided this solid economics background (see chapters: 5, 7 and 8). These chapters are usually difficult to write and often found to be dull reading for most people. Obviously, this background information can be skipped but it would be of huge disservice to you, as the sound economic basis of the facts presented builds the case as to why precious metals are so important for anyone who understands the current level of debt held by the banking system. The current worldwide economic landscape is so incredibly fragile and unprecedented, central bankers have become reckless with monetary policy which is built upon governments that continually spend more than taken in by tax revenue.

One of the best ways to take maximum advantage of a bull market in precious metals is through the purchase of mining shares. Having been through one bull market cycle, the amount of profit made in the previous cycle was truly life changing in some instances. In the 1970s' bull market the South African mining shares led the group, and a handful of top companies were paying dividends equal to the initial investment from years earlier. As an example, a $10,000 investment was paying dividends of $10,000 or more, roughly a decade later. The price appreciation in many of the top companies was at least tenfold.

In this bull market the mining shares have not participated to the level that was suggested by the last bull market. There are several reasons for this, one being that so many other financial instruments are now available that deal directly with metal purchase, leaving the risks of mining to the side. There are several Exchange- Traded Funds and we discuss some of these in the book. Regardless, the opportunity in the mining sector could be a once-in-a-lifetime situation as this book goes to press in early 2015.

We have certainly helped to give exposure to precious metals investing through our first book, but primarily through the Internet, having the silverguru YouTube Channel, @silverguru22 for a Twitter feed, and of course our Web site, TheMorganReport.com.

We have thought that the world was facing the biggest currency crisis in all of recorded history and this is still the prime motivator for all of our work. We have seen so many upheavals in the currency markets in just our lifetime, yet the U.S. dollar has not suffered as badly as many other currencies—yet! It is deliberate to add the word *yet*, because the global financial system is largely tied to the U.S. dollar and as it goes so goes the financial system as a whole. Certainly, the BRICS countries are moving away from the U.S. dollar and may be able to isolate themselves somewhat from a U.S. dollar crisis, but this is unlikely because international trade is so interconnected that to escape what is coming will be impossible.

As in many books, we wanted to summarize or perhaps offer some type of conclusion for the reader. But the essence of the authors is to be open minded and lifelong learners. The best education for us has been life itself and, often, making mistakes. So, the chapter "Beyond Silver" does not offer solutions to the current trajectory for humankind, but rather presents areas to be explored further by the reader. Our highest purpose is to truly be of value to our fellows and be in alignment with the idea that we the people have and will always have the ability to live the paradox of serving others by also serving ourselves.

It is impossible for the government to have monopoly control of "money" and freedom to exist in society, as these are mutually exclusive. We wish to make certain we can help educate as many as possible to take wealth protection precautions. However, it is just as important, if not more so, to instill the idea that the ultimate value for mankind is freedom! This idea can never be taken from you because ideas are bulletproof—but to maintain freedom, the course of history has proven at times that action is required. Are you prepared?

Lastly, it is our quest that individual freedoms are secured again after being stripped away piece by piece. History has illustrated that sound money and freedom go hand in hand. This lies in an even deeper belief of ownership of self and our ability to exercise our natural-born rights, which after all are at the core of our humanity.

Chapter 1: A Monetary History of Silver – 3,400 B.C. - 1792

"Money itself is an object of commerce, a form of wealth precisely because it has value and because any value exchanges in trade for an equal value (ex-ante)." –Anne Robert Jacques Turgot

The question of whether or not gold and silver are money is even more important now than perhaps at any other time in history. The simple and short answer is yes, making the real question: *Why* are silver and gold money?

It is important to first point out that silver and gold have been monies dating back more than 5,000 years. It is also worth noting that every inconvertible fiat[1] (paper money) monetary system in history so far has collapsed, with each "monetary unit" returning to its intrinsic value of zero[2]. It could be argued that not all of them went completely to zero, but as a practical matter the devaluations were so harsh that the currency was abandoned by the population as a medium of exchange—effectively making it worthless.

The average fiat monetary system has lasted roughly 35 years, which ironically, is seldom if ever pointed out in academia. Is it just coincidence that an economic event (hyperinflation[3]) came about at nearly the same time that fiat money came into existence? Hyperinflationary episodes have occurred more than 50 times in the 20th century, compared to just one time throughout the rest of history, with that being in pre-revolutionary France when it decided to adopt the Assignat.

Various economists have answered the question regarding why silver and gold, as opposed to other commodities, are considered money. A. J. Turgot[4], Richard Cantillon, Carl Menger, and others have pointed out that it is because these two precious metals have the most marketability or salability.

Aristotle named the attributes that the most ideal (commodity) money should have. It should be scarce, durable, malleable, divisible, homogenous, and transportable (having a high value to weight ratio). These virtues almost perfectly describe silver and

---

[1] Fiat money simply means a currency that derives its value from government regulation or law, such as paper money.
[2] Voltaire.
[3] Most commonly defined as beginning in the month in which monetary inflation has caused consumer prices to increase greater than 50%.
[4] "Turgot argues further that, while almost all commodities may more or less conveniently serve as money, gold and silver have been chosen as the 'universal money' because they possess in the greatest degree the various physical properties which peculiarly suit them to that role." –Joseph Salerno, *Money, Sound and Unsound*

gold. We will briefly summarize just how intertwined silver and money have been throughout history, which is necessary to understand because silver has two demand drivers. The first is the industrial demand component, which we break down between fabrication (jewelry, photography, and silverware) and that for industrial uses (electronics, batteries, brazing alloys and solders, photovoltaic, etc.). The second is investment or monetary demand.

Investment demand hit a record in 2013 and looks to have done the same again in 2014. Investment demand should continue to set new records nearly every year until the current fiat money house of cards implodes or a worldwide monetary reset occurs, as soon as this decade. This is for several reasons, including but not limited to:

- Investment demand in both China and India continued at an extremely robust pace. India in particular really drove investment demand in 2014. As of the end of December 2014, net silver imports stood at a whopping 7.063 tons for the year, an increase of well over 15% year-on-year[5]. This puts India on track to import 27%-28% of world mine production (assuming total world mine production increased to 842m oz. in 2014).
- American Silver Eagle Sales set another record high in 2014, reaching the 2013 threshold with a month left in the year. Remember this is immaterial but gives us insight into what the smart money is doing.
- Others will be discussed in greater detail in Chapter 4.

At some point in the next five years, the price of silver is destined to reach triple-digit prices, or over 6 times greater than the present (~$17-$18 in early 2015). With silver, the potential is exceptionally strong because of required industrial consumption, which will greatly augment the coming effects of significantly higher investment or monetary demand. This means the price of silver should rise sharply as total demand far outstrips supply. But its value shouldn't be looked at in currency terms, rather in terms relative to other commodities.

To fully grasp the concept of the origination of money, it is necessary to start at the beginning, answering such questions as: *What is money? Why is money necessary? What is its function? Who chooses what constitutes money?* And lastly, *what makes a chosen monetary system sound or unsound?*

Money is a medium of exchange and a unit in which prices are expressed[6] but it is not, as many people think, a measure of value. This is because exchange is an action that expresses preferences; that is, he who acquires a good or service values it more highly than what he pays for it. Market participants use cardinal numbers to measure such things like space, time, weight, and mass. This begs the question as to what technical or economic need there could ever be for a measure of value, given its

---
[5]Koos Jansen, *India Silver Import 6,789t YTD*, Bullionstar.com, December 19, 2014.
[6]Anne Robert Jacques Turgot, *Reflections on the Formation and the Distribution of Riches*, p. 36, London: Macmillan & Co. 1770 (reprinted 1898).

subjective nature. If one were to assume money could measure value, meaning the price paid for a good represents that good's cardinal value, this should then be applicable to money if it were a measure of value. And this brings up the question, "What is the value of this measure of value?" This is essentially a circular argument as it would be absurd to say the value of a unit of money is 5. Value then must be expressed in ordinal terms[7].

The Origin of Money

Starting from the most basic monetary system, a barter economy is when a person engages in direct exchange with another individual, lacking a standard unit of account. This problem is solved by the development and usage of indirect exchange. Naturally problems arise when exchanging one good for another in a barter economy, because the market is constantly changing due to an individual's ever-changing subjective values of needs and wants. Furthermore, exchanges only take place if each party in the proposed transaction has a direct, personal need for the good he/she receives in exchange and views the good he/she receives in exchange as more valuable than what they have to give away for it.

Every economic act involves a comparison of values[8], not a measurement. When a society develops and expands, a standard unit of account arises and a monetary unit is needed to facilitate exchange, which after all is the primary basis of our economic life. In other words, direct exchange becomes extremely difficult and inefficient, bringing about indirect exchange—an extension of the division of labor[9]. Market participants preferring more goods over less eventually identify the higher productivity of a system of division of labor. This knowledge and self-interest therefore explain the emergence of a commodity money in a free society (not confined to a single commodity and therefore could be said as bringing about commodity monies)[10].

This is not to say that money doesn't measure objective prices or ratios of exchange[11]. It is important to realize that it is impossible to measure subjective values, but not objective values. We note this because it is widely accepted that the government must have monopoly control of the (mint) printing press or equivalent (electronic system) in order to provide a unit of account by which to measure goods and services. The problem with this, however, is that when giving government monopoly control, monetary catastrophe is always the end result. This is precisely why a true free market money, absent of government interference, has proven necessary throughout recorded history:

"It is impossible to grasp the meaning of the idea of sound money if one does not realize that it was devised as an instrument for the protection of civil liberties against

---

[7]Hans Herman Hoppe, *The Economics and Ethics of Private Property*, pp. 179-180.
[8]Ludwig von Mises, *Theory of Money and Credit*, p. 38, Yale University Press, 1953.
[9]Jörg Guido Hülsmann, *The Ethics of Money Production*, p. 22, Ludwig von Mises Institute, 2008.
[10]See in particular Carl Menger, *Principles of Economics, 1981,* in Hans Herman Hoppe, *The Economics and Ethics of Private Property*, p. 176.
[11]Ludwig von Mises, *Theory of Money and Credit*, p. 49, Yale University Press, 1953.

despotic inroads on the part of governments. Ideologically it belongs in the same class with political constitutions and bills of rights[12]."

Some could argue the question of whether fiat money can arise as a natural outcome of human interaction between self-interested parties or if it is possible to introduce it without violating justice or causing economic inefficiency. The answer, as we've discussed up to this point, is a resounding "no"; it cannot. As we will discuss in this and the following chapter, fiat money allows fractional reserve banking to be possible, which can easily be refuted on ethical grounds.

What makes a monetary system sound? A clear and concise answer is, "any monetary system that a government is not involved with." A sound monetary system inherently rises in a market economy, with checks and balances that prevent monetary inflation. A more detailed answer, which history has shown us time and time again, is that the market would choose a commodity money, notably gold and/or silver. This shouldn't be confused with the monetary system of the U.S. during the period of 1913 to 1971 as this wasn't a true gold standard.

One of the great things with the presence of a 100%-backed commodity standard is that such a standard is synonymous with freedom. The inherent nature of government is to usurp as much power as it can in an economy, or said differently, attempt to control all or as many as possible factors of production, the most important being monopoly control of the currency, communication, and transportation.

The irony here is that government and central banks are the cause of the boom-bust cycle (business cycle) by distorting interest rates, which relay important information to every individual, instead of letting the market determine interest rates. A common fallacy is that modern day business cycles (1913-present) are commonplace and, as Alan Greenspan would say, are "Economic Phenomena."

Interest rates relay such information as to what part of the structure of production capital will be most efficiently allocated. It reflects society's savings/investment-to-consumption preference and acts as a signaling mechanism to capitalists as to whether they should invest capital to maximize accounting profits. Artificially manipulating interest rates downward, combined with fractional reserve banking (see: Chapter 7), induces an artificial economic boom in the first place, which is followed by a natural bust, or cleansing, of the imbalances from the economy created by the artificial boom.

Looking at Turgot's contribution to monetary theory—more specifically, how exactly the market adapts and has adapted silver and gold as the ideal money—the following quote from Turgot is ingenious, with an obviously deep understanding on the origins of money:

"Individual actions generate a spontaneous and self-reinforcing market process whereby silver and gold evolve into money[13]. Market participants, realizing this, will become increasingly eager to acquire and hold stocks of these metals for the purpose of

---
[12] *Ibid.*, p. 454.
[13] Anne-Robert-Jacques Turgot, *Reflections on the Formation and the Distribution of Riches*, p. 38.

being used in exchange at a later date. This demand for silver and gold and the corresponding market values of each will be augmented by this development, further enhancing their usefulness as a medium of exchange. Once this is accomplished and universally becomes the preferred medium of exchange and traded against every other good in the market, the metal weights become the standard unit in which all market values or prices are expressed[14]."

Sadly, in order to have a natural money circulate as the predominate medium of exchange, private property rights must at all times be acknowledged and protected! To the degree that private property rights aren't acknowledged, the money that comes into use is forced money, a clear violation of private property rights. Forced money therefore has one feature—it owes its existence to violations of private property rights[15], which violates free market principles. In reality (as opposed to theoretically), there is nothing in the middle of capitalism and socialism, thus if government has monopoly control of the mint, it is anything but free market capitalism, and sadly, this is what exists in every major economy today.

Just how pronounced has silver's monetary role has been throughout history? The very word for silver is *money* in many languages. In Italian, Spanish, and French, the words can be interchanged. In Hebrew, the word *kesepph* means both silver and money. Even in Early-American slang, the word *silver* was often used to signify payment: "Grease my palm with silver!" To be precise, among more than 250 million people in over 50 countries, the word for money is identical to the word for silver. Many Europeans refer to both silver and money as "argent," while Spanish-speaking people the world over use "plata" to mean silver, money, or both.

Another greatly misunderstood concept is that of deflation and how mainstream media and market pundits exhibit such great disdain for it. It could be because central bankers do the same, but history has shown that economic forecasts by members of the Federal Reserve Open Market Committee are generally inaccurate and always inaccurate for medium to long periods of time. These forecasts aren't just wrong, but, at times, so significantly inaccurate as to be almost comedic when looked back upon.

Is Deflation Really a Bad Thing?

Why would market pundits and "expert" economists appearing on the popular financial channels be so scared of the deflationary boogeyman? The truth is that deflation is commonplace in a market economy and is synonymous with liberty. A perfect example is in the U.S. during the 19th century (as a whole, given various periods of high inflation or deflation due to vast inflows/outflows of specie). Over the period 1800-1895, deflation caused the purchasing power of the dollar to roughly double. This amounts to an average annual rate of deflation just over 0.72%. This of course refers to the modern-day definition of deflation that is a drop in consumer prices.

---

[14]Ibid, p. 38.
[15]Jörg Guido Hülsmann, *Ethics of Money Production*, p. 27, Ludwig von Mises Institute, 2008.

While there were periods of very high inflation, overall, prices declined. If we just think about the repercussions of our monetary units increasing in purchasing power, it is a benefit to society at large and is proof that efficiencies (production improvements) are being made. In fact, declining prices generally indicate an increase in the standard of living. Ironically, high inflation isn't considered to be any better than deflation, but a little inflation is deemed to be ideal. If society as a whole becomes more productive, it makes sense that consumer prices will fall as increased productive capacity allows for goods and services to be produced more efficiently, thereby increasing the standard of living for society as a whole. This is a natural and healthy effect in a market economy. This is not to say severe deflation is a good thing except when following a Fed-induced economic boom, as it speeds up the cleansing of the imbalances or misallocated capital from the system, thereby making the economy and in particular the productive structure readjust in the timeliest manner[16].

Every economic principle, if valid, should be the most beneficial when taken to the extreme. Clearly this is not the case, as academia has not dealt with economic theory this manner. Instead it determines an arbitrary inflation rate as "ideal." This begs the question, why is a little inflation good? The naïve economist would say it boosts economic activity and is necessary as the population grows, preventing a shortage of money.

The truth is there is no optimum quantity of money other than that determined by the market. If we look back on the ideal commodity money, one characteristic that is key is that of divisibility. If prices fall 1%-5% every decade, the simple answer is to make smaller denominations of money every so often, referring back to Aristotle's characteristics of the ideal money in that of divisibility.

Academia and "expert" economists preach that a small rate of inflation is ideal so that the central banks can inflate the supply of money and credit with ease, whereas in a sound monetary system, this is much more difficult. In particular, governments with large debt burdens "hate" deflation the most because those that have accumulated a significant debt burden (governments) want it to be easy to pay back debt. Inflation makes it easy for governments to pay back in "cheaper" real terms, but deflation makes it very difficult.

This is because the purchasing power of each monetary unit will be lower (significantly for longer duration securities) than at the time of its issuance. It is for this reason as well as countless others, such as cost-of-living adjustments to social security, that government overwhelmingly prefers and in fact fully embraces inflation. The U.S. Federal Government and Federal Reserve do their best to convince the public that deflation is a dangerous circumstance precisely because of the nation's vast debt burdens (the U.S. being the largest debtor nation in the history of the world), including gross federal debt but just as importantly its $60T+ in unfunded liabilities (which will be discussed in further detail in Chapter 8).

---

[16] Jörg Guido Hülsmann, *Deflation and Liberty,* pp. 13-14.

Adam Smith was wrong when he said paper money could serve as a medium of exchange just as well as natural monies but with much lower production costs. In fact, it is precisely because of this fact that precious metals serve as the most ideal monies. Silver and gold are costly to produce, eliminating any possibility of replication at will by governments or other individuals. In other words, because of their relative scarcity, there is a built-in natural insurance against depreciating the purchasing power of money[17].

There are two popular myths regarding money, the first of which is money being neutral, and the second of which is stable prices. When new money (metal or otherwise) begins to circulate in an economy, there are wealth redistribution effects—meaning those who receive the new money first, benefit, relative to those who receive it later. These effects are greatly minimized when a market-generated money is in place, as the cost of mining is a factor, reducing the flow of new money into the economy.

Thinking that prices should remain stable is illogical. If a certain commodity such as gasoline is in high demand in an economy, the price would rise, but this is not inflation because under the assumption of a fixed money supply, the price of another good must necessarily fall. Over longer periods of time, there will be slight monetary inflation (to the degree that a metallic money can be mined) with concurrent consumer price deflation. This is because increases in productivity and lengthening of the production structure would more than offset rather negligible monetary inflation.

Silver's Use as Money: a Brief History

While it is unclear who the first people to mine silver were, we can trace silver mining and silver used as money back to 3400 BC in Mesopotamia (although some argue that silver mining began before that, in Hungary, closer to 4000 BC). This was also beginning of writing, and correspondingly, journal entries. These entries were for local trade, which had various standards as a unit of account, such as silver and animals, amongst several other goods, illustrating that even 5,000 years ago, the market chose silver as a medium of exchange. While this money system was very primitive and remained so until coinage came about, it didn't stop other societies from using silver as a monetary unit nor did it impede the advancement of the monetary system.

The first instance of bimetallism, actually the use of three metals, began 1,400 years later (2000 BC) in Egypt. The monetary system evolved and had definitive weights for trade purposes as well as exchange rates against one another. The unit of weight (deben) and monetary unit (sha) were the following:

- A deben of gold was worth 12 shas
- A deben of silver was worth 6 shas
- A deben of lead was worth 3 shas
- 1 deben = 7.5 grams of gold, 15 grams of silver, or 75 grams bronze/lead

---

[17]Adolph Wagner, Die russische Papierwahrung-eine volkswirtschaftlich und finazpolitsche Studie nebst Vorschalgen zur Herstellung der Valuta, pp. 45-46.

Amazingly, by today's standards the gold-to-silver ratio was 2:1, followed by a gold-to-silver ratio of 5:3 (1.66:1). It is important to note that the gold-to-silver ratio was so low because trade with other territories was very limited until the Phoenicians (those from modern-day Palestine, parts of Syria, and Lebanon) started to advance and dominate trade in the Mediterranean. Trade became a comparative advantage for the Phoenicians as they created trading posts and began to explore outside their region. The advancement of the monetary system continued, and in 1500 BC, monetary units of the same metal had varying weights. The Hittites reverted to a monometallic standard, using silver as a medium of exchange. It is also important to point out that this was prior to the advent of coinage, which came 800 years later.

- Shekel ~ 8.41 grams of silver
- Stater ~ 16.82 grams of silver
- Mina ~ 500 grams of silver, or 15.5 ounces
- Talent ~ 30 kilograms, or 933 ounces

The Lydian System

An immense advancement in the monetary system was made by the Lydians, who were the first to utilize coinage (silver and gold) for monetary purposes, which first occurred around 700 BC. The Lydians were the first to not only coin money but to also develop the first system of coins, initially making them from gold and silver alloys. They were also the first to establish retail shops. Some argue it was King Alyattes who developed and then first coined the stater, while others argue it was King Gyges who first circulated this coinage[18].

These small oval nuggets circulated throughout the East. As you can see, the oval nuggets were not 100% homogenous, so technically could not be called coinage.

King Gyges ruled from 690 to 657 BC, while King Alyattes ruled from 610 to 550 BC. Historians tend to link King Gyges with the first coinage and system of coins. These coins were actually not silver or gold, but rather an alloy of the two. Later, the son of King Gyges, King Croesus, greatly improved the smelting technique of his predecessor via separating silver and gold from the electrum. While either King Alyattes or King Gyges came up with the first coinage and system of coins, King Croesus originated the first bimetallic system of coins, with an exchange rate between the two, as follows:

---

[18] Cyrille Jubert, *Silver throughout History*, p. 20.

- 1 gold stater = 8.17 grams of gold
- 1 silver stater = 10.89 grams of silver
- 1 gold stater = 10 silver staters
- (8.17) x (1) = (10.89) x (10) OR
- Gold-to-silver ratio = (108.90/8.17) = 13.33

The Lydian system spread like wildfire through the East, then to Greece and all of Mediterranean Europe. Greece was able to develop its economy thanks to silver-lead veins running south of the city. The first mines exploited easily-obtained surface veins, which is silver closest to the earth's surface.

This was the start of the first large-scale mining industry, which included more advanced ore refining. As a result, Athens sported a strong currency and advanced trade, but it then made one fatal flaw—initiating the Peloponnesian War.

Athens society and political philosophy were more capitalistic than its neighboring city, Sparta. Sparta had almost the exact opposite philosophy, one that would be regarded as Socialist in today's world. Athens instigated the war in 429 BC and to their detriment did not foresee it lasting 27 years. This brings us to the first instance of government manipulating/debasing its currency. In 407 BC, the government debased its currency by adding copper to the coinage, therefore causing a face value that was less than the value of its metal content. Another devaluation occurred just two years later in 405 BC. During the biblical times of Jesus, notably the betrayal by Judas, we know Judas was paid 30 silver "pieces" for this betrayal. It is unclear as to what weight of silver these 30 pieces equated.

"Then one of the twelve, who was named Judas Iscariot, went to the chief priests and said, 'What will you give me, if I give him up to you?' And the price was fixed at thirty bits of silver." Matthew 26:14-15

There is evidence of two different monetary units (denier and shekel) as well as varying weights of both during this time. At the creation of the denier, it initially weighed 4.51 grams of silver but the silver coin created in 212 BC became devalued and by 140

BC, weighed 3.96 grams of silver. But although the evidence that Judas was paid in "shekels" is much stronger, therein lies another problem. At the time, there were different variants of shekels, "biblical shekels," "Tyrian shekels," and the basic "shekel."

- 30 denier/denarii x 3.96 grams or .127 troy ounces = 3.82 ounces
- 30 biblical shekels x 6 grams, or .193 troy ounces = almost 5.79 ounces
- 30 shekels x 11 grams, or .35 troy ounces = 330 grams or 10.61 ounces
- 30 Tyrian shekels x 14 grams, or .45 troy ounces = 420 grams or **13.50 ounces**

The Tyrian shekel was used over the time period in Jerusalem and they were specifically referenced in the book of Matthew. Due to the fact that a shekel of a specific weight was mentioned (Tyrians) in the book of Matthew (21:12) and it was the medium of exchange used to pay temple tax in Jerusalem, Judas' payment for betraying Jesus was most likely approximately 13.50 ounces of silver.

However, this is a bit confusing, given that the biblical shekel was 6 grams, which naturally sounds as if that were the shekel referred to in the Bible. When the first shekel was coined in 600 BC it weighed almost 11 grams (10.89). Further complicating the issue is the denier/denarii, which is also referenced in the Gospel of John as well Luke (10:25).

The Roman monetary system fell apart when the denier as a weight of silver was reduced as silver coins were recast over and over again with each emperor. Over the period 158 AD to 284 AD, Rome had 20 different emperors, most of whom debased its currency. Starting with Nero in 158-167 AD, the weight of silver in a coin was 2.19 grams. Then in 282-284 AD under Emperor Carus, the weight of coin dropped to 7.47 grams and only included .04 grams of silver. In other words, the silver content in each monetary unit was less than 1/54 of what it was 115 years earlier.

Year	Emperor	Silver Weight in Coin	Depreciation
156-167	Nero	2.19	
167-170	Marcus Aurelius	1.57	-28.31%
191-192	Commode	0.92	-41.40
212-217	Septimius Severus	1.16	26.09%
224-227	Caracalla	0.88	-24.14%
235-238	Maximanus I	0.74	-15.91%
238-244	Gordian	0.61	-17.57%
244-249	Phillip	0.87	42.62%
261-268	Gallian	0.4	-54.02%
268-270	Claude	0.26	-35.00%
282-284	Carus	0.04	-84.62%

The Medieval Period

This period primarily involves Charlemagne, who became king of Gaul and Germania in 771, after the death of his brother. Charlemagne went on to expand his empire by defeating the Saxons to the north, followed by Austria and then Northern Italy. Charlemagne decided to replace the previous worthless currency with a new one, a currency strictly minted in silver. The names of the monetary units were nearly the same, the basic unit being called the Roman denarius. This weighed 1.70 grams, with the next monetary unit being the obol, weighing 0.85 grams. A popular unit was the penny, being worth 12 denarii, as well as the pound, worth 240 denarii. This monetary system was on a monometallic standard (silver), partly due to the fact it was the only one relatively plentiful among the Franks. Charlemagne is important in monetary history because his change to monetary policy would be influential throughout Europe for many decades.

This monometallic system lasted for four centuries. In Venice 400 years later, the first "sequins" were minted. Sequins were first called ducats, which weighed 3.60 grams of gold (3.495 grams of fine gold), thereby replacing the monetary system Charlemagne had put in place. Venetian bankers imposed an exchange rate on gold (manipulation) in order to control its inflows.

In 1275, the prevailing gold-to-silver ratio was 8, increasing to 15 just 50 years later. This along with trade with the Mongols and what was essentially a monopoly on gold mines pushed Europe onto a monometallic monetary system, but this time using gold. The gold-to-silver ratio was reduced as the emperor of Mali undertook a journey to Mecca, bringing with him 60,000+ men and more than 10,000 slaves. In every city this journey took them through, they paid generously in gold for the needs of all the journeymen. Due to the influx of gold, Venice reestablished the gold-to-silver ratio, from 15 to 1, to 9 to 1 by 1345.

Florentine bankers were ruined by the gold manipulation of the Venetians. Their fortune prior to the manipulation was primarily in silver and the increase from 8 to 15 per Gresham's Law drove silver out of circulation. This caused 60% of the silver to be driven out of circulation by 1345, and fractional reserve banking (multiple claims on one

---

[19] Cyrille Jubert, *Silver Throughout History*, p. 35.

monetary unit in specie) or lending out more money than it actually held in deposits caused a financial meltdown. This crisis, also known as the "systemic crash of 1345," led to a substantial spike of inflation.

The results were extreme poverty and famine among the masses, the recipe for a wave of epidemics due to the immune system becoming substantially weakened. It was known as the Black Plague. In five years, it wiped out roughly 40% of the total European population. This, along with the Hundred Years' War, resulted in a century of silver shortages and economic stagnation, or in other words, set back economic progress for more than a century.

China: The birthplace of paper money

The first use of pseudo-fiat money was 2,000 years ago by the Chinese Emperor Wu-ti, as he was caught up in a series of wars and needed financing to fund his battles. He tried numerous money substitutes, most of which were very odd, with one of these being deerskin money, which was exactly like it sounds. This money at the time was highly ritualistic. While this use of deerskin money was successful in financing Wu-ti's campaigns, it didn't last very long. To get an idea just how valuable this was in society, a deerskin monetary unit was equivalent to 480 ounces of silver[20]!

The Tang Dynasty

During the Tang Dynasty (618-906) in China, paper money widely circulated and "religious paper" that corresponded to silver, gold, copper, and silk was not money that circulated in commerce, but was just religious offerings. Copper coins were the primary circulating medium of exchange and for brief intervals of time, silk rolls were used in exchange for medium- to large-sized transactions. Gradually, silver gained preference as the common monetary unit among the people. Three types of credit institutions existed, one being a money shop, which was a concept similar to a bank.

By 750, *fei-ch'ien*, or "flying money," illustrated the advancement of the Chinese monetary system. Today it would be considered an instrument used in credit exchange, similar to a credit card transaction. It could be argued that this is comparable to a warehouse receipt used in "classical" deposit banking, as it was a negotiable draft note. It became commonplace to keep metal on deposit somewhere and draw notes against it (known as debiting the metal on account). It is important to note here that this system arose from the market, not government.

By 812, flying money came to an end as government prohibited private fei-ch'ien as the fee for using fei-ch'ien, similar to credit card fees today (fees were raised from 3% to 10%[21]).

"Chinese histories attribute the origin of ch'ao-pi, or paper money, to the fei-ch'ien 'flying money,' of the Tang period. The 'flying money,' also known as pein-huan, 'credit exchange,' was essentially a draft to transmit funds to distant places; hence it may be

---

[20]Yang, *Money and Credit in China*, p. 51.
[21]Ralph T. Foster, *Fiat Paper Money*, p. 7.

considered a credit instrument but not money. This history of paper money and that of other credit instruments, however, is so closely woven together that the 'flying money' forms a logical starting point for our account[22]."

Paper money was used in Szechwan in 1011, which was called Chia-Tzu. There were problems from the start as the three most prominent money and credit institutions (pawnshop, co-op loan society, and money shops) had control over issued notes, either shortchanging their customers on deposits or even completely ruining them. It only took 11 years from the start of this first paper money experiment until it collapsed due to a loss in confidence, causing the government to close the private note shops. There were and still are a myriad of contradicting explanations regarding why this system collapsed.

The Song (S'ung) Dynasty

Not too long following the first fiat collapse, the Chinese again experimented with fiat money, with the Song (S'ung) dynasty being the second to issue paper money (1024), which was called Chiao-Tzu. As is typical, the prevailing government began abusing this new concept. The notes in circulation did have an exchange rate against gold, silver, and silk, however, convertibility was prohibited.

Initially, all notes would be redeemed after three years and replaced by new notes at a 3% service charge. This, however, began to be abused as the government stopped this practice and instead just printed more and more notes, inflating the inconvertible fiat paper money. Shen Kuo, the minister of finance, explained to the emperor how the economy prospers with more money in circulation in 1077:

"The Utility of money derives from circulation and loan-making. A village of ten households may have 100,000 coins. If the cash is stored in the household of one individual, even after a century, the sum remains 100,000. If the coins are circulated through business transactions so that every individual of the ten households can enjoy the utility of the 100,000 coins, then the utility will amount to that of 1,000,000 cash. If circulation continues without stop, the utility of the cash will be beyond enumeration[23]."

His logic is astoundingly ridiculous and quite comical. Inflation at that time took a bit longer to be recognized as the S'ung dynasty was cautious at first and only issued small amounts, such that the chiao-tzu held its value for seven decades[24]. Inflation, nonetheless, became a big problem around 1085-1090. For a time, fiat money and sound money both circulated, but then the government started demanding taxes be paid, at least in part, by inconvertible fiat paper money.

The government also introduced various laws, which essentially forced individuals to use fiat in a plethora of situations. Less than a century later, the inevitable happened and inflation became an issue. The dynasty was fighting the Mongols (the Yuan dynasty) and the increasing cost of fighting the war made inflation very apparent. The S'ung dynasty eventually lost the war early in the 13th century (1217).

---

[22]Yang, *Money and Credit in China*, p. 51.
[23]Yang, *Studies in Chinese Institutional History*, p. 69.
[24]Foster, *Fiat Paper Money*, pp. 12-13.

From the start in 1106 through 1217, several other fiat systems were tried, but they failed, due to lack of faith from society as a whole.

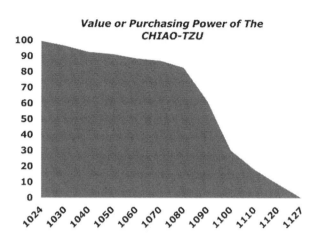

The Chin Tartars

The Chin Tartars gained control of the Northern China Empire, and the S'ung dynasty continued to reign over the empire, which makes up modern-day Southern China. The Chin brought back paper money in the form of Chiao-ch'ao in 1153. The Chin currency maintained its purchasing power for 40 years because the currency was believed to be fully backed by silver and gold as the Chin emperor proclaimed; however, even while he was saying such things, all the precious metals that backed the currency were either redeemed or sold.

Merchants relied heavily on silver[25] to sustain commerce, despite the government trying to do everything in its power to prop up inconvertible fiat paper money by prohibiting the hoarding of metals, imposing a maximum drawdown on silver and gold from the imperial treasury, and eventually inflating the money supply to finance the war.

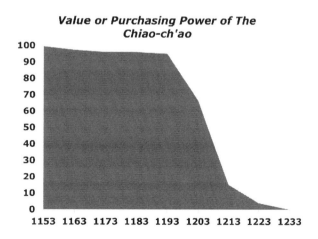

---

[25]Schurmann, *Economic Structure of the Yuan Dynasty*, p. 131.

Coming back to the S'ung dynasty in Southern China, the old S'ung leaders again took charge and introduced paper money after this failed the first time. This time it was in the form of Hui-Tzu, to circulate in everyday commerce. The society reluctantly accepted the new paper money because the collapse of the S'ung currency in the north had been just a few years prior.

Like the paper monies in China before it, the hui-tzu eventually was worth its intrinsic value of zero. For the first 50 years, this paper money was more or less stable—that is, until the government's management of the currency became reckless. This paper money hoax that began in China is in practice in EVERY other government throughout history. More notes came into circulation and the purchasing power declined, followed by an attempt in 1204 (after the currency had lost roughly 20%-22% of its purchasing power) to increase confidence in the monetary unit by calling the newly issued paper note a "gold, silver, and cash communicating medium." Hu Zhiyu criticized the currency, declaring it worthless and stating that only precious metals backing gave paper value . . . in other words, blaming the inconvertibility. He ascribed a great analogy between paper and precious metals as paper money being the child, which is dependent on the mother, precious metals[26].

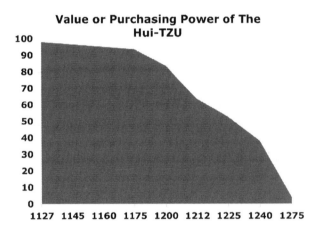

The Yuan Dynasty

The Yuan dynasty fared better with fiat money relative to the S'ung dynasty, due to the actions of Kublai Khan, who followed the recommendation of Yeh-lü Ch'u-ts'ai, his most prognostic advisor, and instituted a conservative ratio of paper to backing by silver[27]. Further inspiring confidence in the Chung-t'ung currency, in 1268 the government established the Equitable Ratio of Treasuries. These bureaus served only as a place where convertibility of paper money to silver and gold was processed.

At this point it could be stated that the Chinese had learned from their failures experimenting with paper fiat money. It was clear the government learned something,

---

[26] Ralph T. Foster, *Fiat Paper Money, Fountain of Fortune*, pp. 19, 46, 63.
[27] Schurmann, *Economic Structure of the Yuan Dynasty*, p. 132.

albeit not in full, from the mistakes made in monetary policy from the recent past, as Minister Liu Hsuan said the following:

"If there was the slightest impediment in the flow of paper money, the authorities would unload silver and accept paper as payment for it. If any loss of popular confidence was feared, then not a cash's worth of the accumulated reserves of silver and gold in the province concerned would be moved elsewhere. At that time, still very little paper money was issued without a reserve to back it, and it was therefore easy to control . . . For seventeen or eighteen years the value of the paper money did not fluctuate[28]."

Liu accompanied this by also warning of the dangerous risks in inflating the money supply and stressed the necessity of confidence in a currency, which was brought about by precious metal backing and/or convertibility.

The economy improved at first, most notably in agriculture, water irrigation, encouraged silk production, and a vast improvement in monetary affairs, while he made paper money even more widespread but backed the money by specie. This led to more active commerce with the construction of roads, improved canals, and a postal system.

This, however, got the economy into trouble after some time, due to excessive spending on public works programs that persisted after Khan's reign. His successors fared no better and began engaging in currency manipulation, higher taxation, and several other economic shenanigans that were both unpopular and unsuccessful.

Peasant uprisings began to occur after the government tried to exploit them in various manners, and a series of over 30 very harsh winters caused the existing economic problems to worsen. The Yuan currency morphed into a fiat currency due to the vast expenditures on public works programs, and the Mongols undertook numerous unsuccessful military and naval excursions.

It wasn't one single event but rather several that caused the dynasty to go broke. Several incredibly large naval fleets were destroyed by typhoons, and countless other small events put pressure on the system. Price inflation took off due to massive printing of inconvertible and unbacked paper money, causing society at large to accumulate precious metals. Minister Liu Hsuan was very outspoken in his opposition to the printing of paper money.

---

[28]Elvin, *The Pattern of the Chinese Past*, p. 160.

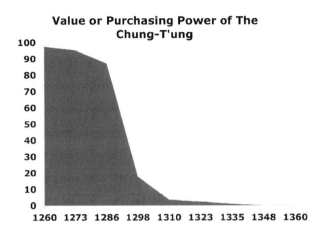

The transition from the Yuan dynasty to the Ming dynasty was a result of the peasant uprisings combined with the harsh winters and other natural disasters. The Ming dynasty arose from the collapse of the Yuan dynasty caused by wars among the Mongol imperial heirs. In 1368, Zhu Yuanzhang became the emperor; he was a Chinese peasant and former monk turned rebel army leader.

The Ming Dynasty

The Ming dynasty brought back paper money, purportedly because it lacked the wealth to instill a sound monetary unit. The Ming dynasty managed to inflate the money supply to such a degree that over a 75-year period (1375-1450), the purchasing power of the Ta-Ming pao-ch'ao was reduced to 1/1,000 of its original strength by the end of this period, relative to the start.

In 1375, one ounce of silver was worth one string of paper. By 1450, one ounce of silver was worth 1,000 strings of paper[29]. The Chinese finally had enough and before the 16th century, silver was far and away the most popular medium of exchange. By the end of the Ming dynasty, the people rejected all attempts by the government to bring back paper money.

Silver Fever in Asia

Lastly, the Manchu dynasty (1645-1911) flourished as it became even more liberal (in the classical sense) than the West, with much more freedom from state interference[30]. Silver ingots overwhelmingly dominated exchange in both domestic and world trade as well as in everyday use in commerce. It could be stated that China had "silver fever" during this time as well, accounting for a whopping 25% of world population. It is important to note that during the first experiments with a "pseudo-fiat" monetary system, the Chinese had eventually realized that such a monetary system would not work and would inevitably fail. In this sense, economic knowledge has not only been lost, but has actually regressed!

---

[29]Yang, *Money and Credit in China*, pp. 67-68.
[30]Goldstone, *Revolution and Rebellion in the Early Modern World*, p. 16, citing Myers, *Customary Law, Markets, and Resource Transactions in Late Imperial China*.

At this point in history, the Europeans realized the Chinese civilization was advanced relative to theirs, and had little desire for most European goods; however, the Europeans desired Chinese products, most notably, silk. Gold had no real monetary value in China, so a significant amount of trade with the Chinese was done using silver as the primary monetary unit. Silver became much more highly valued in the Eastern world (China and Japan) and, because of the combined populations, had an uncanny ability to absorb the metal. From the 15th through the 17th centuries, the gold-to-silver ratio in China averaged 6-6.5:1 and roughly the same in Japan. Starting in the 17th century, the gold-to-silver ratio began to climb in the Eastern world. By the mid-17th century, the gold-to-silver ratio had increased to 13-14:1.

It has been said the value of silver in real terms peaked over the period 1450-1489 as the Hundred Years' War came to an end. Since silver was in short supply during this period, the government once again resorted to debasing its currency. This backfired, driving individuals to hoard silver, naturally exacerbating the shortage.

The Renaissance and Discovery of the Americas

This period was marked by several innovations, notably in navigational instruments (compasses, maps, etc.) and in mining. In 1451, new methods were discovered for the extraction of silver (increasing the recovery rates) by adding mercury, salt, and copper sulfate. Furthermore, new hydraulic processes were implemented to "de-water" underground mines.

These two occurrences allowed for increased extraction of silver from both copper and silver ore. Mining became a more viable industry, which attracted many financiers to invest in both mining and refining. This increased investment and superior mining methods soon resolved the silver shortage issue.

This brings us to a major currency crisis in England known as "The Great Debasement," as Henry VIII debased the English coinage by first re-smelting the coins so they contained less and less silver. The market soon realized that this was a 75% depreciation. Thus, as a consequence, rampant inflation occurred in short order. The British currency quickly reversed course when Elizabeth the 1st took the throne and named her financial advisor, Sir Thomas Gresham. This is where the fairly popular term "Gresham's Law" originated among free market economists. It can be explained in different ways, but broadly speaking, it means "bad money drives out good." In those days, it meant that if two currencies are in circulation, the undervalued one will be hoarded/exported and driven out of circulation while the other will be used in everyday transactions. Seigniorage, the right to coin money, was considered a source of income; thus, newly minted coins were overvalued relative to their weight in silver. Each new minting of a given metal resulted in inflation or confirmed Gresham's Law and was driven out of circulation.

We then move to the discovery of "the Americas," in particular, the West Indies and the Caribbean, as Christopher Columbus and the conquistadors were looking for a new route to India. Initially, only gold was shipped backed to Spain from South America.

It wasn't until more than five decades later that silver mines were discovered, bringing with them, unprecedented wealth.

The first major discovery was made in modern-day Bolivia, part of Peru at the time. The Potosi Mines were discovered in 1545, being the first large silver mines discovered in the "New World." These mines were in the Andes Mountains and contained very pure and high-grade silver ore. During the first 20 years of mining at Potosi, 60 tons were produced, followed by an average annual production of 240 tons per year for the next 115 years[31]. This amounted to 170,000,000 oz. of silver over the life of the Potosi Mines.

Production after 1680 saw a sharp drop off, because once the extremely high-grade surface veins were fully exploited, grade and prevalence declined at depth. Thus we can conclude these were epithermal deposits, although this knowledge wasn't known at the time, so it naturally was surprising to the miners. During the period of mining at Potosi, other smaller scale deposits were discovered both in Peru and Bolivia. However, the next big mines would be found in Mexico.

The silver mines in Mexico were discovered and exploited relatively soon after that in Bolivia, and by 1650, silver production in Mexico exceeded that of Peru and Bolivia combined. Prior to the significant innovation in silver mining, exploration, extraction, recoveries, and refining developed during the 20th century, Mexico's peak production came in 1780, totaling 22,000,000 oz. Today, Mexico produces roughly 120,000,000 oz. This too will see a significant increase a decade from now, as explained in Chapter 3.

This took place during the reign of Charles V, who, along with his successors, received the "Royal Fifth," or 20%, of all the gold and silver extracted. Added to this was the seigniorage tax for producing money. Naturally, these taxes became too burdensome and many evaded them by smuggling, shipping, and selling metal to Asia, among other things.

The "Royal Fifth" was changed to the "Royal Tenth" after the Spanish realized what was actually happening. Over time and around the world, the price of silver fell, due to the vast increases in supply from the Americas. This can be seen through the increase in the gold-to-silver ratio, depicted in the chart below. For example, in England, wages increased to 4.1 grams from 3.4 grams over the period 1600-1650 from 1550-1599. Each 50-year period, the same thing happened through 1800. Wages increased to 5.6 grams, 7.0 grams, and then to 8.3 grams by 1800.

---

[31]Cyrille Jubert, *Silver Throughout History*, p. 80.

GSR Over History	GSR
Menes, 3200 B.C.	2.5
Egypt, 2700 B.C.	9
Mesopotamia, 2700 B.C.	6
Egypt, 2000 B.C.	2
Egypt, 1000 B.C.	10
King Croseus, Lydia, 550 B.C.	13.33
Persia under Darius	13
Plato, 445 B.C.	12
Xenophon	11.66
Menander 341 B.C.	10
Greece, 333 B.C.	15
Greece, 300 B.C.	10
Rome, 207 B.C.	14.5
Rome, 189 B.C.	10
Rome, Julius Ceasar 40 B.C.	7.5
Rome, Claudius	12.5
Constantine The Great	10.5
Theodosian Code	14.4
Medieval England	11.1
Medieval Italy, 1275-1300	8
Medieval Italy, 1301-1325	15
Medieval Italy, 1326-1345	9
Spain, 1497, Edict of Medina	10.07
China: 1400-1600	6.7
Japan: 1400-1550	4.8
Japan: 1550-1650	9.6
France: 1500-1650	13.9
Germany, 1500	10.05
1600-1620	12.1
1700-1720	15.1
1800-1840	15.3
1850 Japan	5

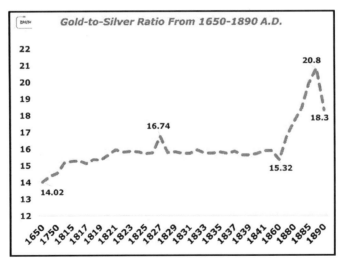

The Mississippi Bubble—A Look at Early Experiments with Paper Money in the Western World

John Law was behind the first widespread use of fiat money, defined at the time as inconvertible paper money or paper money backed by the nation's land. But in reality it was backed by nothing except an empty promise. Law, who obviously lacked an understanding of the basics of monetary theory, thought increasing the supply of money and credit would boost trade and increase employment and therefore production. Law was of the mindset that the hard-money tradition was entirely incorrect in terms of efficiency and soundness. Anne Robert Jacques Turgot would destroy Law on an intellectual level years later, because of Law's theory of money—that is, money just being a government creation, having no intrinsic value as a metal. The sole function was to be a medium of exchange and anything but a store of value. The following is from Turgot and is mentioned above but important to understand and is just one of many criticisms relating to Law:

"Thus, then we come to the constitution of gold and silver as money and universal money, and that without any arbitrary convention among men, without the intervention of any law, but only by the nature of things. They are not, as people imagine, signs of value; they have a value themselves. If they are capable of being the measure and pledge of other values, they have this property in common with all other articles that have a value in commerce. They differ only because being at once divisible, more unalterable, and easier to transport than the other commodities, it is more convenient to employ them to measure and represent the values[32]."

Our contention is that John Law lacked the ability to differentiate cause and effect. He went so far as to assure both England and France that an increased supply of money and credit wouldn't cause any ill effects, such as consumer price inflation. In simpler terms, his thinking was so circular that he believed monetary inflation didn't equate to price inflation[33].

Another criticism of Law's monetary theory is that inflating the money supply would lead to an outflow of gold and silver, per Gresham's Law, equating to a negative balance of trade. Furthering our contention of bordering on lunacy is Law's response to this criticism; he declares that increasing the money supply expands employment and therefore output, increasing exports and leading to a positive balance of trade with gold and silver flowing into the country. All strong economic principles can and should be brought to extremes, and reinforcing the action has the same reaction. In this case, constantly increasing the supply of money and credit should lead to a nation quickly becoming the dominant economy of the world and far and away the wealthiest. Furthermore, Law equated low interest rates with prosperity. However, once again he illustrated his vast lack of economic knowledge by confusing cause with effect.

Holland at the time was on a hard-money standard while also sporting low interest rates. Law took notice of the Dutch prosperity, high savings rate, and higher standards of living, and determined they were a result of low interest rates, when in fact this thinking was completely backwards. He also dismissed that Dutch prosperity had resulted from high production and export, which in turn brought about an influx of silver

---

[32] Anne Robert Jacques Turgot, *Reflections on the Formation and the Distribution of Riches*, p.39.
[33] Inflation, truly defined as an unnecessary increase in the supply of money and credit, whereas the definition used today is most commonly defined as a general increase in consumer goods. The latter is actually a symptom of inflation.

and gold coinage. Law looked at the latter as being the cause, not the effect, of prosperity.

Law was soon appointed as the head of France's central bank, after an outright failure instituting his policies in England. Prior to this, Law headed the Banque Generale in 1716, which had a monopoly on bank notes that could be redeemed in silver. Of course, this quickly ended and he also became the head of the Mississippi Company and director general of French Finances. Notes issued by the Mississippi Company were said to be backed by undeveloped land in North America, hence the "Mississippi Company." Law's new bank was solely responsible for the first modern boom-bust episode known as the "Mississippi Bubble."

The supply of money and credit ballooned quickly, followed by rising consumer and commodity prices (which tend to lag inflation for a brief period) as well as a remarkable and abnormal increase in the stock market. This was followed by a "bust," or inflationary depression, in 1720. Richard Cantillon[34], Law's partner and skeptic in the Mississippi Company, was widely considered the founder of modern economics in his book, *Essay on Economic Theory* (American translation). Cantillon was a brilliant man, realizing beforehand what John Law was going to do and the results of his actions. He knew the theory of money just as well as Turgot did (and in fact Turgot was influenced by Cantillon's book), illustrated by the following quote:

"Gold & Silver were highly valued before they were used as money. They hold many advantages such as durability, divisibility, transportability, and homogeneity. These are the reasons which led gold and silver to be chosen as money, not 'fancy' or common consent[35]."

It was during the Mississippi Bubble that the term "millionaire" was coined. Naturally, Richard Cantillon exploited the fact he knew a boom would occur followed by a corresponding bust. He rode the stock market up and exited early, lending out his money to various individuals with an inflation premium. When these loans were repatriated they included an effective interest rate of up to 55%.

It may be worth noting that many in the mainstream consider Adam Smith the father of economics; however, if you read Richard Cantillon's book, *Essay of Economics in General*, and then read Adam Smith's *Wealth of Nations*, it is very apparent that Adam Smith took quite a bit from Cantillon. Several decades earlier, Cantillon had first developed the main ideas that Smith presented in *Wealth of Nations*. In short, Richard Cantillon was the founding father of free market economics, although very few realize this.

---

[34]Cantillon strongly voiced his opposition to the enacted policies but realized he could be more effective trying to limit the damage instead of being ousted from monetary affairs altogether.
[35]Richard Cantillon, *Essay on Economic Theory*, p. 103

Chapter 2: A Monetary History of Silver in America

The U.S. Constitution: Notable Sections and Articles

Article 1

Section 10: No State shall enter into any Treaty, Alliance, or Confederation; grant Letters of Marque and Reprisal; coin Money**; emit Bills of Credit; make any Thing but gold and silver Coin a Tender in Payment of Debts;** pass any Bill of Attainder, ex post facto Law, or Law impairing the Obligation of Contracts, or grant any Title of Nobility.

Section 8: Provides **Congress** with the right to coin Money, regulate the Value thereof, and of foreign Coin, and fix the Standard of Weights and Measures;

Section 8: To provide for the Punishment of counterfeiting the Securities and current Coin of the United States.

Have the Federal and State Governments been in violation of the Federal Constitution since the signing of the document? Beginning with Article I, section 10, it states: no STATE shall enter into any Treaty…..coin Money, emit Bills of Credit; make any Thing but gold and silver Coin a Tender in Payments of Debts. Thus the several states at the founding were restricted but did this wording leave some room for the Federal Government to manipulate the meaning?

In order for anything but gold and silver to serve as the <u>only</u> mediums of exchange would Article 1, Section 10, need to be amended? This question has been debated any questioned in court by many and the result has been an upholding of the "legal tender law."

Certainly within the confines of the U.S. gold and silver coins minted by the U.S. Treasury are silver valid in payment. However, there is a problem with this since the amount of "dollars" (read Federal Reserve Notes) varies on a daily basis whereas the coins themselves are only accepted officially at stamped value in "official" transactions. For example to buy a roll of stamps at a U.S. post office with a silver eagle (one troy ounce 0.999 fine silver) it would be accepted at the stamped value of "One Dollar" when in fact the market price could be near $20 Federal Reserve Notes.

To think about this even more deeply the current minted silver coin is exactly one troy ounce, whereas the 1792 coinage act defines a weight of silver as a dollar which is 371.25 grains and is closer to 3/4 troy ounce. Simply stated the modern department of the Treasury clearly ignored or did not even know this simple fact.

We can then move on to Article 1, Section 8 of the Constitution which provides Congress the right to "coin Money", not print money. You cannot coin paper! The Federal Constitution provided Congress with the right to coin Money, regulate the Value thereof, and of foreign Coin, and fix the Standard of Weights and Measures. This power was never granted to a Central Bank.

For a full discussion of the above matter let us suggest reading Pieces of Eight by Dr. Edwin Viera on what the legalities of the monetary system of the U.S. is compared to what the foundational agreements stated.

Bimetallism and Gresham's Law

Bimetallism, while not even known by many who advocate a commodity-backed monetary system, is the most ideal monetary system. (Some could argue trimetallism). If we look back in history, bimetallism has a track record of one failure after the next; however, every instance of this, including that used in the U.S. early in its infancy, implemented a bimetallic standard **incorrectly**, as it were as if Gresham's Law was understood by no one. In fact, the problem throughout history was **fixing** a ratio between silver and gold.

Each time this fixed ratio was applied it had to be assumed the market was static, but markets are incredibly dynamic. Thus this implies that the gold-to-silver ratio is ever-changing. It can then be deduced that a bimetallic standard on a fixed ratio could never work for long periods of time and inevitably would cause Gresham's Law to come into effect. Monetary history bears this out as the undervalued monetary unit would flow out to other countries or be hoarded by individuals, while the overvalued monetary unit would circulate in the economy. The U.S. was unable to maintain a bimetallic standard precisely because the government fixed silver and gold to one another.

Why a bimetallic standard, not a monometallic standard? As we've seen throughout the past 5,000 years, the market has chosen this standard more often than a monometallic standard. The instances of a monometallic standard have always been fiat based or made legal tender by the government.

It is outside the scope of this book, but having a monometallic standard that is a gold standard with the banks in control of that one metal, history bears out that the system eventually morphs into a paper-backed "gold" system and eventually into a completely unbacked currency.

Bimetallism also provides a larger monetary unit (gold) or paper redeemable in specie and a smaller monetary unit (silver) or paper redeemable in specie. (Copper could be added in a trimetallic system). The former would be used primarily in large purchases and world trade while the latter would be used in everyday commerce.

While a monometallic standard would provide for a sound monetary system (assuming no fractional reserve banking), a bimetallic standard puts some tighter checks and balances on the monetary system. In the case of a monetary system that government involves itself with, it could inflate notes redeemable for specie; per

Gresham's Law, one metal would be driven out of circulation and this would be noticed by the public. The logical deduction can be made that an outflow of specie which causes the gold-to-silver ratio to become detached from the world market ratio must always be a result of government intervention.

This is because the effects of inflation cause all commodity prices to rise, but not in lockstep with one another. There are several albeit other negligible checks/balances that bimetallism would provide under various scenarios (a worldwide or multi-countrywide sound monetary system versus a single-country sound monetary system). And although minor, they are nonetheless superior, precisely because the market has often chosen a bimetallic standard only to witness the banking establishment move on to a gold-only standard in favor of gold and leaving the (public) silver owners losing purchasing power due to the banks' pronouncement.

Bimetallism, assuming no government intervention in the monetary system, would be implemented by first defining a "Dollar" as a specific weight of silver or gold, not both. The metal not defined as a weight per "Dollar" would then freely-float against the other metal, thereby establishing a parallel standard. This would allow both metals to continuously circulate without having to worry about Gresham's Law driving the undervalued money from circulation. The ability for one metal to freely-float against another would cause the ratio of one metal against another to remain aligned with the world market ratio.

Silver and Gold in the United States (Revolutionary War-Present Day)

In the Colonial era, as the economy grew, silver and gold became more common as a monetary unit replacing beaver fur, wampum, rice, and especially tobacco. Massachusetts issued fiat money in 1690 and this was the first time since the Chinese back in the S'ung and Yuan dynasties. (There were instances such as the South Sea Bubble, Mississippi Bubble, and pre-revolutionary France where a fiat paper money was issued but was purportedly backed by real estate.) As the government issued this fiat paper, it made a pledge to ensure paper would be the accepted medium of exchange: it would redeem paper in silver or gold from tax revenues and these issuances of more fiat would end in just a few years. This pledge amounted to be mere words, as in 1691, the Massachusetts government declared it had "fallen far short" of its issuance and proceeded to issue €40,000 (the U.S, was still part of Great Britain) to repay its debt. In 1692, the government made paper money compulsory and the natural disappearance of silver occurred, with concurrent inflation.

To put this into perspective in 1690, before the "orgy" of fiat money printing began, €200,000 redeemable in specie as silver was available in New England but just over two decades later, New England issued €240,000 paper but silver had nearly completely disappeared from circulation.

This inflation continued and drove out all the silver from circulation, so the government reacted by stating the new issuances were to be backed by real estate.

Eventually the government had inflated the money supply to such a level it resulted in dramatic consumer price inflation, which propelled the people to begin to turn against paper money.

This experiment of inflating fiat money spread throughout the colonies and resulted in numerous boom-bust periods, which eventually led to Great Britain prohibiting any more paper issuances in 1751. This prohibition was followed by a further extension, and in 1764, the New England colonies resumed payment of silver and retired the inflated money supply.

The Revolutionary War: The First U.S. Fiat Money Collapses in the Continental

Inconvertible fiat paper money funded the Revolutionary War with no pledge of redemption but the promise (broken) of retiring this money in seven years. Prior to the Revolution, the money supply was estimated at $12,000,000. Even before the first full year (1775), $6 million had been printed, amounting to a 50% increase in the money supply. This fiat money was known as the "Continental" and was inflated, continuing from 1775 through spring of 1781, as follows:

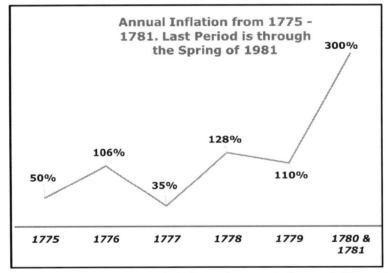

Note: The Continental did not hyper-inflate, falling short of the widely held definition.

Some historians suggest that Great Britain had a hand in increasing the money supply by counterfeiting the Continental, and although this could be the case, the fact remains that counterfeiting by legal or illegal means results in disaster at some point. With this event fresh in their minds, the founding fathers were well aware that a fiat monetary system wasn't sustainable.

Thomas Jefferson was held in high regard by President Washington and asked Jefferson whether the Constitution allowed congress to create a national bank (central bank). He told Washington "No" in addition to his belief that a central bank would assume powers not granted to it, violating the 10th amendment. It was Jefferson's strong belief in private property rights and civil liberties, in addition to being close friends with economist Jean-Baptiste Say. Jefferson ardently opposed a national bank altogether that enabled him to accurately predict a central bank would assume powers not granted to it.

While Thomas Jefferson was a strong believer in the principles outlined in the Constitution, he was also very aware of the severe problems which could arise.
"Our Country is too large to have all of its affairs directed by a single government" and if ever the powers of the state governments should become concentrated in the general government "it would become the most corrupt government on earth.[36]"

While parts or the Constitution as a whole are studied in law schools today as well as in some undergraduate and graduate classes, the discussion of whether paper money (which the Constitution forbids) is seldom discussed. Oddly enough, the standard unit/money of account of the United States remains both constitutionally and legally the "Dollar," defined as 371.25 grains of fine silver! This fact, however, is conveniently overlooked by the monetary authorities and the financial system at large.

Coinage Act of 1792

Alexander Hamilton recommended Congress pass the Coinage Act of 1792, which was enacted. While this only established a de facto bimetallic standard, the act illustrates that the U.S. was founded on a silver standard. This act did put a bimetallic standard in place, in which a **fixed gold** (24.75 grains of fine gold) to silver (371.25 grains of fine silver) ratio of 15:1, but a dollar of silver, was forever undeniably fixed and established as the standard money of account in the United States of America. This corresponded to the gold-to-silver ratio as determined by the market in the 1790s. But the prices of both metals were constantly changing; therefore, fixing the ratio was a poor idea. Due to the massive increase in the annual mine production of silver in Mexico over the following three decades, the market ratio of gold-to-silver had to increase.

In 1760, the market ratio was just 14:1 but the following took place: The extra mine supply caused the market ratio of silver against gold to fall (or the gold-to-silver ratio to rise) as the market ratio was 15.75 (by 1805) but the fixed ratio had remained unchanged, causing gold to disappear from circulation.

From 1810 to 1834, only silver coin circulated in the U.S. At the time the U.S. allowed foreign silver coins to circulate in the economy and fractional Spanish silver coins tended to weigh the same or more as U.S. coinage except for fractional dollar coins but traded at face value, which became significantly overvalued (half-dollars, quarter-dollars, dimes, and half-dimes). In other words, American fractional dollar coins were undervalued relative to their counterparts in the U.S. fractional dollar coins. The Spanish silver fractional coins served as the major U.S. currency, as the U.S. silver fractional coins were driven out of circulation.

---

[36] Jefferson to Gideon Granger, August 13th 1800, Thomas Jefferson: Writings, p. 1079

The First Bank of the United States: 1791-1811

Alexander Hamilton argued for a central bank but not based upon an understanding of free market economics, specifically money. It was as if he had put the knowledge of John Law's money fiasco in England completely out of his mind. History is replete with those who "think" their plan will be executed in a superior manner or a new regulation will prevent the problem from arising again. But history is clear—a bad idea no matter how well intended is still a bad idea. Further, as Albert Einstein defined insanity is *"doing the same thing over and over, expecting a different result."*

This led to the creation of the first central bank in the U.S., the First Bank of the United States, in 1791. The rationale Hamilton used was that there was a shortage of silver and gold money, further illustrating a complete ignorance regarding basic economic principles. The central bank of course did what one would expect, that being to inflate the money supply by printing more paper money. Economist Murray Rothbard sums up the First Bank of the U.S. in this way:

"The Bank of the United States promptly fulfilled its inflationary potential by issuing millions of dollars in paper money and demand deposits, pyramiding on top of $2 million in specie. The Bank of the United States invested heavily in loans to the United States government. In addition to $2 million invested in the assumption of pre-existing long-term debt assumed by the new federal government, the Bank of the United States engaged in massive temporary lending to the government, which reached $6.2 million by 1796. The result of the outpouring of credit and paper money by the new Bank of the United States was an inflationary rise in prices. Thus, wholesale prices rose from an index of 85 in 1791 to a peak of 146 in 1796, an increase of 72 percent. In addition, speculation boomed in government securities and real estate values were driven upward. Pyramiding on top of the Bank of the United States' expansion and aggravating the paper money expansion and the inflation was a flood of newly created commercial banks. Whereas there were only three commercial banks before the founding of the United States, and only four by the establishment of the Bank of the United States, eight new banks were founded shortly thereafter, in 1791 and 1792, and 10 more by 1796[37]."

Luckily, the bank's charter expired after its initial 20-year term. Just the establishment of the First Bank of the Unites States (central bank) brought up criticism, especially from the Jeffersonians. Their contention was that the Constitution gave no power to the Federal Government to establish a bank in the first place. This, however, did not hold up in court as *McCulloch v. Maryland* (1819) sided with the Hamiltonian interpretation, in that the Constitution "implied" the Federal Government had the power for carrying out national goals. The total number of state banks reached 117 by 1811, by the time the First Bank's charter expired. When it came time for re-chartering of the

---

[37] U.S. Department of Commerce, "Historical Statistics of the United States, Colonial Times to 1957," pp. 116, 119-121.

Bank of the United States, it was narrowly defeated by one vote each in the House and Senate.

As is typical during times of war, there came a significant inflation of the money supply. The previous war saw the currency collapse in the "Continental." The War of 1812 saw inflation of the money supply occur and the corresponding increases in goods and services. The significant monetary inflation resulted due to a suspension of specie payments or the ability of paper money to be exchanged by silver and gold and fractional reserve banking. The U.S. Government borrowed heavily to finance the war. Interestingly Maryland passed a compulsory par law in 1819, forbidding the exchange of specie (hard money) for bank notes.

The Second Bank of the United States 1816-1836
Andrew Jackson (Old Hickory) vs. Nicholas Biddle:

"Finally, for the first time in American history, and for one of the very few times in human history, the people had chosen one of their own to govern them."
–On Andrew Jackson Being Elected President

Instead of following the path of sound money in 1816, which was championed by the Old Republicans, the Democratic-Republicans turned back to the old Federalist path and created a new central bank. The Second Bank of the United States started with a national paper currency redeemable in specie (at least initially).

It seemed the central bank's goal was to support that of the state banks on its inflationary endeavors, as opposed to cracking down on these policies. Politics prevailed as the Second Bank of the United States lacked the discipline to insist on payment of its notes from state banks, piling up a large balance against them at the central bank to the tune of $2,400,000.

Many influential people at the time had stock in the state banks and the public in general were motivated to keep the banks in an easy money policy to originate additional loans. The Second Bank never held more than $2,500,000 in specie, while the total notes and deposits amounted to $21,800,000, or an 11.46% reserve ratio. Again, embarking on another significant round of inflation of money and credit, state banks rose from 232 in 1816 to 338 in 1818 (a 45.69% increase).

In just two years, the money supply ballooned to a whopping $90,000,000 from $67,000,000. However, in mid-1818, both the U.S. Government and the Second Bank realized what the consequences would be, following this prolonged period of money and credit expansion. This caused the Second Bank of the Unites States to embark on a series of money and credit contractions. The bank forced a curtailment of loans and contractions of credit in both the southern and western states. It also began to purchase a million dollars of specie (silver and gold) from abroad and ousted what would be referred to today as the chairman of the central bank, William Jones. This brought about a widespread economic depression, causing banks to fail and private banks to become much more prudent when originating loans, as well as suspending specie payments in the majority of the country.

The number of banks initially remained rather flat, followed by a steep decrease over the following three years. In mid-1819, there were 341 banks, falling to 267 by mid-1822. The national supply of money contracted significantly, inclusive of the U.S. Treasury contracting its note balances from $8,810,000 to $0 by 1819. In short, the money supply fell over 28%.

This contraction in the supply of money resulted in a large wave of defaults and bankruptcies of various businesses and manufacturers, and all of the misallocated capital from investments made during the "boom" period was cleansed from the system. This, however, was healthy for the economy in the medium and long-term as it corrected the imbalances that prevailed in the economy due to Nicholas Biddle of the Second Bank of The United States inflating the supply of money and credit.

Second Bank of The U.S.	Specie	Money & Credit	Expansion/(-Contraction)
1817	$2,500,000	$2,600,000	-
1818	$2,360,000	$21,800,000	$19,200,000
1819	$2,360,000	$11,500,000	($10,300,000)
State Banks	**Specie**	**Money & Credit**	**Expansion/(-Contraction)**
1817		$64,700,000	$38,400,000
1818		$72,200,000	$7,500,000
1819		$62,700,000	($9,500,000)
Entire Banking System	**Specie**	**Money & Credit**	**Expansion/(-Contraction)**
1817		$67,300,000	$27,400,000
1818		$103,510,000	$36,210,000
1819		$74,200,000	($29,310,000)

[38]

The Rise of the Jacksonian Movement and Hard Money in the U.S.

After the successful victory of the revolutionary war, chronic economic problems persisted due to the lack of any uniform currency as well as protectionist trade measures between various states. This led to the 1787 Constitutional Convention. During the Constitutional Convention of 1787, paper money was destroyed, at least for a short period of time. The Constitution stripped states of having any monetary authority except that of naming a legal tender, which was restricted to silver and gold. Silver was preferred to gold because it was the most common medium of exchange in commerce.

Coinage Act of 1834

Each dollar coin contained 41% of a dollar of silver while accounting for the silver at the full constitutional standard. The gold-to-silver ratio became too low in the years

---

[38]Murray Rothbard, *A History of Money and Banking in the United States: The Colonial Era to World War II*, pp. 87-89.

leading up to 1834 and in that year, it was adjusted to reflect the world market ratio of 16:1. The Coinage Act of 1834 brought with it two companion coinage acts[39]:
1. Being hard money or "sound money" advocates, the Jacksonians thought specie was specie and saw absolutely no reason foreign gold or silver coins should not circulate in the exact same way as American-minted coins.
2. A dollar as defined by the Coinage Act of 1792 is a weight of 371.25 grains of fine silver (.999 fine). This definition allowed for a specific weight not a particular mint mark. One other important section of the Coinage Act of 1792, is section 19:

*"And be it further enacted, That if any of the gold or silver coins which shall be struck or coined at the said mint shall be debased or made worse as to the proportion of fine gold or fine silver therein contained, or shall be of less weight or value than the same ought to be pursuant to the directions of this act, through the default or with the connivance of any of the officers or persons who shall be employed at the said mint, for the purpose of profit or gain, or otherwise with a fraudulent intent, and if any of the said officers or persons shall embezzle any of the metals which shall at any time be committed to their charge for the purpose of being coined, or any of the coins which shall be struck or coined at the said mint, every such officer or person who shall commit any or either of the said offences, shall be deemed guilty of felony, and **shall suffer death**."*

Andrew Jackson ran on the platform of Liberty, following a Jeffersonian tradition. A stern believer in personal and economic freedoms, Jackson wanted the Federal Government to be extremely limited in scope. He believed the government did not have the right to embark on reckless spending such as public works as the Constitution prohibited. Jackson opposed the national debt entirely and in 1835 managed to pay it down in full. Furthermore, Jackson pushed the Federal Government to give up ownership of public lands, which is true free market thinking. Lastly, he believed the government had no business meddling in monetary policy, which he thought should be managed by the marketplace.

Jackson managed to accomplish something no other president has been able to do, abolish the central bank. Jackson believed the country was being controlled by a congressional-financial-bureaucratic complex in which the needs and concerns of the people were ignored and benefited the political and other elites[40]. He articulated that Second Bank of the Unites States (the modern day central bank) was "the embodiment of unfair privilege."
"I was aware that the Bank question would be disapproved by all the sordid and interested who prized self-interest more than the perpetuity of our liberty, and the blessings of a free republican government. I foresaw the powerful effect, produced by this moneyed aristocracy, upon the purity of elections, and of legislations; that

---
[39] Martin, *Metallism*, p. 436.
[40] Jon Meacham, American Lion, p. 120

it was daily gaining strength, and by its secret operations was adding to it. I have brought it before the people and I have confidence that they will do their duty.[41]"

The Coinage Act of 1837 changed the standard fineness of both silver and gold coins to 90%, which had the effect of lowering the weight of a dollar coin while maintaining the weight of silver at 371.25 grains and a slight increase in the weight of fine gold to 232.5 grains from 232 grains. This has a small impact on the gold-to-silver ratio but not enough to be noticed as the ratio fell to 15.988 from 16.002.

The Gold Rush in California and a scarcity of silver in early 1849 prompted the Coinage Act of 1849. Congress provided for the minting of double eagles ($20 pieces), weighing .9675 of fine gold and gold "dollar" coins, each to be the value of one dollar. Each gold dollar contained 23.2 grains of fine gold (.0483) troy ounces.

The Coinage Acts of 1853 and 1857

While most, including Congress, continued to think gold would continue to appreciate against silver due to significant gold discoveries in California and Australia, the opposite happened. The ratio fell to 15.7:1 and silver was forced out of circulation because the market value of bullion was greater than the legal tender value. The world market ratio continued to fall, reaching 15.5:1, which led individuals to hoard it and arbitrageurs to melt (silver dollars) and export silver. The Coinage Act of 1857 stated foreign gold and silver coins would no longer be considered legal tender.

The primary driver pushing silver out of circulation was a sudden influx of gold when the California Gold Rush caused a surge in annual world mine supply, the majority of which occurred in the latter half of the 1840s through the first few years of the 1850s. This, in turn, wasn't accounted for in the fixed gold-to-silver ratio (as seen in the falling ratios in the second chart below) and Gresham's Law went into action, driving silver out of circulation due to the undervaluation while keeping gold in circulation (overvalued on a relative basis).

Annual Gold Production in $'s		Increase
1720-1830's	$12,800,000	-
1840's	$38,200,000	198.44%
1850's	$139,000,000	263.87%
1853 (Peak Until 1890's)	$155,000,000	11.51%

Market Ratios	
170-1830's	15.97
1850 Average	15.7
1851 Average	15.46
1853-1860	15.32

---

[41] Ibid, pp. 121-122.

While it could be argued that the U.S. never had sound money since its founding, the monetary policies the Jacksonian's put in place were as close as the U.S. came to a factually sound monetary system. Although Andrew Jackson desired a sound money policy, he was unable to abolish fractional reserve banking during his time in office.

In reaction to the experience from 1819, there arose the Jacksonian Movement and the corresponding war on the central bank. This movement was exemplified by absolute dedication to both hard money and the abolition of fractional reserve banking. The Jacksonian movement (which included two terms as Jackson holding office followed by Martin Van Buren for one term) further deplored the national debt.

Andrew Jackson in particular was a hard money convert and wanted nothing less than 100% reserve banking. The Jacksonian's could be considered libertarians, favoring free enterprise and free markets. The Jacksonian's would today be considered minarchists, in that they favored very minimal government in everyday life, both at the federal and state levels. In other words, they **believed the government only need serve one purpose, acknowledging and protecting private property rights**!

When it came to monetary policy, the Jacksonian's believed in a complete separation of government from the banking system altogether. They were knowledgeable regarding the consequences of fiat money and would accept nothing less than 100% reserve banking, backed entirely by specie. The Jacksonian's faced a huge obstacle to reform the current monetary system at that time into that which the forefathers had directly outlined in the Constitution and those ideals held by the Jeffersonians.

For most of the second decade of the 19th century, the U.S. essentially had a one party system, the Federalists, adopted by both Democrats and Republicans. Martin Van Buren (successor to Andrew Jackson) was in large part responsible for the founding of the new Democratic Party (which would be considered the libertarian or Tea Party Republicans today, not to be confused with what are socialist democrats of today).

Van Buren was quickly converted by the Jacksonian's to free market economics founded on sound money. He had paved the way for the *New Democrats* by solidifying past alliances with the Old Republicans of Virginia among others but needed a charismatic leader in order to have a fighting chance at displacing incumbent John Quincy Adams, and he chose none other than Andrew Jackson. Jackson, first elected president in 1828, set out to accomplish the following in his two terms:

- Significantly decrease tariffs
- Pay down the gross federal debt
- Reduce government programs and enact various parts of the Jacksonians free market economic program
- **Most importantly: Abolish the central bank and fractional reserve banking**

Jackson was successful at accomplishing all his goals except ridding the banking system of <u>fractional reserve banking</u>. He viewed the central bank as the major source of inflation[42] and not, as many think, to allow the state banks to initiate inflationary expansions of their own. The first step was to abolish the central bank and then deal with ridding the state banks of fractional reserve banking.

Nicholas Biddle, the modern day central bank chairman in 1831, filed for renewal of the bank's charter. Jackson reacted aggressively, vetoing the bill passed by the National Republicans and the non-Jacksonian Democrats, which Congress then failed to pass it over his veto. Re-elected in 1832, President Andrew Jackson wasted no time to begin breaking the back of the central bank, when in 1833, he removed the Treasury deposits from the central banks and placed them into a plethora of state banks throughout the country. He further spread these deposits into 91 state banks by the end of 1836[43].

Historians, for the most part, blame Jackson for the 52% rise in wholesale prices from April 1834 to early 1837 and illogically conclude that the boom during this period occurred precisely because Jackson abolished central banking. But that wasn't the case in the least; price inflation[44] really began earlier, reaching a low in mid-1830, then proceeding to rise 20.7% in the following three years[45].

Total Money Supply	
1830	$109,000,000
1833	$159,000,000
3-Year CAGR	15.30%
3-Year Percentage Increase	45.87%

Second Bank of The United States	
1830	$29,000,000
1832	$42,100,000
2-Year CAGR	20.49%
2-Year Percentage Increase	45.17%

---

[42]Murray Rothbard, *A History of Money and Banking in the United States in the United States: The Colonial Era to World War II*, p. 92.
[43]Hammond, *Banks and Politics*, p. 420.
[44]Inflation properly defined as an increase in the supply of money and credit. Consumer Price Inflation/Price Inflation merely means a rise in consumer prices. It is therefore a symptom of inflation, not the definition of.
[45]Hugh Rockoff, *Money, Prices, and Banks in the Jacksonian Era, In the Reinterpretation of American History*, pp. 448-458.

End of Year	Money Supply	Specie	Reserve Ratio	Proportion of Money Held As Specie
1820	$85	$41	32%	24%
1822	$81	$32	21%	23%
1824	$88	$32	27%	13%
1826	$108	$32	20%	12%
1828	$114	$31	18%	11%
1830	**$114**	**$32**	**23%**	**6%**
1832	**$150**	**$31**	**16%**	**5%**
1834	**$172**	**$51**	**27%**	**4%**
1836	$276	$73	16%	13%
1838	$240	$87	23%	18%
1839	$215	$83	20%	23%

[46]

This rampant influx caused the supply of money to swell from $85m in 1820 to an enormous $240m ($155m growth well of the money supply) or an increase of 182%. The prevailing consumer price index bottomed in mid-1830 at 82, increasing to 99 in 1832. In the first chart above, the total money supply can be seen expanding by an average of 15.30%. But what was to blame for the continuing increase in the money supply from $150,000,000 in 1832 to a whopping $276,000,000 just four years later?

One might assume that the reserve ratio of 16% was lowered, but that wasn't the case[47]. Instead, it was a remarkable influx of specie into the nation's banks[48]. This inflow of specie was so expansive that by 1833 it was just $31,000,000, increasing to an astounding $73,000,000 four years later, or an increase of almost 142% (23.88% four-year compound annual growth rate).

It is important to point out that inflation is an increase in the "money" supply even if it is sound money, as noted in the previous paragraph. During this period, the general public became more risk adverse, choosing to hold 13% of its money in specie, compared to just 5% prior to this period. This was because banks increased their notes and deposits at the same rate as the increase of specie flowing into the banking system as a whole. Some of this would have been prevented if Jackson had been able to move more rapidly in returning the banking system to a 100%-specie basis, as he could have used the influx of specie to ease the monetary contraction that is natural when returning to pure specie money. But logically and constitutionally, once a standard is set, it cannot be changed. That simply is the nature of a standard. Dr. Edwin Vieira sorts out this confusion in his classic legal-monetary history of the United States, *Pieces of Eight*.

---

[46] Peter Temin, The Jacksonian Economy, p. 71
[47] Temin, *The Jacksonian Economy*, pp. 68-74.
[48] Result of two factors—large influx of silver coin from Mexico and reduction in exports to the Orient in favor of opium. Influx from Mexico due to Gresham's Law and paper money inflation. Also attributed to possible increases in mining productivity but a hard contention to make because the inflow stopped permanently in 1837. –Murray Rothbard, *A History of Money and Banking in The United States The Colonial Era to World War II*, p. 98.

Pursuant to the Constitution, Congress in the Coinage Act of 1792 set the standard at 371.25 grains per "dollar" of silver, and regulated the value of the gold coin according to that standard. Later coinage acts only serve to buttress this conclusion, since all but two (the 1870 and 1985 acts) conform to the same standard, and even the other two acts do not purport to alter the ancient dollar standard.

Congress's confusion is aggravated by the public's confusion in referring to the "price" of silver in "dollars." A "dollar" of silver is not, strictly speaking, a price, but a weight: 371.25 grains of fine silver, or 1.2929 dollars to the troy ounce. To quote the price of silver in dollars confuses the unit of measure ("dollar") with the thing measured (a fixed quantity of silver).

The "price" of silver in dollars makes about as much sense as the pricing of milk in quarts. Legally, the quotation of silver ought to be turned exactly upside down, for the real question is not the price of silver, but the price of paper money. The price of Federal Reserve bank notes constantly fluctuates and depreciates. A "dollar" of silver still contains the same 371.25 grains of fine silver it contained in 1792, while the Federal Reserve Note, to put it most charitably, is nothing but an empty promise[49].

Martin Van Buren, Andrew Jackson's successor, although not as popular as his predecessor, championed the same ideologies, notably that of liberty, minimizing the size and reach of government and that of sound money. He helped rid the political economy of "The Era of Good Feelings" which arose following the war of 1812. This era was very corrupt and essentially single-party rule.

In July 1836, Jackson issued a "Specie Circular" requiring payment for public lands be in silver and/or gold. The Democratic Party had two factions regarding the Specie Circular. One on side, Democrats advocated for a complete separation of the national government and all banks, which is of the free market capitalism mentality. On the other side Democrats believed credit expansion promoted economic growth and maintained the relationship between government and banks was a necessity.

Just two months in office, a major financial panic arose bringing the Specie Circular debate to the forefront. Van Buren obviously sided with sound money and maintained "all former attempts on part of the Government" to "assume the management of domestic or foreign exchange" always "proved injurious." What really made Van Buren stand out during this period was his call for a total and complete separation of bank and state through an Independent Treasury, making the most fundamental requirement being government hold all monetary balance in specie (silver and gold).

Many thought by and hoped that as the now independent treasury via eliminating government support for bank notes (paper money) would drive them out of circulation entirely, which in effect would make fractional reserve banking much more difficult.

Martin Van Buren had to deal with the Panic of 1837. He did increase government expenditures in 1837 to $37.20m from just $30.90m the prior year but over his one

---

[49] James Blanchard and Franklin Sanders, Silver Bonanza, p. 18,

term as president, spending declined by 21% to $24.3m in 1840[50]. At the end of four years, Van Buren was able to avoid heavy debt financing, with total national debt of just $5m. This was in the face of his unwillingness to raise taxes[51].

What is interesting to note here is that the U.S. went on to have an economic contraction during the period of 1839-1843, and this is more in line with the natural order as it generates the liquidation of unsound investments, debts, and banks. Deflation over this period mirrored that of the U.S. in 1929-1933. The key take-away from this is that the U.S. Government greatly exacerbated the contraction now known as "The Great Depression," which could have been much similar to that the period of 1839-1843.

Year	Money Supply	Consumer Prices	Gross Investment	Consumption	GDP
1839-1843	-34%	-42%	-23%	21%	16%
1929-1933	-27%	-31%	-91%	-19%	-30%

[52]

Although many blame deflation for the magnitude and duration of the Great Depression, it was actually the central bank and federal government's attempt to fight this deflation that greatly exacerbated the economic contraction. In this way, unsound investments and economic imbalances were not able to liquidated and cleansed from the system. The contraction in 1839-1843, was not met inflationary monetary nor fiscal policy, therefore the natural cleansing of mal-investments was able to occur and the economy recovered rather quickly in addition to the economic contraction being much less violent.

Free Banking Era

The "Free Banking Era" or "Wildcat Banking" prior to the Civil War has in fact been misinterpreted by most monetary scholars. Fractional reserve banking (legalized counterfeiting) was possible to the <u>degree each bank bought state debt</u>. In other words, these bonds were considered the reserve base upon which each bank could pyramid an amount of money.

So the more state debt a bank owned, the more they could expand the number of bank notes issued. This was an enormous moral hazard because banks could originate more loans and make more money if they monetized state debt.

But this was not the case, due to the market's inherent self-regulating actions, or "market process." If a bank did engage in fractional reserve banking and if any of those

---
[50] John Denson, Reassessing The Presidency, p. 188
[51] Richardson, Messages and Papers of the Presidents, Vol. 3, pp. 1824, 1828
[52] Murray Rothbard, A History of Money and Banking in the United States Before the Twentieth Century, p. 103

who did the same were unable to pay someone on demand and/or went bankrupt, they would lose a significant portion, if not all, of their business. A bank that maintained a 100% reserve requirement would garner a reputation as the safest bank and its business would increase. This was the result of competition amongst private banks following the Civil War. Fractional reserve banking did take place and those banks who held low reserve ratios went under or simply lost customers. Other banks did as well but maintained high reserve ratios, with many having 100% or very close to it.

Some would ask, how can a bank make money in this way? Banks could engage both in deposit and loan banking, which, without going into too much detail, would allow the bank to use some customer's money to loan out and pay them a higher interest rate (with loan banking the customer realizes this), thereby the bank would make the spread on what interest rate it was charging on the loan it made and the interest rate paid to those customers.

The Free Banking Era could be considered a vast improvement over the monetary system of today. While it is far from ideal and wouldn't be as stable, relative to a fully backed commodity based monetary system, free banking did place checks and balances on the monetary system.

During that era the banks could experiment in making the system sounder and did so when they created the Suffolk system. In the simplest of terms, this was a creation of a free market or private central bank. The bank kept a check on inflation and allowed for a stable monetary system in New England.

The Constitutionality of Fiat "Paper Money"

A fiat monetary system began with the introduction of the "Greenbacks" in 1862 and the Legal Tender Act which provided that bank notes should be lawful money and legal tender in the payment of all debts. This was the first time (following adoption of the Constitution) the U.S. Government forced its citizens to accept paper money as legal tender. Fortunately it was declared unconstitutional[53] in Hepburn v. Griswold but was reversed a year later by packing the court with those who held the opposite view in Knox v. Lee[54]. It begs the question how the Supreme Court could reverse its decision over such a short interval.

Chief Justice Chase said the following after the Hepburn v. Griswold decision:
"It has not been maintained in argument nor indeed would anyone, however slightly conversant with constitutional law, think of maintaining, that there is in the Constitution any express grant of legislative power to make any description of credit-currency a legal tender in the payment of debts."

The court held, that while the issue and use of government notes as a currency was absolutely suitable for such things as carrying on war, regulating commerce, or

---

[53] Francis Brooks, Fiat Money: A Review Of The Decisions Of The United States Supreme Court As To Its Constitutionality , *p. 4*
[54] Ibid, p. 7

borrowing money (confined to war time measure), government notes in no way could be considered legal tender in the payment of public and private debts[55].

Prior to the passage of the Legal Tender Act, it was made undeniably clear that payment of paper money were contracts to pay in gold and silver coin; and that as a very large proportion of the property of civilized men exists in the form of contracts for money, it would be inconsistent with the spirit of the United States Constitution to hold that Congress had been designedly vested with the power of injuring or destroying the private property rights of the people, the control or protection of which was a logical deduction belonging to state governments[56].

The Founding Fathers, those who framed the Constitution expressed an extreme hostility and for a few, extreme hatred for the issue of paper money both by state governments and the Federal government as going to show that no paper money power ought to be incorporated into the Constitution by implication or construction.

While this initially was only a "wartime measure," it set a frightening precedent. It was so alarming because Congress acted as though it did have the authority to emit bills of credit and declare them legal tender in the payment of some public and private debts, if redeemable in specie, which the U.S. Constitution specifically does not give them authority to do. The Constitution only gave Congress the authority to "*coin money.*" The aforementioned *Knox v. Lee* decision, however, reversed the *Hepburn v Griswold* decision with Justice Strong explaining this decision:

"The fundamental question, that which tests the validity of the legislation [The Legal-Tender Act], is, can Congress constitutionally give to treasury notes the character and qualities of money? Can such notes be constituted a legitimate circulate medium of exchange, having a defined value?"

In addition to commenting:

"It might be argued that the grant to the United States of the power of coining money and regulating the value thereof and of foreign coin, was understood as conveying general power over the currency; the power which had belonged to the States and which they surrendered."

This decision, no matter how the constitution is read, does not say the congress has general power over the currency. Furthermore, this decision was the foundation of the Federal Reserve (1913) and its ability of regulating the value of the currency, therefore making fractional reserve banking legal when the Federal Reserve came into existence.

Crime of 73'

Because the U.S. Constitution and the Coinage Act of 1792 established 371.25 grains of silver as the constitutional money standard, it could never be changed in law. It could, however, be changed in practice. In other words, silver was demonetized. The

---

[55] Ibid p. 5
[56] Ibid, pp. 6-7

Bimetallic War, or "Crime of '73," also known as the Coinage Act of 1873, was enacted by Congress, embracing the gold standard and demonetizing silver. This put the U.S. on a gold standard (although it remained on a de facto bimetallic standard almost three decades thereafter) and it wasn't until 1900 that the U.S. adopted the gold standard, although silver was used in coinage until 1965. All other major nations had already adopted a gold standard, with only China continuing on a silver standard until 1935.

In 1890, the Sherman Silver Purchase Act was passed and while it did not allow for free and unlimited coinage that the "Free Silver" supporters desired, it did increase the amount of silver the government was required to purchase on a monthly basis to 4.5 million ounces[57]. Ironically, this act was passed in response to the growing complaints from two interested parties, the farmers and the miners. Farmers became overextended financially and were unable to pay off their debts, which was made more difficult due to the overproduction of agricultural goods, driving down the price of agricultural products.

Augmenting this problem was the fact that mining companies had been extracting vast quantities of silver from the West, resulting in an increase in supply to the degree that, in most cases, mining operators were at break-even on each ounce of silver mined.

The Sherman Silver Purchase Act was passed concurrently with the McKinley Tariff of 1890, by which, in accordance with said act, the federal government purchased millions of ounces of silver per year. It required the government to purchase an additional 4.5 million ounces a month[58] in addition to the $2 million-$4 million that was required following the passage of the Bland-Allison Act of 1878.

This produced consequences as the silver would be purchased by special issues of Treasury notes, which were redeemable in specie. Per Gresham's Law, the people redeemed these notes in gold, depleting government gold reserves as gold was undervalued on a relative basis and the overvalued or "bad money" (silver) drove out undervalued or "good money" (gold) from circulation. A run on gold was one of the causes of the panic of 1893 and President Grover Cleveland oversaw the repeal of this act.

Advances in mining technology and innovation to increase annual output came along at a sluggish pace until the 20th century. Then, in an 82-year period, the worldwide silver mined exceeded that which was mined in the previous 5,000 years.

Another key point in silver's monetary history came during deflation, devaluation and the Depression of the 1930s. Silver's price fell lower and lower, finally bottoming at 25 cents in 1933. However, the Thomas Act of 1933 allowed foreign debtors to pay the U.S. in silver coin at 50 cents per ounce, twice the unofficial price, and silver soon strengthened worldwide. The price rallied to 44 cents by the end of 1933, a 75% increase above the Depression low, but it could still be said that silver was clearly in a state of monetary confusion. (The Thomas Act also authorized a reduction in the gold content of the U.S. dollar). The dollar was debased relative to gold. Prior to FDR

---

[57] Homer E. Socolofsky and Allen B. Spetter, *The Presidency of Benjamin Harrison*, p. 59.
[58] *Ibid*.

depreciating the dollar, one ounce of gold cost $20.67, which was then depreciated 69.33% such that it cost $35/oz. of gold.

At the request of insolvent bankers, all banks were closed, an embargo was put on gold sales, and the dollar was allowed to float. In the same year, the Banking Act, commonly known as Glass-Steagall Act, was passed, which maintains there needs to be a separation between commercial and investment banking. This, however, was repealed in 1999 but what it had intended to prevent was essentially made legal by the central bank. It also established the FDIC at that time. The Social Security Act was passed in 1935, as FDR continued his "social programs."

Silver Purchase Act of 1934

The next major monetary adjustment for silver resulted from another political action. The Silver Purchase Act of 1934 directed the Secretary of the Treasury to purchase silver both at home and abroad until the market price reached the official monetary price of $1.29 per ounce. This political action quickly inspired still another political action. The U.S. Treasury issued an edict that taxed domestic silver transactions at 50% in order "to capture the windfall profits created by the Treasury." Over the next four years, the U.S. acquired 3.2 billion ounces of silver—including the physical confiscation of so much actual silver stock that it became impossible for the Commodity Exchange of New York (COMEX) to function.

Coinage Act of 1965

From 1934 until 1955, the U.S. Treasury support price for silver remained above the actual market price. After 1955, however, the market price began to exceed the Treasury price, with silver users (largely in the photographic and electronics fields) buying silver from both domestic mines and the Treasury. Faced with dwindling supplies and increasing market prices for silver, the Coinage Act of 1965 moved through Congress, boosted by a letter dated June 3, 1965, from President Lyndon Johnson, which declared his support for the elimination of silver from coinage in the United States. These were then referred to as Johnson slugs.

Silver lasted longer than gold as a medium of exchange (real money) for the people, surviving until 1965, whereas gold ceased to circulate among the population in the U.S. in 1933, being reserved for balance of trade payments until the gold window was closed in 1971. And to properly understand what President Johnson did, you need to know something about the rule of law. A contract is considered sacred and cannot be broken—but Johnson essentially urged Congress to break the contract with the American people that is printed on all silver certificates. Some Americans, aware of what was really going on, saved every 90%-silver coin they could get their hands on.

Furthermore, the claim that too little gold or silver was left to be used as money is an argument often stated but seldom explained and is invalid. The correct observation is that too many paper claims have been issued against the currently existing amount of real money. In a true gold standard, many financial planners would be out of business. If the monetary system were based on honest weights and measures, a person would know, when first entering the workforce, exactly how much he or she would need to have saved by the time of their retirement. Why? Because their purchasing power would remain constant and in fact increase, insofar as society as a whole realized gains in productivity. Under an honest monetary system, interest rates are much more stable, relative to those of today, and stable, long-range planning is simplified.

In a true gold standard, purchasing power actually increases over time so that an ounce of gold would buy more after thirty years, for example, than it did when one originally entered the workforce. It must be stressed that the U.S. has never been on a true metallic or bimetallic standard in its history. As we will discuss in a later chapter, fractional reserve banking combined with a central bank or government having monopoly control of the mint is at the root of destruction in ANY monetary system. This would be simple to resolve would the banking system only back all its reserves 100% by silver, gold, or both!

Obviously, a true gold standard is not perfect, and there are still problems associated with human interaction. The potential buying power of gold has importance for determining silver's usage as money. For example, if gold reaches a price in U.S. dollars of $2,000 per ounce, then the smallest practical coins, being the one-tenth-ounce pieces, would have a value of roughly $200. This is far too large for a great many daily transactions such as buying bread, milk, or gasoline. If coins were to be used in commerce, it would require a smaller denomination currency unit, which could be silver. The United States of America was conceived in liberty with each individual guaranteed natural rights given by the Creator and secured by the Constitution. Additionally, the U.S. was founded on sound money (silver standard) but just as importantly the first nation was based on quasi-free market capitalism. As time went on, individual freedoms were stripped away, an early example being when the John Adams signed the Aliens and Seditions Act. These acts were comprised of four different bills passed by the Federalists and signed into law.

The Naturalization Act increased the residency requirement for American citizenship from 5 to 14 years. The Alien Friends Act allowed the president to imprison or deport aliens considered "dangerous to the peace and safety of the United States" at any time. This is entirely subjective augmenting the stripping of civil liberties during that time. The Alien Enemies Act authorized the president to do the same to any male citizen of a hostile nation, above the age of 14, during times of war. The controversial Sedition Act restricted speech which was critical of the federal government.

Economically, free market capitalism began to erode with the founding of the First Bank of the Unites States and the Second Bank of the United States, which set back progress and development due to exaggerated central bank induced boom-bust cycles.

The rise of the Jacksonian movement reversed much of the central bank meddling for quite some time. Jackson's successor essentially abolished the U.S. Treasury, moving back toward the Founders' original intent.

Moving ahead to the Crime of 1873 when silver was demonetized, indicating the U.S. was moving away from its roots even though the country was on a de facto bimetallic standard for the following 26 years, in 1900, the U.S. was on a gold standard de jure. We then come to the founding of the Federal Reserve, the timing of which coincided with the increasing severity of boom-bust cycles to present day. The founding of the Federal Reserve officially marked the change of America from one of quasi-free market capitalism to one of statism, which has grown increasingly worse over the last 100 years.

What is probably most disturbing nowadays is a part of the fairly recent institution of the National Defense Resources Preparedness Act. According to the **second chapter of title 12, of subchapter IV, section 95A, the Federal Government can confiscate gold and silver**, but only under the following circumstance:

> "DURING THE TIME OF WAR, THE PRESIDENT MAY THROUGH ANY AGENCY THAT HE MAY DESIGNATE, AND UNDER SUCH RULES AND REGULATIONS AS HE MAY PRESCRIBE, BY MEANS OF INSTRUCTIONS, LICENSES, OR OTHERWISE—
>
> "(A) INVESTIGATE, REGULATE, OR PROHIBIT ANY TRANSACTIONS IN FOREIGN EXCHANGE, TRANSFERS OF CREDIT OR PAYMENTS BETWEEN, BY, THROUGH, OR TO ANY BANKING INSTITUTION, AND THE IMPORTING, EXPORTING, HOARDING, MELTING, OR EARMARKING OF GOLD OR SILVER COIN OR BULLION, CURRENCY OR SECURITIES. . . ."

Concluding these first two chapters regarding silver's use as money throughout history and the United States in particular, was that the political importance of Andrew Jackson's railroading of the Second Bank of the United States and was of great significance as it showed that a central bank could be broken by the proper ideology, that of freedom. Could a return to sound money take place today with the current bureaucracy?

It is important to note here that critics of the gold standard point to period from the founding of the Federal Reserve through Nixon closing the gold window but this wasn't a true gold standard. The monetary system was unstable because initially bank deposits only needed to have 40% gold backing. This allowed the central bank to induce an artificial economic boom (the roaring 20's) and the corresponding bust, The Great Depression. FDR the devalued the dollar against gold, allowing the central bank to inflate the supply of money and credit. This was followed by more abuse including the Bretton Woods monetary system and further removed the monetary system from even coming close to a true gold standard. In other words, those who talk about the gold standard and its flaws by pointing out the U.S. during this period of time are naïve and this wasn't close to being representative of a true 100% gold standard.

Chapter 3: Silver Supply Dynamics

Silver, symbol Ag on the periodic table, naturally occurs by itself in nature and is usually derived from copper, lead, and zinc refining. The majority of silver comes from base metal mines, particularly lead-zinc, and is found in various base metal concentrates. Over 60% of annual world mine production of silver comes from primary base metal mines.

The Changing Composition of Silver Production by Type of Mine

Beginning in 2014 through the rest of the decade, silver production from primary silver mines relative to total silver production will increase substantially as a host of world-class mega and large primary silver mines reach production. There is also a looming supply deficit in primary zinc-lead mines, with some of the largest mines contracting and/or becoming depleted through next decade. As can be seen in the adjacent graphic, primary lead and zinc mines produce the majority of silver, in relation to any other type of mine. Silver production from primary copper mines will also increase, however, given the increase of primary silver production, it will only add an additional 1.40% over the period (2018-2020) vs. (2012-2014).

Note: Other studies could vary, perhaps significantly, as some mines may be classified differently from our own. We define a primary silver mine as the majority of revenue being derived from silver. Zinc and lead are so often found with one another that we group them together. Below has been more or less the primary consensus over recent years, with 24%-25% coming from primary silver mines, 13%-14% from primary gold mines, 23%-25% from primary copper mines and 36%-38% from primary lead/zinc mines.

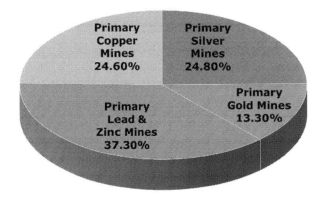

2012-2014 Avg ~ Breakdown of Silver Production by Type of Mine

- Primary Copper Mines 24.60%
- Primary Silver Mines 24.80%
- Primary Gold Mines 13.30%
- Primary Lead & Zinc Mines 37.30%

The silver byproduct mining activity began to change at the beginning of 2014 and will transition over the next 10 years, as shown in the next chart. The decline in silver produced from primary lead and zinc mines will be rather small at first and increase as we enter the second half of this decade through the first half of the next (mines such as Brunswick and Perseverance were fully depleted by mid- 2013), while silver production will increase at an annual rate anywhere from 1.4%-2.5%, at least through 2022.

Silver production will see a significant boost from primary silver mines, as many large mines are in development, being constructed, and/or ramping up production. One of these is Escobal, currently ramping up, producing roughly 20m oz. Ag per annum starting in 2015 and coming close in 2014. Silver produced from primary gold mines will also increase as well as silver produced from primary copper mines. The latter include large copper mines such as Oyu Tolgoi (Open pit and underground a few years later), Las Bambas, Toromocho, and Mina Ministro Hales, Cobre-Panama as well as medium size mines such as Constancia, Rosemont, and others. Also included are numerous mine startups, expansions and development projects owned by silver behemoth Fresnillo PLC. These include: Saucito II [8.4m oz.], San Julian [10.3m oz.], Fresnillo Expansion [5-7m oz.] and Pyrites Plant [5-5.50m oz.] and Juanicipio [14.1m oz.].

2015-2017 Avg ~ Breakdown of Silver Production by Type of Mine

- Primary Copper 25.30%
- Primary Silver Mines 27.10%
- Primary Gold Mines 11.90%
- Primary Lead & Zinc Mines 35.70%

This next chart is what the addition of numerous large primary silver mines and a falloff in silver produced from zinc/lead mines due to closure or contraction. There are two reasons silver from primary gold mines will fall so much, the first being a contracting gold-to-silver ratio (thereby making many primary gold mines with significant silver credits, a primary silver mine, such as Hycroft, Peñasquito, San Dimas, to name a few); secondly, by the time they reach production, many mines in development that are currently primary gold mines will become primary silver mines.

Why is silver production from primary silver mines going to increase to such a degree? The answer is an increase in mining generally due to the commodities boom in the early 2000s. Only recently have the majority of large primary silver mines started reaching production or begun development.

While silver production from primary copper, zinc and lead, and gold mines will increase in this period, some will all fall as a percentage of total silver production due to such a remarkable increase in silver production from primary silver mines. As discussed later in the chapter, this leads up to our projection of "peak silver." This is because roughly 5-10 years following peak silver, the falloff in silver production will really start to gain steam, for several reasons. Many more of the primary base metal mines will become depleted, and many of the primary gold mines that produce silver byproducts are epithermal deposits, meaning that over time and at depth, silver production will fall off by varying degrees. Lastly, many of the of existing primary silver mines and those which will reach production this decade will start to produce less silver, as many of them are also epithermal deposits.

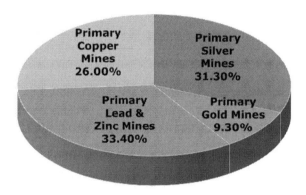

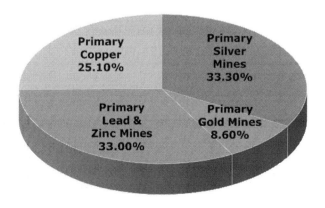

Potential New Mines

Mine Type	Mine	Capacity	Production
Near Term Mine Startups			
Primary Ag	**Escobal**, Gaocheng, Rosario, **Saucito II**	27,100,000	*Ramping Up*
Primary Cu	**Mina Ministro Hales, Toromocho**, Constancia	18,740,000	*2014-2015*
Primary Pb/Zn	Santander and Caribou	1,550,000	*2014-2015*
Primary Cu	Oyu Tolgoig O/P, Las Bambas	5,100,000	*2015*
Primary Pb/Zn	Tuva, Don Roman	2,900,000	*2015*
Primary Au	Cerro Negro, Parral, Inmaculada, Xietongmen	8,200,000	*2015*
Expansions	***Various	7,700,000	*2014/2015*
Medium Term Mine Startups [Q4 2015-2017]			
Primary Ag	**San Julian**, Pulacayo-Paca, Kempfield	13,700,000	*2015-2016*
Primary Ag	Flame & Moth, San Sebastian	6,500,000	*2016-2017*
Primary Ag	Avino, San Felipe, Fuwan, Pyrites	12,200,000	*2015-2016*
Primary Pb/Zn	Halfmile, Stratmat, Prairie Creek, Ozernoye	6,800,000	*2016-2017*
Primary Ag	Santa Ana, La Joya, Bulldog	8,600,000	*2016-2017*
Expansions	***Various	9,350,000	*2016-2017*
Medium-Longer Term Mine Startups [2018-2023]			
Primary Ag	**Pitarrilla, Juanicipio**, Gavilanes, Mangazeisky	32,200,000	*2018-2019*
Primary Cu	**Oyu Tolgoi U/G**, Angangueo, Rosemont	14,000,000	*2017-2021*
Primary Au	*****Hycroft**, Cerro Morro, San Luis, Cerro Gallo	23,600,000	*2017-2020*
Primary Au	******Pascua-Lama**, Yenzipar, Armutbel	36,500,000	*2018-2022*
Primary Ag	**Hackett River**, Hermosa, Rock Creek, **Navidad**	38,000,000	*2018-2021*
Primary Ag	Corani, Montanore, Bowdens, **La Preciosa**	21,200,000	*2017-2019*
Primary Pb/Zn	Tulseqhah Chief, Dugald & Bilbao	3,500,000	*2017-2018*
Primary Ag	**Metates & Malku Khota**	32,000,000	*2019-2021+*
Expansions	***Various	10,300,000	*2017-2020*
Total Potential Silver Production		339,740,000	
Adj Gross Silver Production Growth		217,641,800	
Silver Production From Primary Silver Mines		122,067,060	
Silver Production From Primary Copper Mines		40,840,000	
Silver Production From Primary Gold Mines		34,421,560	
Silver Production From Primary Lead/Zinc Mines		20,313,180	

*Hycroft is a Primary Silver Mine w/GSR= < 46, **Pascua-Lama is a Primary Silver Mine w/GSR=< 38

***Expansios Include that from San Dimas, Fresnillo, Endeavour, First Majestic, Pan-American, Fortuna, Great Panther, Hecla and others

Given the recently depressed metal price environment, peak silver won't likely occur according to our original forecast and have therefore included two alternative scenarios. In the chart above, there are a few select mining projects that will be developed no matter the economic outlook because they are either absolutely world-class projects and will be developed and/or owned and operated by mining giants with very deep pockets. These include:

- Escobal – Roughly 15-17m oz. Ag in 2014 and 20m oz. Ag in 2015
- Saucito II, San Julian and Constancia – 8-11m oz. Ag in 2015, 16.5-18m oz. Ag in 2016 and 20.5m oz. Ag in 2017.
- Mini Ministro Hales, Inmaculada, Toromocho, Caribou – 11-14m oz. Ag in 2015 and 17-21m oz. Ag in 2016
- Fresnillo Expansion, Pyrites Plant, Cienega Expansion, Juanicipio, Del-Toro, La Preciosa, La Pitarrilla, Metates and Corani – 10-15m oz. Ag in 2016, 15-20m oz. Ag in 2017, 30-45m oz. Ag in 2018 and 60-75m oz. Ag in 2019 or 2020.

In the near-term there are two large primary silver mines that will produce large quantities of silver. First, Escobal has completed ramping up production, achieved an annualized rate of 18-20m oz. in Q4 2014. Saucito II will add 8.4m oz. at capacity, which will be operated by Fresnillo, who will then bring on San Julian in mid-2015, which will add 10.3m oz. of silver production at capacity. Additionally, Fresnillo will undertake an expansion at its cornerstone Fresnillo Mine, Cienega Expansion, and bring the Pyrites plant project and Juanicipio into production, which together will produce an additional 23m oz. of silver, or 41.7m oz. of silver in aggregate. This will bring Fresnillo's total silver production between 70-80m oz. The Shafter Mine owned by Aurcana has the capability to produce 5m oz. of silver. Other large primary silver mines that will reach production in the medium-term are Fuwan (4-5m oz.), La Preciosa (9.1m oz.), Santa Ana (5m oz.), Corani (6.0m-8.3m oz.), and La Pitarrilla (10-15m oz.). In the longer-term (2018 or later), there is Hycroft (21m oz.), Pascua-Lama (35m oz. first five years, 26m oz. thereafter), Navidad (19.2m oz.), Hackett River (11m oz.), Montanore (6m oz.), Bowden's (4.5m oz.), Malku Khota (14m oz.), Hermosa (6m oz.), and Metates (19m+ oz.).

    These alone will increase silver production by nearly 200 million ounces. Obviously some projects will be delayed and some may not materialize as projected but this is accounting for large silver mines and not medium and smaller mines. There are also expansions of existing primary silver mines—large, medium, and smaller—that could add to the silver supply.

Largest Silver Producing Mines

Mine	Status	Production	Type of Mine
Mega Silver Mines [15m+ oz.]			
Penasquito	Producing	28m	Primary Gold-Silver
Cannington	Producing	28m	Primary Lead-Zinc
Fresnillo	Producing	22m	Primary Silver
Dukat	Producing	18m	Primary Silver
Escobal	Ramping up	20m	Primary Silver
Rudna Copper	Producing	16m	Primary Copper
Hycroft	2018E Start	21m	Primary Gold-Silver
Pascua-Lama	Community Issues	28m	Primary Gold-Silver
Navidad	Awaiting Permit	19.1m	Primary Silver
Metates	Exploration	20m	Primary Gold-Silver
Large Size Mines [9m - 14.9m oz.]			
Juanicipio	2018 Start	14.1m	Primary Silver
Antanima	Producing	13.5m	Primary Lead-Zinc
Oyu Tolgoi	2016-2018 Start	13m	Primary Copper
Pallancanta	Producing	12.5m	Primary Silver
La Pitarrilla	2018 Start	10-15m	Primary Silver
Polkowice	Producing	11.2m	Primary Copper
Uchucchacau	Producing	10.4m	Primary Silver
San Julian	2015 Start	10.3m	Primary Silver
Mina Ministro	2015 Start	9.6m	Primary Copper
Lubin	Producing	9.6m	Primary Copper
La Preciosa	2018 Start	9.1m	Primary Silver
Medium Size Mines [6m - 8.9m oz.]			
Toromocho	2015 Start	8.7m	Primary Copper
Saucito II	2015 Start	8.4m	Primary Silver
Palmarejo	Producing	7.5-8m	Primary Silver
Pirquitas	Producing	7.5-8.5m	Primary Silver
San Dimas	Undergoing Exp	8m	Primary Gold-Silver
Gumuskoy	Producing	8m	Primary Silver
Corani	2017-2019 Start	7-9m	Primary Silver
Del Toro	Ramping up	6m	Primary Silver
Mt. Isa	Producing	6.8m	Primary Lead-Zinc
Chunger	Producing	6.5m	Primary Lead-Zinc
La Colorada	Undergoing Exp	7.5-7.7m	Primary Silver
Zhezkagen	Producing	8.6-8,8m	Primary Copper
San Jose	Undergoing Exp	6.4m	Primary Silver

The above chart lists new mines that will reach production, and it notes some of the expansions, planned startups, and currently producing mines but is not all inclusive. San Dimas recently completed the first of a two-phase expansion, increasing silver production just over a million ounces. In 2015, San Dimas will increase silver production to roughly 6.8m oz. and in excess of 8m oz. per annum once the second phase is complete. First Majestic's Del-Toro Mine is ramping up production from roughly 2.6m oz. in 2013 to 5.6+ oz. in 2016. Pan-American will undertake expansions on La Colorada and Dolores, which will add an additional 4.8m-5.7m oz. combined, incrementally through 2018.

Fortuna Silver will begin mining a higher-grade area as well as expanding mill and mining capacity by 50%, which will increase production by 2.8m oz. over 2013 production. When this will occur is still to be determined but it is likely to be undertaken sooner rather than later. Other junior primary silver producers including Santa Cruz Silver, Avino Silver and Gold, among others, will add a healthy portion of silver production by the end of the decade.

First Majestic plans on expanding at least two of its operations, bringing Plomosas and La Luz into production. Hecla Mining will be expanding its Lucky Friday Mine, adding an additional 2m oz., and Endeavour will expand El Cubo and bring its San Sebastian Mine into production later this decade.

When Alexco Resources bring Flame & Moth into production mid-late 2015, the Bellekeno, Lucky Queen, and Onek mines will come with it. As Alexco generates cash flow and its cash position builds, it will expand Lucky Queen, a high quality deposit with the capability of producing 5-6m oz.+ once fully optimized. As time goes on, Alexco could bring numerous additional mines into production at Keno Hill, given that many are just one to two years from production. These include Elsa Tailings, Bermingham, Silver King, McQuesten, Husky-Elsa, Hector-Calumet, and Sadie-Ladue.

After discussing the increases in silver production it may seem that silver investment in the mining sector might be a poor decision. However, this is only part of the story, as all mines end in failure—meaning they are depleted over time and the mining activity ends. Thus miners are constantly looking to replace reserves and many silver mines either are reaching depletion, contracting, or as in the case of some of the larger mines, are beginning a three- to five-year ramp-down.

This ramp-down is the case most notably in primary lead/zinc mines and began last year with the Brunswick and Perseverance mine closures. Those two mines used to produce over 6m oz. Ag combined, which isn't that much but marked the start of a 10-year period in which primary lead/zinc mines alone will begin their demise, therefore ending the silver component as well.

Another issue to consider is Mexico's royalty tax, which may cause the marginal quality mines to not be constructed. Increasing capital and operating costs will cause more projects to be deferred or scrapped altogether until a reasonable profit can be generated. On the financing side, the cost of equity is high at this time for the industry. This leaves only the highest quality projects available to obtain financing.

The mining industry, as does the whole commodity sector, goes through cycles. At this time we have seen a boom in the sector from roughly 2000 to 2010. After that 10-year boom, we have seen a three year slump and the longer silver remains under $25 and $30/oz., the less silver supply will come on-line in the future to varying degrees. It simply is bad business to start a business that is not profitable, and primary silver mines all-in costs are roughly $22 per ounce currently.

Those who are new to the industry must understand that "cash costs" are only one part of many that determine the true cost. This is discussed in detail in the chapter regarding appraisal of a mining company. The Mexican royalty tax basically punishes a precious metals miner. The end result will be opposite to the stated purpose of benefiting the Mexican citizens. The increased tax won't just affect some construction decisions on various deposits but, more importantly, will also divert capital invested for exploration purposes, which in the long-term could prevent a very high quality or potentially world class silver deposit from being discovered. In other words, this new tax will actually decrease the tax revenue especially long-term, which is the opposite effect of the rationale for imposing this royalty tax in the first place.

This royalty tax for a precious metals miner can be explained as follows:
- A 0.5% royalty tax on total revenue derived from precious metals.
- A 7.5% royalty tax on EBITDA (Earnings Before Interest, Taxes, Depletion, Depreciation, and Amortization).
- This is more devastating than it sounds as a typical royalty tax is placed on EBT (Earnings Before Tax), which is always a much lower number, as depletion, depreciation, amortization, and interest serve as tax shields.
- The corporate tax rate is 30% instead of 29% in 2014 and 28% in 2015, which was the rate of corporate taxation that was initially supposed to occur.
- Exploration costs on non-producing mines cannot be expensed and have to be capitalized. Therefore exploration costs are not tax deductible.
- In aggregate, these primary effects (there are several more that either impact mining directly or indirectly albeit to much lesser degrees) have the impact of raising the corporate statutory rate from 28% (as we're close to 2015) to an effective 42%-44%.

Again, this is especially destructive for the more marginal mining companies. Free cash flow (the real measure of profitability) will be much lower than it would otherwise be and therefore an impediment to further mine development.

There are various measures of profitably, notably in the resource sector. Net income is representative of profitability, yet only a starting point. There are two measures of profitability—operating cash flow, defined as net operating profit (net income +/- one-time expenses and/or gains) plus depletion, depreciation, and amortization (a non-cash charge) less sustaining capital investment and exploration on currently producing properties. Equipment wears out and thus mine and mill need reinvestment in maintenance, parts, etc.; this is accounted for in the statement of cash flow. Operating cash flow is more representative of profitability because in order to continue generating cash flow, a certain amount of reinvestment is required each year. The absolute measure of profitability, meaning that which can be paid out to shareholders in the form of dividends (though it does not necessarily have to be) is free cash flow. This is nothing else but operating cash flow—expansionary/growth capital investment.

Let's look at an example. If a mining company currently has two mines in operation and one that is being developed, the operating mines generate operating cash flow of $60m each; however, the cost to construct the third mine is $140m over a two-year period, with investment in the first year of $85m and $55m in the second. The free cash flow in Year 1 would be ($60m x 2) - $85m = FCF, = $120m - $85m = $35m, FCF = $35m.

From this example it is clear that the ability for a company to expand and optimize operations and/or develop additional mines is not an easy task. The Mexican royalty tax will make the mining industry less viable, at least in Mexico, which is important to the supply of silver because Mexico is the largest silver producing country.

The True Cost of Mining

We did a study in 2013 regarding the true costs of mining an ounce of silver. Costs rose substantially from early 2009-to-early 2014 before stagnating. Energy costs have retraced significantly, which account for 20-25% of the operating costs of a mining operation. This does not mean the all-in-sustaining costs of mining operators with fall by this percentage, rather the mining and processing costs will decrease by roughly this amount. Commodity prices in general have trended lower, however, all-in costs amongst the lowest cost primary silver producers remain around the levels in 2012. Our study showed the all-in costs to be around $20.50/oz. of silver. It included over a dozen of the lowest cost producers, meaning all those included in the study were in the bottom half of the industry cost curve and more than half in the lowest cost quartile. Operating costs will likely bottom in Q1 2015, if not Q2, but this is almost all for naught, especially for those which have operations in Mexico due higher cost courtesy of the Mexican royalty tax (which impacts the entire industry as it is the largest silver producing country) and the accompanying increase in the corporate tax rate.

The following chart outlines "cash costs" which mining companies reported in the past and range from 45-to-65% of the true cost or all-in costs. The second graphic is a basic example of a low cost producer. $9.70 was more or less the average "cash cost" in the industry in 2013.

*Environmental Duty (0.5% x Revenue)
Mining
Processing $9.70 ← "Cash Costs"
Labor
*Mexican Royalty Tax (7.50% x EBITDA)
G&A
Interest Expense
Other Royalties
Corporate Taxes
Sustaining Capital
Exploration Expense on Producing Properties
*Exclusive to Mexico

Silver Price	$25	
Production	3,000,000	
Low Cost Producer: Example		
Revenue	$75,000,000	
*Environmental Duty (0.5% x Revenue)	($375,000)	($0.13)
"Cash Costs"	($29,100,000)	($9.70)
G&A	($9,100,000)	($3.03)
Mexican Royalty Tax	($2,731,875)	($0.91)
Taxes (28% Statutory Rate)	($9,434,075)	($3.14)
Sustaining Capital	($7,200,000)	($2.40)
All in Cost	($57,940,950)	($19.31)

 The all-in costs of producing an ounce of silver for primary silver mines is upwards of $20-$21/oz. for the lowest fifty percent of producers on the Industry cost curve. This is distorted as mining companies have only recently begun to report this number, instead reporting "cash costs" which is only the cost of extraction, mining, processing and labor. The companies is the lowest quartile on the cost curve have all-in costs between $16-$19/oz. with some outliers such as Fresnillo, Avino Silver and Gold, Tahoe Resources and a few select others. These have one thing in common, high silver grades and varying degrees of byproduct credits.

 The industry as a whole has all-in costs well in excess of $25/oz., Primary zinc/lead and copper mines have all-in costs per ounce of silver below that of primary silver mines, however, it is only a few dollars lower. This is worth pointing out because the price of silver over in 2014 was below the all-in costs of production. Does this make sense given investment demand for all intents and purposes reached a new record and industrial demand was very strong?

 Goldcorp has already said it will defer a significant amount of exploration capital to other countries due to the aforementioned Mexican royalty tax. A material amount of byproduct silver will begin to wind down and become depleted starting in 2015 through 2023-2025. Australia's Cannington Mine will become depleted in 2025-2026, with silver production beginning to fall off in 2019. This mine is known as one of the largest silver producers and has produced an average of roughly 33m oz. Ag over the past five years.

Peak Silver

"Peak silver" is close and is highly likely to occur sooner rather than later due to the current global economic condition worsening courtesy of increasingly reckless monetary and fiscal policy. Of course, our forecast has to be adjusted if conditions warrant, as there are so many variables that could change our forecast. The following is a brief list of the most impactful variables:

- Mine permitting
- Various geopolitical issues
- Financing
- Economics—metal price vs. rising capital and operating costs

We have applied our own methodology to determine our forecast. It is based on individual mines rather than a methodology that is applied to the industry as a whole. It is because of this fact we refrain from discussing how we determine each contribution/subtraction for each mine. The biggest factors used are either discounting production to various degrees and/or discounting a mine altogether or changing the timeline in which large-scale operations reach production due to the underlying uncertainty of mines obtaining permits.

Silver's future mine supply needs to be calculated by taking production from the most current year and then adding expanding mines and mines that are or will be constructed and subtracting mines that will become depleted.

In order to determine an accurate idea of the future of silver mining it is necessary to calculate net additions/subtractions to worldwide mine production. Over the next eight to ten years, new silver production will predominately come from primary silver mines followed by primary copper mines, but silver production from both primary gold, lead/zinc mines will not be substantial.

We will forecast peak silver for primary supply (mine production) while excluding secondary supply, as the latter has already been produced. We still forecast what secondary supply (recycling/scrap, coin melt) will be, in order to get a full picture of the coming depth in the silver deficit.

Each year there are two significant silver studies, one produced by the Silver Institute and the other by CPM Group in New York City, New York. Briefly we wish to point out how difficult it can be to determine all aspects of the silver market, as these two main publications vary as illustrated. We will examine the 2013 release of both publications as the 2014 Silver Yearbook typically is released late March-April.

CPM - Supply	
Mine Production	819.1
Secondary Supply [Scrap + Coin Melt]	230
Total Supply	**1049.1**

GFMS - Supply	
Mine Production	819.6
Scrap	191.8
Net Government Sales	7.9
Net Hedging Supply	**-41.3**
Secondary Supply	158.4
Total Supply	**978.0**

D&C - Baseline Supply	
Mine Production	819.35
Scrap & Coin Melt	207.80
Net Government Sales	7.90
Secondary Supply	215.70
Total Supply	**1035.1**

On the supply side, we took the average from both studies with just a 500k oz. difference, and a mid-point at 819.35m oz. Secondary supply differed significantly, most notably in scrap/recycling. We tend to think GFMS is more accurate, given that recycling silver at an average price of $31.15/oz. (2012 average) versus $23.79 (2013 average) is far less economical, as well as the fact that old photography stockpiles are running low or have become fully depleted.

We do, however, take a weighted average and overweight the GFMS number slightly higher than that of CPM. In any case, our baseline total supply is much closer to CPM's relative to GFMS's. It is 14m oz. lower than CPM and 57.1m higher than GFMS. GFMS calculated total supply by including "Net Hedging Supply," which we excluded for obvious reasons and in our opinion vastly understated the total supply at 978m oz.

Our forecast for Peak Silver would be depicted in the following two charts, however, due to depressed metal prices in 2013, 2014 and 2015 (the latter remains to be seen just how much of the year), numerous projects have been scrapped, shutdown or deferred. We have included three scenarios: Base Case, Alt #1 and Alt #2 (the latter being that depicted below).

We conducted a study regarding the all-in costs for primary silver producers and amongst the bottom quartile on the industry cost curve. The average all-in costs, now with the Mexican environmental duty and increased royalty tax, came to be slightly over $20.50/oz. This is calculated by taking the basic cash costs number (which is net of byproduct credits) + selling general and administrative + exploration costs (confined to properties which have an operating mine) + interest (if any) + taxes + royalties + sustaining capital investment = all-in costs. For producers in Mexico, this would include the 0.50% on revenue + 7.50% tax on earnings before interest, taxes, depreciation, depletion and amortization (EBITDA).

The chart below is one of three alternatives we provide for peak silver. This assumes that metal prices rise such that the majority of projects become economic or at least the percentages similar from 2004-2010. The chart immediately below is the "best-case" scenario.

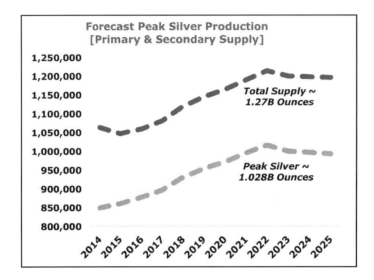

Due to the scrapping of mine projects, mine shutdowns and deferral of numerous projects, the timing of peak silver will varies, perhaps significantly. In our three scenarios below, peak silver ranges from 936.27m – 1,028m oz. sometime between 2019-to-2022.

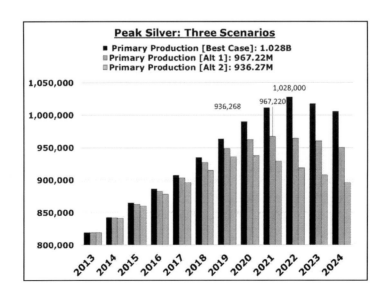

In each of the three scenarios, annual primary (mine) production growth varies, depending on the year. This is net of production that will go offline as base metal, gold and primary silver mines become depleted.

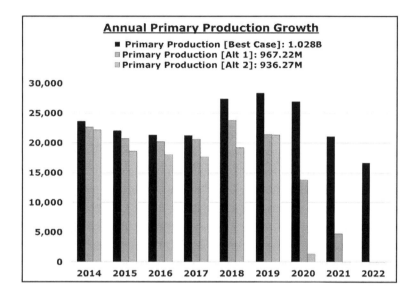

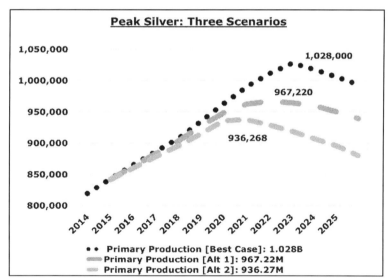

Silver Production Growth Key Region – The America's
North & Central America

North and Central America will account for a greater share of total silver production growth over the medium and long-term. This has to do with several variables, including the fact mentioned earlier in this chapter that Mexico has numerous large, primary silver mines coming into production over the next eight years or so (Saucito II

(8.4m oz.), San Julian (10.3m oz.), La Pitarrilla (12.5-15m), La Preciosa (9.1m), Juanicipio (14.1m oz.), Pyrites Plant (5-5.5m) and possibly Metates (19-20m oz.) and many others as well as numerous expansion projects on existing mines.

The U.S. has short, medium, and longer-term drivers of production growth, including the Hycroft expansion, which when complete will increase silver production 17-18m oz. per annum. Aside from that, the U.S. has the Lucky Friday expansion, increasing production from 1.5m oz. in 2013 to roughly 5m oz. in 2016. Lastly the U.S. has four other mines, of which at least one or two of these will fail to get fully permitted in a timely manner. There are also many mine which need its final permit including Rosemont (2.9m oz.) and Montanore (6m oz.).

Canada is quite surprising over the medium and long-term as it has Flame & Moth in the prolific Keno Hill District reaching production in 2015-2016. The production from this is just 3.1m oz., however, Flame & Moth mine and milling capacity will definitely be expanded before the end of the decade. Keno Hill already has one fully developed mine, one that is 95% developed, and another that is 85%-90% developed. In other words, this one district alone has ample capacity to increase production by a material degree. Canada also has Hackett River, which is owned by Glencore and will produce 11m oz. annually once in production. These are all on top of the Escobal mine, which will increase silver production in 2014 roughly 15-17m oz.

South America

Like Central and North American, South American also has vast potential for a substantial increase in silver production. South America, however is plagued with much more risk, either by the government or the local communities. It has the Pascua-Lama mine in Chile/Argentina, which will produce (35m oz.) for the first five years once in production and (26m oz. thereafter), Navidad (19.1m oz.), Malku Khota (14m oz.), Corani (6-8m oz.), Santa Ana (5m oz.) and others.

Note: These are just potential additions to silver production. Below is a list of the some of the mines mentioned in the above list but have certain characteristics which greatly reduce development risk. For example, in the first of the three charts, Escobal is up and running at capacity, Saucito II and San Julian are and will be ramping up, followed by two large primary copper mines with significant silver byproduct credits in Toromocho and Mini Ministro Hales. Constancia is currently in pre-commercial production, while Del-Toro continues to ramp up toward 5.5-6m oz. per annum. Lastly, the Pyrites Plant is just 12-16 months away from Fresnillo, owned in large part by Penoles. Just this small group of mines which are ramping up, producing or will soon reach production and ramp up to capacity add a hefty 70m oz. Ag when all mines are up operating at initial design capacity. Stripping out 2013 production, that added to beyond 819.35m oz. is roughly 48-54m oz. by 2H 2016.

Near-Term Highly Probable		
Mine	**Current Status**	**Production Capacity**
Escobal	Operating at Capacity	20m
Saucito II	Ramping Up	8.4m
San Julian	Q1-Q2 Ramp up	10.3m
Pyrites Plant	12-16 months from Production	5.5m
Mina Ministro Hales	Production mid-2015	9.6m
Toromocho	Production mid-2015	8.7m
Constancia	Pre-Commercial Production	2.4m
Del-Toro	Ramping Up	5.4-6.0m

Our forecast is that because of severely depressed metal prices for the last 6-months of 2013, all of 2014 and it is currently looking at least through the first quarter of 2015. This will and already has been enough to cause companies to defer development projects indefinitely. For this reason, it is looking more and more as if primary silver supply continued to grow at 2.80% +/- in 2014, with another strong year (2.50-2.60%) in 2016. Beginning in 2017, through 2020, we do expect production to rebound given the numerous world class mines which will reach production 2017-2020. 66.5m 26, 77.1m ounces.

Near-to-Medium-Term, Probable		
Mine	**Current Status**	**Production at Capacity**
San Dimas Exp	Ramping up, Exp comp Q2 2016	6.8m (2015) and 8.05m (2017)
Penasquito Exp	Primary + 1/2 other projects	26m (2015) 30m (2017)
Bowdens	2017 Start	4.5m
Prairie Creek	2017 Start	2-2.2m
San Felipe	2016 Start	2.3-2.4m
Pulcayo-Paca	2016 Start	2.5m +/-
Rosemont	2017 Start	2.9m
Fresnillo Expansion	2016-2017	7m

While there are multiples of low risk, world class primary silver mines than it depicted below, this gives a good feel for all the mega-primary silver mines which will be and could be developed.

Medium-to-Semi Long-Term (8-years), Probable		
Mine	Current Status	Production at Capacity
La Pitarrilla	2018 Start	12-15m
Juanicipio	2018 Start, Capacity in 2019	14.1m
Hycroft	2018 Start	18m
Metates	2019-2020 Start	19m
La Preciosa	2018 Start	9.1m
Corani	2018-2019 Start	6-8m

These less risky, very lucrative mining operations and/or development projects would increase primary supply by 170m oz. Ag. If we just take these mines and use other new mines to make up for those which become depleted, this comes out to 2.385%. While this seems much too high, remember this is gross primary silver production. Net primary silver production would negate the effect of many large silver projects listed above. There are also countless new mines that will come-online that are not listed as well as various mines that are and will undergo expansions.

Chapter 4: Silver Demand Dynamics

Silver has two demand dynamics. First, as discussed in the first two chapters of this book, is its monetary aspect, which dates back over 5,000 years; but also, because it is or was essentially an industrial metal "ahead of its time," it will soon show how vital it is for its many uses in industry. The potential future use in industry is so significant as to be essentially unlimited. We will be looking at the industrial aspect, followed by the fabrication and monetary aspect and forecasts.

Before proceeding further, we cannot stress enough that it has only been since the turn of the century that silver has really begun to be used in industry to a material degree. Yes, previous to this time, a significant amount of silver was used in photography. However, the vast potential this "miracle metal" possesses has only recently begun to be exploited in the last 15 years or so. It is essentially a metal in its infancy! As global technology advances worldwide over the next 5, 10, 20, 50, and 100 years, silver will be the metal of choice due to its unmatched properties. The existing, growing and novel would have been growing post-2008, however, the absence of any real recovery has muted growth for its use in industry. Despite a global economy which is just as weak as it was in 2008 (at least in ALL major industrialized countries), silver's use in industry is picking up.

Silver has very dynamic physical characteristics, which are greatly overlooked by almost all investors but not by most sectors of the electronic industry as well as various other industries that will be discussed in detail later. Probably the most notable physical attribute is the fact that silver possesses the highest electrical conductivity of ANY element, as well as the highest thermal conductivity of any metal. Platinum and palladium can be considered substitutes in many cases, but that price differential would have to narrow very significantly. It wasn't until roughly the mid to late 2000s that silver began to be used in increasing amounts outside of electronics. Alternative applications include photovoltaic, batteries (both non-rechargeable and, more recently, rechargeable), solid state lighting (OLED, LED), super-capacitors, and other small contributors.

The photography impact was addressed in my (David Morgan) first book, *Get the Skinny on Silver Investing*, and will not be addressed here. Suffice it to state that the idea that silver was "dead" because of digital photography was a myth.

Silverware sales have been fairly flat for quite some time, yet each year a reasonable amount is purchased regardless of economic conditions. In the future, however, as the Eastern world is recognized as having the world's economic superpowers, these economies such as China's will undergo significant structural changes, which are healthy and normal. Currently, China is a producer and savings-based economy, but this has already started to change (albeit slowly) and at the turn of the decade a few years from now should become a much more balanced economy in terms of production and consumption. This involves, in part, increasing its society's standard of living, which will most likely involve, to some degree, ownership of silverware.

Let's put silver's industrial demand growth into perspective and explain why it has unique dynamics unlike most other investments. In 1990, industrial demand totaled roughly 275,000,000 ounces. Just nine years later, industrial demand surged over 36% to 375,000,000 ounces. This means the compound annual growth rate was just over 3.5%. Over the next decade, ending 2010, industrial demand surged roughly 115,000,000 ounces to 510,000,000 ounces, or 36% +/- or 3.12% compound annual growth rate. Note that this was in the face of a rapid silver elimination from the photography industry, making it that much more impressive.

Silver's use in industry is on pace to increase another 30,000,000 ounces by the end of 2015, or 18.36% to 540,000,000 ounces (1.15% CAGR). The compound annual growth rate has been flat-to-increasing relative to the previous decades and the total demand growth for industrial uses. Growth in industrial uses has been rather stagnant following the 2008 financial crisis as the world economy has been weak and certainly much weaker than portrayed in the mainstream media. Growth will resume in the short and medium-term even in the face of a renewed downturn in the world economy.

Longer-term, the opportunities for new or novel uses for silver in industry, given its unrivaled conductivity characteristics and recently the characteristics involved in using silver in nanotechnology, are very substantial. While we view an average annual growth rate in excess of 5%-6% as excessive unsustainable, we do view an average annual growth of 1.5%-2.5% as a very real and a likely possibility. By this, we are referring to the long-term, not just over 1, 5, or even 10 years out, instead more like 20,40, and 60 years from now. We say this because we expect investment demand for silver to absolutely explode in the years ahead due to the first failure of a fiat monetary system on a global basis, which will drive the price to levels so high that the use of silver in industry simply will not be worth the cost for select uses, at least for a period of time.

We break down demand into three categories, the first being fabrication, which includes photography, silverware, and jewelry. The second is industrial demand, which includes everything outside fabrication and investment demand, including electronics, batteries, brazing alloys and solders, photovoltaic, novel uses and other industrial demand.

Investment demand is broken down as follows: coinage, small silver bars (100 oz. and less), large silver bar (commercial bars), and ETP (Exchange-Traded Product) flows.

Fabrication numbers are derived from the two silver studies mentioned in this books acknowledgements with some "bias" on our part, meaning that we strive to maintain an objective view but also determine which numbers fit best, not for the most bullish case but for the reality of the silver market as a whole.

Photography demand as reported by CPM provides for basic photography, X-ray, graphic arts, and motion pictures. Jewelry and silverware demand are incredibly difficult to determine even with significant resources to utilize.

Silver Studies

CPM - FABRICATION DEMAND	
Photography	82
Jewelry & Silverware	266.5
Total Fabrication Demand	**348.5**

GFMS - FABRICATION DEMAND	
Photography	50.4
Jewelry & Silverware	248.8
Total Fabrication Demand	**299.2**

D&C FABRICATION DEMAND	
Photography	71.4
Jewelry & Silverware	257.65
Total Fabrication Demand	**329.05**

In other words, we picked various line items from both studies multiple times and came up with roughly the same number each time in many categories, yet there were differences such as the following regarding industrial demand:

CPM - INDUSTRIAL DEMAND	
Electronics & Batteries	218.4
Photovoltaic	69.5
Other Uses	219.9
Other Countries [smallest countries]	9.5
Total Industrial Demand	**517.3**

GFMS - INDUSTRIAL DEMAND	
Electronics & Batteries	233.9
Photovoltaic	50.3
Other Uses	189.7
Brazing & Alloys	62.4
Total Industrial Demand	**536.3**

D&C INDUSTRIAL DEMAND	
Electronics & Batteries	218.4
Photovoltaic	69.5
Other Uses	169
Brazing Alloys & Solders	62.4
Total Industrial Demand	**519.3**

Investment demand surged to record levels in 2013. Ironically, the CPM Silver Yearbook claimed investment demand fell, while acknowledging silver coin demand set an all-time record high. This is likely to reverse course when the 2014 study is released. Regardless, we believe GFMS to be more accurate on the investment demand picture as a whole.

As of December 2014, silver investment demand illustrated it was well on its way to setting a second consecutive record year of investment demand. Furthermore, ETP flows, as of the November 2014 were 25m+/- oz. higher (depending on the data is looked at).

The discrepancy is that we define total investment demand as silver coin demand + silver bar demand (100 oz. and less) + silver bar demand (commercial 1,000-oz. bars) = total investment demand(1) + ETP flows = total investment demand(2). Our reasoning is a few of the ETFs have very questionable auditing—specifically, the largest silver ETF, SLV. Augmenting this fact is that JP Morgan is the custodian of this particular ETF, which has been maligned as the biggest silver manipulator for years by many Internet commentators outside the mainstream.

This is not mere theory, as verification can be obtained by studying the Commitment of Traders Report, which is reported every week by the CME and the Bank Participation Report. There is little doubt, with any objective analysis, that JP Morgan has significant influence in the silver market. However, as important as this may be, we must maintain the fact that the numbers that can be verified above are NOT as significant as the Over-the-Counter Market (OTC), which does not require any disclosures. It is largely recognized by those within the industry that the OTC market is vastly larger.

Since only the coinage and commercial bars are discussed in detail by CPM, we viewed GFMS (Gold Fields Mineral Services) silver bar demand as more accurate but not complete.

CPM reported (-30.8m) in commercial bar demand (1,000-oz. bars) due to institutional sellers in 2013. In our baseline number below, we use both the CPM and GFMS silver bars demand. GFMS reports coin and bar demand at 245.60m oz., which gives an implied investment demand for silver bars of 127.10m oz. Instead of taking this number as well as CPM's 30.80m from individuals, institutions, etc., selling commercials bars into the market, we decided to err on the side of being conservative. We did this by taking GFMS's number for coinage and 100-oz. and less bar demand 245.60m and subtracting out CPM's coinage number of 136m oz., leaving us with 126.75m in coinage and 109.60m in silver bar demand (100 oz. and under) less CPM's commercial bar sales of (30.80m).

This yields 126.75m + 109.6m − 30.80m = 205.55m oz. for investment demand (1). The ETF flows from both studies were fairly close, with CPM reporting net outflows of (-2.50m), while GFMS reporting inflows of 1.60m. However, CPM goes through a more in-depth discussion as well as showing the contribution of each ETP. In all, the two studies in relation to our baseline look as follows:

CPM - INVESTMENT DEMAND	
Coinage	136
Silver Bars	**(30.80)**
Total Investment Demand (1)	**105.2**
ETP flows	**(2.50)**
Total Investment Demand (2)	**102.70**

GFMS - INVESTMENT DEMAND	
Coinage	118.5
Silver Bars	127.2
Total Investment Demand (1)	**245.70**
ETP flows	1.60
Total Investment Demand (2)	**247.30**

D&C INVESTMENT DEMAND	
Coinage	126.75
Commercial Bars	**(30.80)**
Silver Bars	109.6
Total Investment Demand (1)	**205.55**
ETF flows	**(2.50)**
Total Investment Demand (2)	**203.05**

Let us look at the most recent fundamental data regarding supply and demand. We will rely most heavily on our baseline numbers in our analysis following the charts and short summary of what each shows. The biggest impact of our forecast is investment demand, beginning in 2015-2016.

Although industrial demand is important and certainly needs to be considered the fundamentals of silver, investment demand is the main driver as there is an unlimited "demand" for currency. We will come back to this most important premise in later chapters. The silver balance according to each study is as follows:

CPM - SILVER BALANCE	
TOTAL SUPPLY	1049.10
TOTAL DEMAND	968.5
Silver Balance	**80.60**
ETP INFLOWS/-OUTFLOW	(2.50)
Balance W/ETP FLOWS	**78.10**

Silver Is In a Surplus

GFMS - SILVER BALANCE	
TOTAL SUPPLY	978.0
TOTAL DEMAND	1081.20
Silver Balance	**(103.20)**
ETP INFLOWS/-OUTFLOWS	1.60
Balance W/ETP FLOWS	**(104.80)**

Silver is in a Deficit

D&C-SILVER BALANCE	
TOTAL SUPPLY	1035.05
TOTAL DEMAND	1053.90
Silver Balance	**(18.85)**
ETP INFLOWS/-OUTFLOWS	(2.50)
Balance W/ETP FLOWS	**(16.35)**

Silver is in a Deficit

The silver balance from both studies differs with 89-97m oz. discrepancies. We did consider net hedging, which GFMS includes. Net hedging supply, however, has little to do with actual physical supply, and instead is a paper contract that at times settles in physical, but this is seldom the case. Oddly enough, by applying our own methodology, we essentially ended up at the mid-point between the two studies.

Scrap supply takes many forms, and at one-time (1999) was primarily photographic waste. However, now the bulk is made of up electronics that are being recycled.

The year 2013 witnessed record sales of American Eagles, Canadian Maple Leafs, and Austrian Philharmonics—all well-recognized bullion coins. The Shanghai Exchange, which is new to the precious metals world, has seen robust physical demand for both gold and silver. The London Bullion Metals Association is primarily a paper trading market with some deliveries occurring but at a mere fraction of the amount "traded" on paper.

We also know India started buying much more silver than has been typical, due to the gold import duties. From a longer-term perspective, India has been a huge silver purchaser for monetary purposes, having moved more into the gold market as the country on balance became wealthier. The purpose of analyzing the two studies is to try to get a feel for the market. In other words, the silver balance that GFMS came up with and our baseline numbers suggest the silver market is getting tight, although not quite tight enough to suggest a significant upward price increase just yet.

Investment demand remains bullish, as it was in excess of 200m oz. and enough to put silver in a deficit for 2013. We wish to look at industrial demand starting with the 1990s and onward to present day. Then we forecast industrial demand from present day through the end of 2018. The graphs (throughout the chapter) are simple supply and demand graphs, which are sufficient to represent silver during the '90s. During the 90s industrial demand was not dominated by the electronic world, as the global technology revolution was just beginning. The biggest demand component at that time was silver's use in photography.

During the 2000s, silver began to be used in new applications. This increased at an accelerating rate for most of the decade but it started from a low level. The industrial demand was robust enough to send the price from a low of $4/oz. in 2002-2003, to a high in early 2008 of $21/oz. This is an increase of 400% in six years (+/-). Early in the 2000s, silver demand was almost entirely due to industrial use. As the Federal Reserve began to inflate the money supply, the price of silver began to increase due to investment demand picking up and increasing every year until the 2008 crisis.

We still maintain it is monetary demand at the margin that will really determine the ultimate silver price. As an example, investment demand may have accounted for $30 of the $48 peak in 2011, as compared to roughly $6-$9 during the 2008 high. Since 2011, the real inflation rate is has been running 9- 10% per annum using John Williams work at Shadowstats.com. This is not some new proprietary method, rather the inflation rate based on how it was calculated in 1980. This is important, as it suggests the Fed is losing control of inflation.

Silver and gold have yet to attract attention from the mainstream in a significant way, and most of the reporting is more designed to extol the virtues of paper assets. Gold and silver have virtually outperformed most conventional assets over the past decade up through the end of 2012. The primary driver of the silver price will be investment demand; silver demand for investment purposes has picked up significantly in the East, which so far in 2014 is keeping or perhaps exceeding that in 2013.

This extremely robust investment demand will put pressure on above-ground stockpiles that have increased from their low in 2005. Eventually a tipping point will be reached, causing the price to be determined by the physical market, rather than being controlled by paper contracts. The West has continued to increase the purchase of silver coins significantly the past four years, setting new records. More importantly, central banks in the Eastern world have been buying precious metals hand over fist, including China, India and Russia. It is very difficult to determine just how much China is buying because at the start of 2014, it no longer took delivery from the exchange, instead importing it into several different cities. Regardless, the private buying on the exchange speaks for itself. Silver inventory at the Shanghai Gold Exchange was decimated in 2014, with those taking delivery making it difficult for the exchange to have inventory levels comparable to early 2014 and 2013.

The foundation has been laid for the world at large to move into the precious metals, as inflation is unavoidable at this point. It is our experience that the amount of real precious metals investors may move from the current (less than) one percent of the population to perhaps two percent. But this is a doubling of investment demand and thus a significant increase especially for silver, since the amount of investment silver is actually a smaller amount than gold.

The heavily doctored Consumer Price Index has become a tool to convince the U.S. public that inflation is not a concern. It is important to remember that the C.P.I is nothing but an artificial construct and is detached from reality. This could be insulting to the public in light of the facts as to how the CPI is presently calculated:

- Geometric weighting (which by definition reduces the weighting of goods rising in price and increases the weight of those falling in price or increasing the least)
- More frequent re-weightings of the basket of goods used (re-weighting now occurs every two years instead of every ten years)

Prices in Year T

1st	$1.59	$5.99	$9.99	$16.99	$36.00	$58.00
2nd	$7.27	$13.46	$22.09	$44.00	$64.00	$89.99

Prices in Year T + 1

1st	$1.67	$6.34	$10.29	$18.39	$40.99	$60.99
2nd	$8.09	$14.09	$25.39	$44.99	$66.66	$92.99

Group 1

Arithmetic Mean Change in Price	6.86%
Geometric Mean Change in Price	6.11%

Group 2

Arithmetic Mean Change in Price	6.77%
Geometric Mean Change in Price	5.39%

Group 1 & 2

Arithmetic Mean Change in Price	6.81%
Geometric Mean Change in Price	5.74%

- Hedonic adjustments, which are entirely subjective and a blatant attempt to alter the CPI lower. In a nutshell, if the government deems an item in the basket of goods in the CPI has increased in quality, the prices are adjusted lower to offset the perceived high quality.
- On-going re-weightings (using prices from discount/sales outlets versus an average retail price)

- Substitutions—replacing one item for another, such as replacing steak with hamburger meat

As previously mentioned, John Williams of ShadowStats.com calculates the CPI as it was calculated back in 1980 as well as in 1990. Applying the formula used back in 1980, he came up with a CPI inflation rate in excess of 9.00% and of 5.00% using that from 1990.

While the current CPI is completely removed from reality, it presently is starting to move in a way that even the mainstream is having a difficult time hiding. In addition, the recovery that is broadcast continuously by the financial press also is blatantly showing signs of rapid decline. Such things as median household income have dropped to levels not seen since 1995, the labor participation rate continues to decline and headline economic growth only possible to significantly seasonal adjustments and numerous other gimmicks.

The True Money Supply (TMS)

In our view, one of the best measures of the money supply was formulated by economist and historian Murray Rothbard. He includes all "monies "immediately available for use in exchange as part of the money supply. This is a clear and concise definition and there is one simple test that can tell you whether it is part of the money supply. Monies must serve as the final means of payment in all transactions including the extinguishment of debt. There are six components of the TMS, which include the following:

- Currency Component of M1
- Total Savings Deposits
- Total Checkable Deposits
- Demand Deposits and U.S. Note Balances of the U.S. Government
- Demand Deposits Due to Foreign Official Institutions
- Demand Deposits Due to Foreign Commercial Banks

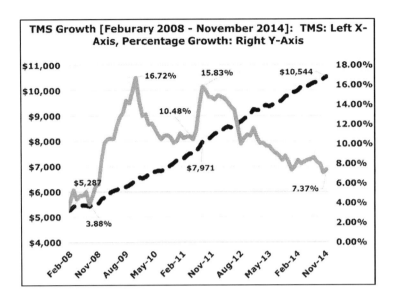

The above chart depicts the money supply growth, which is expressed in absolute terms [$5.29T in February 2008-to-$10.66T in December 2014] as well as in percentage growth [year over year]terms). The money supply has more than doubled relative to the comparative period in 2007. The monetary aggregate, TMS, will be discussed in chapter 8 as economic growth is a function of TMS growth. Note there is a relatively high correlation between growth in the TMS and credit expansion.

Notice, this excludes time deposits, money market mutual funds, money market deposit accounts, and traveler's checks, as these are not immediately available on demand. Starting in the second half [November of 2008] to present day, the TMS has been growing at a compound annual growth rate (CAGR) in excess of 11%! The prices of goods and services are determined (absent all manipulation) by the equilibrium or intersection of supply and demand.

Silver needs to be analyzed differently from gold because there are two demand components. We are referring to Investment Demand I(N) & Industrial Demand I(D). While this may seem a moot point today, for longer-term investors, silver will reach a place in time where prices will either increase or remain strong in any economic environment. The chart below just illustrates this graphically.

Industrial Demand I(D) and Investment Demand I(N)

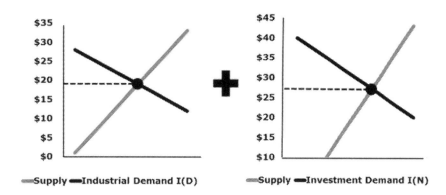

Silver in the 1990s, however, was essentially only composed of industrial demand, given its low price and because of the technological revolution, highlighted by the wide adoption of the internet and relative technologies, along with other macroeconomic events, largely negated the effects of inflation, as it was primarily seen through the rampant increase in the NASDAQ composite.

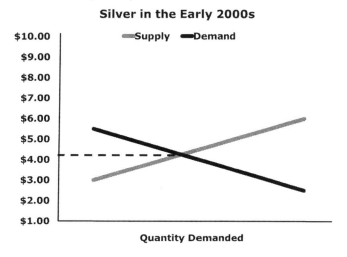

During the mid 2000s, the BRIC countries started to industrialize abroad, causing the industrial demand for silver to increase. At the same time, Alan Greenspan ignited his second consecutive bubble via extremely easy money policy; inflation started to pick up and investment demand was resurrected.

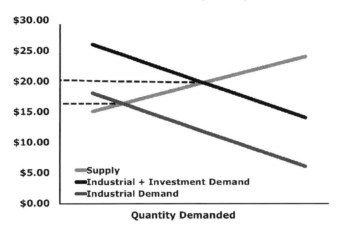

The Federal Reserve began to pump unprecedented amounts of capital into the banking system, which continues presently despite the tapering reported by the mainstream financial press. Quantitative easing and negative real interest rates are also related to growth in the TMS.

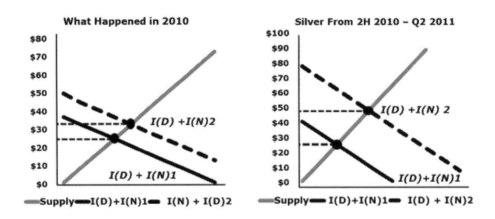

The reason industrial demand is depicted as increasing from roughly $14 to $21 in 2010 over 2008 is that the monetary inflation pushed the price of all commodities higher, following the late 2008-early 2009 lows. Investment demand resulted, thus pushing up the price of silver. The chart on the right illustrates that it was investment demand that had picked up significantly, which caused the price to peak at over $48/oz. in Q2 2011. This price explosion took place after the Federal Reserve announcement of QE2.

The last chart depicts silver under current conditions in which there is essentially no monetary premium. The chart to the right is what could take place to the price of silver if/when the U.S. dollar is either reset or collapses. We must stress that this chart is not using present "value" dollars, rather those in the future, whereby all commodities will increase in price significantly.

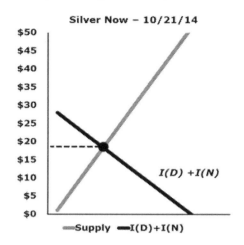
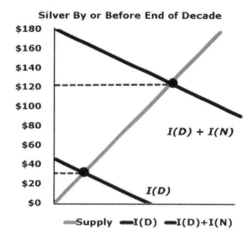

Industrial Demand

The rest of the chapter will focus on novel and growing uses of silver's use in industry. First we will focus on the existing uses, particularly the large components. These include silver's use in electronics and batteries, which make up the largest industrial use.

At this point it is important to note the price of silver is known as price inelastic in economic terms. This means that in almost all applications in industry, the amount of silver used is so small, relative to the overall cost of the finished product, as to be demanded regardless of price. Therefore in the event of the silver price doubling or more, the impact on industrial demand will be immaterial holding all else equal.

This can be illustrated best by example, so let us look at a refrigerator using silver as an essential component. If silver were to go from a price of $20 per ounce to, say, $200 per ounce as an extreme, the refrigerator manufacturer would still purchase silver because there is no substitute, and, more significantly, the amount of silver used—being perhaps one tenth of an ounce per unit—costs the manufacturer an increase from $2.00 to $20 on an item that retails for perhaps $600 or more.

Again, this must be emphasized as silver has been squeezed down to the minimum amount necessary to get the job done, and industry is continually looking for ways to reduce the amount. Yet in practical terms, silver is essential to the end product and must be used and will be used regardless of price. Where silver is not price inelastic is where silver is the MAIN component in an item such as jewelry or silverware. These uses, however, could actually increase should the price of silver rise as it becomes more coveted as fine jewelry or silverware, specifically in the Eastern world because a great deal of wealth has been transferred from West to East. When it comes to China, personal savings is very high unlike the mindset in the Western world where savings is non-existent. At some point in the near-to-medium- term, the Chinese people will want to increase their standard of living.

Silver's use in industry will continue to grow precisely because of silver's conductivity characteristics. Some other large uses are brazing alloys and solders and photovoltaic, which continue to increase albeit at a slower pace than was forecast in 2010. The cost of production has been falling significantly so even when the price of silver is higher, solar panels should still be economical as long as the amount of silver used on each panel continues to decrease.

Silver is largely inelastic on the demand side for almost all industrial uses. However, with a significant and sustained increase in price, it can be forecast that many companies would do their best to further reduce the amount of silver used if possible.

It is actually better for photovoltaic demand to grow by greater volume with less silver used than by less volume and more silver used per unit. Lastly, silverware and jewelry are the last large components of industrial demand, which we classify as fabrication. Other than that, the category "other uses" comprises many other uses.

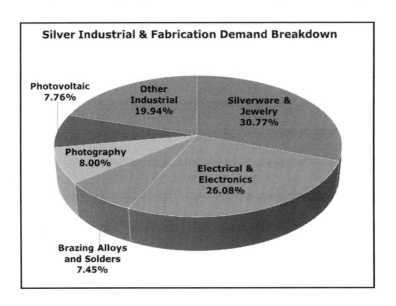

In 2013, fabrication demand (defined by us) accounted for 328.40m oz. Industrial demand on the other hand accounted for 519.30m oz. Fabrication and industrial demand combined accounted for 847.70m oz. Going forward, the primary drivers of industrial demand will remain automobiles, photovoltaic, electronics, ethylene-oxide, batteries in addition to novel uses including solid state lighting, flexible display, interposers, water purification, etc.

The chart above illustrates a rough breakdown of industrial and fabrication demand in 2013. Going forward, electrical and electronics will account for an increasing portion of the pie, along with other industrial and photovoltaic (at least in the short-to-medium-term). However, fabrication has the potential to surprise given that silver and associated jewelry demand could and likely will increase in the latter years of the decade. If our forecast is correct and silver reaches an absolute minimum of $100/oz., it will become more coveted relative to present day. Additionally (as discussed in chapter 7 and 8) some currencies will be inflated more so than others, if not collapsing altogether.

Though unlikely, silverware demand could also increase or remain at current levels for much of the same reasons jewelry demand is likely to increase.

Silver-oxide (non-rechargeable and rechargeable) and silver-zinc batteries (rechargeable) will, over time, increase electrical and electronic uses, perhaps significantly. These batteries have only reached commercial production on a very limited scale to date. This is not to be confused with all the other types of batteries that also contain silver. Before the end of the decade, silver used for silver-based batteries could push upwards of 20m oz.

Silver growth in industry in the short-to-medium term (end of decade) will be primarily driven by products that use the conductive properties of silver in order to make them more efficient, as energy costs across the board have been continuously increasing. The primary drivers will remain electronic, battery, and photovoltaic demand, although more recent "novel uses" could surprise the market, as we will discuss.

Photovoltaic Demand

Solar photovoltaic is currently the third-most renewable energy source, following hydro and wind power. This is an area that should show strong steady growth throughout the decade. The economics of solar power will not be driven or determined by the capital investment needed to build power stations (although it will most definitely remain a large consideration), but rather by the cost of other primary energy sources such as oil and gas. Photovoltaic demand has increased and will continue to increase over the next several years. One study, which will be discussed, forecasts that the consumption of silver for use in meeting photovoltaic demand will reach nearly $110m in 2018.

The European Photovoltaic Industry Association (EPIA) forecasts that solar could provide for more than 9% of the world's population electricity needs by 2030 and over 20% by 2050[59]. Some think the former is achievable as early as the end of the decade. Solar energy is becoming increasingly competitive, as the efficiency of photovoltaics has been increasing while also seeing a consistent price decline. Over a five-year period ending 2012, the average annual price decline has been 11.84%[60]. In order for solar to remain competitive and provide investors with an internal rate of return in the double digits, further cost reductions will need to continue.

India announced that it plans to construct the largest power station in the world. China also has many power stations that are being or will soon begin being built in the near future. It is likely more plans to build additional power stations will be announced over the next several years following its decision to become more "green."

This projection is difficult as governments have subsidized solar in the past (most notably in Germany), although solar at this time is not as efficient as conventional forms of energy. Yet the gap is closing and this is what makes the projection difficult. If solar

---

[59] Solar Photovoltaic Electricity Empowering the World, EPIA.org (22 September 2012)
[60] Renewable energy costs drop in '09, Reuters, 23 November 2009

truly becomes competitive to conventional forms of energy then the market demand could increase significantly and accelerated growth would occur.

Solar competitiveness will soon increase in the world energy market as solar follows what is called Swanson's law, similar to the more well-known Moore's law, which is used in computer hardware and semiconductors whereby performance doubles every 18-24 months. In the case of Swanson's law, it says the cost of production falls 20% for every doubling of capacity[61].

Worldwide capacity stood at 139 gigawatts as of the end of 2013. This is currently projected to increase substantially by the end of the decade. The European Photovoltaic Industry Association (EPIA). In 2013, capacity in Europe totaled 81 GW and projected to increase to 130 GW by 2020 [baseline] or 200 GW [accelerated scenario][62].

Global installations reached a record in 2013, adding 38 GW: however, this is expected to increase in 2014, if not 2015 through the end of the decade. China represents the largest growth market as well as other Asian countries including India. A fair estimate of new capacity coming online through the end of the decade is 440 GW +/-. This dictates that the cost of production per unit should fall 20% sometime in 2016 over 2011-2012 and another 20% in 2019. This is solely through economies of scale, not other optimizations. Other optimizations will undoubtedly occur in the future, augmenting further cost reduction.

While photovoltaic film has two main types—thick and thin—the former is silver intensive while the latter uses very little and sometimes none at all. Thick film, however, dominates its usage, having an 80% market share, due to its technical superiority. In terms of novel uses in industry, currently the primary driver appears to be the growth of silver used in solid state lighting/LEDs, batteries, and other electronically related uses. Then there is potentially an endless list of new technologies that benefit from the thermal and electrical conductivity of silver. While novel uses will increase industrial demand, the main driver, at least for the rest of the decade, will likely be increases in established uses.

Ethylene-Oxide (EO)

The EO industry uses a silver catalyst in order to help combine ethylene and oxygen which is critical in the production of anti-freeze, detergents, plastics, solvents and a broad range of organic chemicals, and is an example of the unmatched importance of silver in industry. Pure ethylene-oxide is a disinfectant that is widely used in such places as hospitals. EO capacity is forecast to increase rapidly as has been the case over the past several years. It is projected that silver consumption for EO application will grow 21% by 2018 over 2013 to 63m oz.[63]

---

[61] Sunny Uplands: Alternative Energy will no longer be alternative, The Economist, 21 November 2012
[62] Global Market Outlook For Photovoltaics 2014-2018, p. 33
[63] CRU International, Glistening Particles of Industrial Silver, p. II

Solid State Lighting, Flexible Display, Interposers

Solid state lighting produces electroluminescent light when a current passes through the electrodes. It uses semiconductors to produce light (LED) or (OLED). Solid state lighting has primarily only been used in traffic lights and car headlamps, until fairly recently. Light-emitting diodes, or LEDs, up to this point in time have been very small. This is because costs have only recently begun to drop at a very rapid pace. Going forward, the growth potential is incredibly significant. There are countless applications solid state lighting can fulfill.

Solid state lighting (SSL) in everyday use such as LED light bulbs has just begun to become known; however, this has gained significant traction, relative to the short time in which such lighting has gained more attention at reasonable cost. Solid state lighting is now significantly cheaper, relative to fluorescent lighting, and continues to become more so as increased efficiency has been recognized while cutting production costs. This trend will likely continue as further research and development is conducted. Silver consumption in SSL has been growing very sharply and will continue to do so throughout the next ten+ years, with the largest market being mainland China.

Recent research conducted by the Lighting Research Center has shown that LEDs make "impressive" progress in terms of light output, color properties, efficacy per electric watt, and potential for long life. This combined with vast cost reduction has resulted in many more applications for consumer electronics, automobiles, and general lighting. More recently, airports throughout the world are transitioning to LED-based solutions at an increasing rate. This is because LEDs are particularly suited for applications in need of colored light, and, due to signals and other visual aids, airports do not require much light output. Early generation LEDs were able to provide suitable solutions, but now, with the potential to improve visibility to pilots, energy savings, and longer illumination life, newer generation LEDs are more desirable[64].

Up until very recently the technology could only produce backlighting and signage, but now this technology will rapidly evolve such that it can be used in higher performance items. This could drive the demand for solid stating lighting to consume a significant amount of silver. Whenever projections are made in advance, estimates are often overstated, but various groups have forecast that over the next decade (ending 2025) it could consume as much as 20m-40m oz. annually.

Longer term, if this is the preferred method of lighting worldwide, this includes but is not limited to the aforementioned lighting in aviation, residential lighting, security lighting, outdoor lighting, health and vision, controls (sensors), automotive, day-lighting and street lighting. Alternatives that are non-silver are far less efficient, notably with dimming and uneven lighting. Solid state lighting also offers more brightness while using less energy relative to that which is consumed by incandescent light bulbs. These are being and/or have been banned in numerous countries, including the U.S., Brazil, Argentina, and most European countries. Perhaps the banning by various governments

---

[64] Jean Paul Freyssinier, "Airfield Lighting: The long-term performance of LEDs," April 16, 2014.

will actually favor a silver-based lighting system most likely unknown to them at this time.

Fluorescent light bulbs currently in use in the U.S. are the quick alternative to incandescent bulbs; however, they use mercury and have rather poor lighting quality. SSL does not produce as much heat, which is an advantage in some applications. Should SSL become more prevalent, as it's likely to do over the second half of this decade and through the next decade, it will consume a very healthy amount of silver. It reduces energy use while concurrently meeting the needs of society. Furthermore, if solid state lighting becomes adopted by the Eastern world, it could add to the silver demand we projected! The average LED light bulb currently lasts fifty thousand to sixty thousand hours, although this will likely be increased significantly over time as there are on-going studies for optimizing the integration of other components to the LED bulb. Despite the higher price relative to a fluorescent bulb, the economics are far superior.

Flexible displays are electronics that possess next generation technology. Like solid state lighting, this also represents a material long-term growth segment for silver consumption in industry, particularly electrical and electronics. Initially, the primary targets will be flexible displays such as in laptop screens, touchpads, and smartphones. But as time passes, most everything with a screen and/or lighting in general will likely be available as a flexible option as costs of doing so will eventually fall. Taking this a step further, this technology could potentially advance in the longer-term, to such a degree that small televisions, laptops, smartphones, touchpads, and the like are able to fold up so small that such products may be able to fit in your pocket or take up a much smaller space. Should this occur, it would be truly revolutionary in terms of industrial demand for silver consumed for a single segment.

Interposers hold considerable promise for silver demand in the longer term. Like flexible displays and solid state lighting, to a lesser degree interposers are also a next generation technology. These have been used in the past with silicon in semiconductor chips; however, silicon has limited performance that is just now being reached. Interposers are crucial for the proper functioning of many computers, medical devices, and countless other applications. Stacking semiconductor chips both saves space and increases functionality, allowing multiple chips to be integrated into a single circuit. This is referred to as three-dimensional integrated circuits (3D IC)[65].

The semiconductor fabrication industry is known as being one of the most aggressive regarding year over year cost reductions. Although silicon (which is expensive) currently dominates the market today, glass is being looked into very closely and is in the pilot stage of production. Glass would be in excess of 40% cheaper relative to silicon. Additionally, however, the economies of scale can further reduce costs, and using glass makes it much easier and cheaper to meet the required thinness. Lastly, glass is more efficient, as it allows electronic signals to travel faster. As in most things, copper poses a threat as a cheaper alternative for the "fill material" in interposers, but

---

[65]Metals Focus, "The Outlook for New Electrical & Electronic Uses of Silver," July 2014.

silver is likely to win out because there is a certain portion of glass manufacturing that is only compatible with silver. The technology using silver is much more advanced and is similar to thick film used in solar cells[66].

Batteries

There are two main types of silver-bearing batteries: silver-oxide batteries, which generally have a low power capacity, and silver-zinc batteries, which are of higher capacity. The characteristics of both include long operating and shelf life, as well as a high performance-to-weight ratio. The former has only recently begun to show the potential for them to be rechargeable (silver-oxide batteries), making the potential growth in this market primarily from silver-zinc batteries (at least in the short-term). Silver consumption is projected to increase 13% by 2018 over 2013, reaching 36m oz.[67]

Silver-zinc batteries currently are the most widely used batteries containing silver. The zinc matrix battery is a rechargeable silver-oxide battery designed by Matrix Power. This newer type of battery consists of zinc, silver, and water, and it is one of the first commercially produced, rechargeable silver-oxide batteries. The comparative advantage versus a lithium-ion battery is that it's free from thermal runaway, also known as overheating and in some cases exploding. In identical sized batteries, the zinc matrix battery stores **twice as much energy** while also weighing less than a lithium-ion battery[68].

The biggest advantage, however, is that the zinc matrix has no "lazy battery effect," in that each time is it recharged it can hold a full charge, in contrast to lithium batteries, which both gradually lose their maximum energy/charge capacity over time and also gradually lose it if the battery only undergoes a partial charge. In other words, silver-oxide batteries are far more cost efficient relative to lithium-ion over the life of the battery, despite the higher initial cost.

Due to robust growth expectations in a number of end products, including smart phones, laptops, and tablets, the potential here is significant due to the pervasive nature of the handheld devices on a worldwide basis. These batteries could be recycled for their silver, but the ramp up in their use could put some noticeable pressure once the public becomes aware of the advantages of a silver-based battery.

Additional uses for silver-oxide/zinc batteries may be the auto industry, specifically in electric cars, although research at present hasn't focused on the exact level of silver consumed per auto catalyst and is steered more toward development of lithium-ion catalyst. We think silver-based batteries will prove to be the overwhelming choice as they will likely prove to be safer and more efficient. The same risks apply here regarding lithium-ion auto catalysts compared to laptop batteries, in that they can overheat and potentially explode. Silver-based batteries have also been billed as a

---

[66] Ibid
[67] CRU International, *Glistening Particles of Industrial Silver*, pp. I-II
[68] Zinc Matrix Battery, see company Web site: Zpowerbattery.com

"clean" technology, due to the fact, as mentioned, that both the silver and zinc can be recycled once the battery life has ended[69].

Super-capacitors

This presents a huge market for silver, longer-term. Super-capacitors are basically batteries in terms of their function. They store and release energy and theoretically last forever with no impairment to performance. What is so spectacular about super-capacitors is that they are the battery of the future yet the technology is here today. Energy intake occurs much more quickly than with a conventional battery while also being able to source energy from wind or solar power, power grids, and even in braking a vehicle when driving. In short, super-capacitors bridge the gap between ordinary conventional capacitors and rechargeable batteries.

Since this is a new technology (at least a newer technology in terms of maximum efficiency, which is still unknown) and a costly one presently, cheaper less efficient alternatives could develop. The projected use could be in the range of five to ten million ounces annually. During the next decade, super-capacitors, primary electronics, photovoltaic, silver alloys, jewelry and silverware, solid state lighting, and other novel uses could put silver back into a deficit (wherein consumption outstrips supply [excluding investment demand], not to be confused with shortage), this will likely remain indefinitely.

Wood Preservatives

Chromated copper arsenate (CCA) was the dominant preservative until 2003, when it was greatly restricted from use because it was toxic. It can take the following forms: silver-oxide, bromide, iodide, chloride, and nitrate, and these have advantages such as protection against fungi, termite damage prevention, and mold inhibition. CCA, however, is costly in comparison to alternatives that cost well below 50% less per liter. The key for CCA to be cost efficient enough is to use less silver and more copper, if a more balanced albeit still efficient preservative can be achieved. The potential of this application is dramatic due to the amount of silver used in the application at the present time. The use is very restricted at this time and used only where necessary, such as wood playgrounds for children.

Automotive

While not a novel use, roughly 56m oz. of silver annually are used in automobiles. Every electrical action in a modern car is activated by silver-coated contacts. The most basic functions of a car are activated using a silver membrane switch, including starting the engine, adjusting power seats, and moving windows up and down. Automotive production in China and India is accelerating and is on pace to drive the automotive sector to consume roughly 70m oz. of silver in 2018. This however, is actually a

---

[69]GFMS, "The Future of Silver Industrial Demand," 2011.

decelerating compound annual growth rate for use in automobiles as it represents a CAGR of 4.4%-4.5% compared to a CAGR of 4.9% over the period 2008-2013.

The active ingredient in anti-freeze is ethylene-oxide, a compound made from silver. Over the next ten to twenty years, the automotive industry will use considerably more silver. Cars are becoming more technologically advanced and many now have touch screens in the dashboard. These use silver and, like everything else, will become increasingly more sophisticated over the coming years.

China is still a production- and savings-based economy and just recently has slowly started transitioning into a more balanced economy. This really cannot happen in full until the Chinese completely de-peg the renminbi (RMB) from the U.S. dollar. This is because once the RMB is able to float against all other currencies, the purchasing power of each monetary unit will most likely increase, at least relative to what is today. When this happens, China's society in general will have the ability to increase its standard of living. This will be very easy, not only because its purchasing power has increased by a fair degree, but also because the personal savings rate is very high. This could spur automobile sales to a large degree.

A little-discussed topic about electric cars is that silver-oxide/silver-zinc batteries may be used in electric cars in the future. Research and development has begun to look at alternatives to the lithium-ion batteries, given the inherent dangers the latter possesses. Silver-zinc batteries have been billed a "green" technology because both components can be recycled. Almost the entire electric car industry is focused on lithium-ion batteries: but do not count silver out—it could be a big leading factor in the electric car industry in the future.

Radio Frequency Identification (RFID)

RFID tags can be used as an alternative to bar codes in tracking inventory and store a significant amount of more data. Passive RFID tags can only transmit data after they are powered from the reader, which sends electromagnetic waves that induce a current in the tag's antenna. Active tags on the other hand have their own power force and can transmit data to the reader independently. While considerable growth is forecast for RFID tags in general, it won't cause any substantial increase in terms of ounces consumed, as very little silver is used. Even if it were to take 100% of the market, the silver used would be minor.

In our earlier work, the amount of silver used was basically an unknown and since the amount to be used varied widely, it seemed possible that RFID tags could impact the market. Now that the subject is well-known, that earlier forecast is erroneous.

Water Purification

There are several ways in which silver can be used for purifying water. The most widely used applications make use of silver's bactericidal properties, in forms including silver-impregnated ceramic filters, silver deposited on activated carbon, silver nitrate, silver chloride, or in tetrasilver tetroxide. Silver is also used as a catalyst for the production of hydrogen peroxide, which is in turn used in water disinfection. It is used in building municipal water supply systems, pools, spas, or personal water purification devices.

In water supply systems, it can destroy bacterial growth in pipes, connections, and tanks; in pools and spas, silver ion filtration canisters treat all components; and in personal purification devices, it prevents bacterial and fungal growth that would otherwise block the active charcoal filter. At present, silver-based water treatments are used more widely in Europe than in the United States. There does not seem to be undue concern regarding the safety of using silver in water purification devices. The World Health Organization (WHO) states that a lifetime intake of approximately 10g of silver can be considered to be the "no observed adverse effect level" (NOAEL).

In public pools, silver is a much more preferable filtration option than chlorine; it possesses all the same characteristics but isn't nearly as bad for the skin. Silver is ideal for water filtration as silver particles locate, oxidize, and destroy negatively charged bacteria and pathogens. While silver consumption for filtration and purification purposes is unlikely to reach any meaningful quantities in any year this decade, there is a very real potential for it to do so near the turn of the decade or soon thereafter (=>10m oz. annually).

Medical Uses

Silver is often an ingredient in wound treatments, dressings, powders, and creams that make use of its antimicrobial action against yeasts, molds, and bacteria. It is used in a variety of forms, including silver sulfadiazine, silver chloride, silver sulfate, and nanocrystalline silver. With regard to wound dressings, studies have shown that dressings containing silver increase the comfort level for burn patients by minimizing adhesion between the wound and dressing, thereby reducing pain when changing dressings. Furthermore, the frequency of changing dressings might also be reduced, owing to the antimicrobial activity of the silver. Clinical evidence also supports the efficacy of silver as an antiseptic (which can take many forms, including gels, sprays, and powders) for infected wounds.

Silver can also be used in catheters, which are made with a silver-based antimicrobial coating, as well as for other medical implantation devices, such as prosthetic heart valves and vascular grafts. In urinary catheters, research has shown that the use of silver alloys reduces the incidence of urinary tract infection (UTI) by as much as threefold, compared to non-silver-bearing types. Despite the initial higher cost of the silver-bearing products, therefore, the longer-term benefits of reduced spending on aftercare may justify the economic cost of using these materials.

With regard to silver demand, current off-take is only a small percentage of total silver demand. To give an indication of the quantities involved, the silver content in bandages is typically measured in mg/100cm2, and in creams in terms of milligrams (μg)/cm2 per application. One of the world's leading bandage manufacturers consumes only around 7,000 ounces of silver per year.

Food Packaging

For its hygiene benefits, silver is often applied as a coating or is embedded in polymers used in some food packaging. Cooking utensils, kitchen detergent, and refrigerators also make use of silver's antibacterial properties, mostly in nano form. Currently there is a lack of clarity regarding the use of nanosilver, which means regulations could be applied retrospectively. Although the EU Food Packaging Regulation covers all materials that come into contact with food or drink, nanosilver has not yet undergone this safety assessment. This is because nanosilver has not been deemed an "existing" product.

In the United States, food packaging containing nanosilver falls under the jurisdiction of both the Environmental Protection Agency (EPA) and the FDA (Food and Drug Administration Agency), with the former regulating the pesticide aspect and the latter the container itself. Notwithstanding these concerns, the food hygiene sector is unlikely to become a major silver consumer.

Industrial demand is looking like it will increase in 2014 over 2013 in excess of 2.5%. Photovoltaic demand was on pace to increase in excess of 11% through June. This could have continued through the rest of the year, although it is more likely to see an annual increase slightly lower and see an 8%-10% growth.

Looking Ahead—2015 and Beyond (Investment Demand)

From the data we were able to obtain, primary silver supply is running more or less along our forecasts through the first half of the year. Meanwhile, secondary supply is running slightly below our forecasts. Secondary silver supply will likely fall 20+/- in 2014, which shouldn't come as a surprise as the economics of recycling silver are greatly reduced when the average price of silver is substantially lower than the previous year. In 2013, secondary supply decreased a material amount as silver's average price was $23.79/oz. In 2014, the average price of silver was $4.72/oz. lower at $19.07/oz.

Investment demand continues to run at a very robust pace, although we are unable to obtain many large components at this time. Investment demand could very well set a second consecutive annual record in 2014 as we think it has done. As of the first week of December 2014, Silver American Eagle Sales set a new record after setting the record in 2013. The U.S. mint did not forecast such strong demand, selling out when demand was surging meaning sales could have been several million ounces higher. Silver American Eagle sales set a record in 2014, selling just over 44m ounces. Canadian Silver Maple Leaf sales were also on pace to also set a second consecutive annual sales record through the first half of the year but these numbers are not yet known.

Silver imports into both China and India continue unabated, although the former is harder to gauge, given that the imports placed on the Shanghai Gold Exchange (SHGE) is information not easily obtained. As of the first week of July 2014, the Shanghai Futures Exchange saw its silver inventories were drawn to just 148 metric tons due to a remarkable amount of contracts that individuals chose to take delivery on. In February

2014, silver stocks stood at 575 metric tons but we don't know the quantity imported from February 1, 2014 to July 1, 2014. The only thing we know for sure is that a minimum of 500 tons has been delivered on the SHFE/SGX in the first half of 2014. As mentioned briefly in Chapter 1, the Shanghai Gold Exchange deliveries for both gold and silver continued its robust pace. Augmenting this fact is the rampant investment demand in India. In aggregate, just these two countries accounted for more than half of primary supply (mine supply), that is industrial, fabrication and investment demand combined. The trend is obvious that a great deal of precious metals is moving into these two countries. Silver for investment demand in India alone accounted for more than 26% of primary silver supply, with net silver imports setting a record at 7,063 tons.

The COMEX recorded more than 6.50x the trading volume relative to the Shanghai Futures Exchange in 2012 but by 2013, volume on the SHFE exceeded that on the COMEX by more than 500,000 metric tons. Last year, the volume on the SHFE exceeded the COMEX by more than 1,500,000 metric tons. If we include the SGE, which increased 17% in 2014 over 2013, the trading volume in China relative to the U.S. is that much higher. Why is this important? It's important because the Shanghai Futures Exchange and Shanghai Gold Exchange are both physical exchanges, whereas the COMEX is nothing but paper. This is not to say the SHFE and SGE don't have a material amount of trading settled in cash, but that these exchanges also have a material amount of contracts settled by one party taking delivery.

Futures exchanges originally were important for price discovery; however it has become immaterial because nearly all trades are settled in cash, at least in the Western world. As the SHFE and SGE gain market share, the price of silver will begin to reflect more accurately, the market price net of all the intervention that took and is currently taking place and thereby causing price distortions. Hopefully, this discrepancy continues to increase, causing the masses who deal in the futures market to ignore the COMEX altogether. Lastly, the ETF SLV, the largest ETF by silver holdings in the world has seen its inflows increase roughly 9.0% even though the largest gold ETF GLD decreased. This amounts to roughly 25m-30m oz. of silver.

Silver for investment demand has been extremely robust in China in 2014. Furthermore, India's silver imports have absolutely exploded, standing at 6,789 tons for the year (through November) or 28% increase over the same period in 2013. November was a new record for silver imports, totaling a whopping 1,254 tons[70]! India finished the year with total imports upwards of 7,063 tons for the full year 2014. Putting this into perspective, this amounts to more than 26% of annual mine supply in 2014 (assuming mine supply totals 842m oz.).

Industrial demand in 2014 was also quite significant. Demand elasticity (to a moderate degree) would likely start impacting industrial demand around the $40-$60 level. Silver demand is incredibly inelastic precisely because it possesses such powerful conductivity characteristics, meaning products that do use silver consume so little that

---

[70] Koos Jansen, India Silver Import 6789t YTD, December 19th 2014, see company Web Site: bullionstar.com

changes in the price only begin to have a material impact on economics at exponentially higher silver prices.

A study was released by the Silver Institute near the end of 2014, indicating that silver demand for industrial uses is projected to increase significantly over the five-year period (2014-2018) by a whopping 37% or 142m oz. for a total of 680m oz. This equates to a (CAGR) compound annual growth rate of 4.90% through 2018. Per this study, total Industrial demand will total 680m oz.[71], excluding fabrication and investment demand and if we use that number and assume fabrication demand remains flat for the lowest number of the two studies, in 2018 silver demand (excluding investment demand) will be 980m. In our view the study prepared for the Silver Institute by CRU International is too optimistic, due to our forecast of continued global economic stagnation which will then be followed by a worldwide economic contraction. Our forecast is for industrial demand in 2018 to be closer to 570m-620m oz.

According to the London-based consultancy Metals Focus Ltd, electrical and electronic uses will increase use in industry from 15 to 20 million ounces by 2018. This will be driven by solid state lighting (OLED) and (LED), flexible displays and next generation of semiconductor chips. These require interposers to enable far greater functionality relative to previous generations. A decade from now, these three components could very well make up a very healthy portion of industrial demand.

Short term (1-4 Yrs):
Photovoltaic, Ethylene-Oxide, **Solid State Lighting LED, OLED, Batteries**, Water purification and other electronics, RFID's

Medium Term (5-10 Yrs):
Batteries, SSL/LED/OLED, Flexible Displays, other electronics, photovoltaic, Water purification, Autocapicitors, Ethylene Oxide

Longer Term (10+):
Batteries, Supercapicitors, Superconductors, **Solid State Lighting**/Led/OLED, **Interposers**, Other Electronics, Autocapicitors, Photovoltaic, and **Flexible Displays**

In summary, the reason silver will see such a dramatic increase in price over the next several years is due to a very sharp increase in investment demand. Investment demand will remain strong likely through the first part of the next decade, though

---

[71] CRU International (Prepared For The Silver Institute), Glistening Particles of Industrial Silver, Dec. 2014

greatly abate from what we will witness at its peak. By that time, due to how price inelastic silver is, industrial demand coupled with peak silver will make for a great longer-term investment. Fabrication and industrial demand will strongly support the supply-demand picture. In particular silver used in electrical devices, electronics, batteries (both basic and silver-zinc), photovoltaic, use in automobiles (which is significant given the urbanization of China and increased pollution controls over the coming years), SSL, novel uses, ethylene-oxide, etc.

- Electrical and electronics will remain a staple in silver's use in industry for the foreseeable future because it has ideal electrical and thermal conductivity properties. As of 2013, accounted for almost 219m oz. of silver consumption. Other studies have this line item in excess of 232m oz.
- Solid State Lighting, Flexible Displays and Interposers are three Novel uses, solid state lighting being the most well-known [LED, OLED bulbs, backlighting, etc.]
- Every day and rechargeable batteries [zinc-oxide] and [silver-oxide]: Silver has been used in batteries in the past and therefore why a material degree is still consumed for this purpose. Silver-based batteries provide unrivaled efficiency in this market, however, it may take several more years to the "go-to" batteries.
- Ethylene-Oxide: This, along with Photovoltaic demand has really been a growth driver regarding's silver use in industrial demand. This is required to make numerous household items. The robust growth in EO catalysts should continue for the next several years.
- Photovoltaic: After taking a brief pause from 2009-2011, Photovoltaic demand has picked up significantly. Last year's 70m oz. of consumption will reach another new record once all the data is known for 2014 and in our projections, this should increase through 2018-2019, surpassing the 100m oz. level.
- Water Purification: Silver have shown its affinity for water filtration numerous times in the past. This includes the ability to fight off legionnaire's disease what a silver water filtration device is used in public pools. Unlike Chlorine, these water filtration systems are not harmful to the skin. This, however, is overshadowed by silver's use to treat unclean water. Silver is used for such things because of its bactericidal properties in silver-impregnated ceramic filters, silver deposited on activated carbon, silver nitrate, silver chloride, or in tetrasilver tetroxide.

Chapter 5: Money & Banking

"It is a sobering fact that the prominence of central banks in this century has coincided with a general tendency towards more inflation, not less. If the overriding objective is price stability, we did better with the nineteenth-century gold standard and passive central banks, with currency boards, or even with "free banking." The truly unique power of a central bank, after all, is the power to create money, and ultimately the power to create is the power to destroy." –Paul Volcker, former Fed chairman

To fully appreciate precious metals manipulation, the origins of the coming currency crisis, and the current economic landscape, we must first address basic yet necessary economic concepts. Therefore we will first focus on money and banking, particularly the process of fractional reserve banking and the various phases of inflation. Basic economic principles dictate price levels of various good and services are determined by the equilibrium where the supply and demand curves intersect. This is also known as clearing the market.

Changing prices are almost entirely determined by the money supply. The exception being gains in productivity, which barring intervention lower the price of goods and services. Price inflation is caused by an increase in the money supply.

Often investors expect an almost instantaneous correlation, but it is important to keep in mind that prices don't rise simultaneously nor evenly. In fact, some prices may decline and some prices may rise considerably. Inflation in its historical sense meant an increase in the money supply, with higher prices being an effect. Simply stated increasing the quantity of the monetary unit in circulation *causes* prices to rise.

The best estimate of inflation is the TMS (True Money Supply), which we have previously examined. Further expanding on the concept of inflation, academia and mainstream economic thought blames stagflation (inflation with economic contraction) as particular rare events for example in the 1970's stagflation was blamed on the "supply shocks" in oil. This in a classic economic sense means that the prices of other goods and services have to decrease because the money supply is unchanged.

Loan Banking vs. Deposit Banking

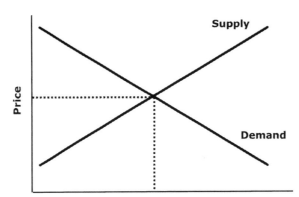

We will examine two primary types of banking, loan banking and deposit banking. By going through an example we wish to make the concepts clear to the reader how these two types of banks function.

Loan Banking
1) Bank XYZ has $1m in retained earnings.
2) Bank XYZ comes to an agreement with Person 1 and they agree on a 2-year, $900,000 loan at a 12% interest rate, paid annually. The IOU is carried as equity and accounted for on the equity and liabilities side of the balance sheet as seen below.
3) The loan is fully repaid with Bank XYZ having been paid back a total of $1,116,000 or $108,000 in interest after year 1 and another $108,000 after year 2, along with the principal of $900,000.

Note: At no time was any <u>money created</u>, although the bank made a loan and recorded that loan plus interest on the balance sheet. In other words, loan banking is usually productive and non-inflationary.

This is how banking would work in a free market as banks would be able to loan increasing quantities of money during the course of building a track record of prudent loans. Banks originate these loans as retained earnings increase, therefore over time a larger quantity of loans would be originated and/or that bank would be able to make larger sized loans. If the bank makes unsound loans, it will show the loss and if it makes too many bad loans then in a worst case the bank is bankrupt and closes. This is actually healthy for the overall economy because in a true free market, ideas, goods and services that fail are taken out rather rapidly and the market is the overall judge.

It seems to be lost in the current political system that in a real free market the "right" to succeed also means the "right" to fail. Further, it must be pointed out that at times a failure may just be a step in the process that leads to a better overall product or service.

A capitalist may have a great idea and the market provides feedback that requires the idea to be adjusted to fit what the market really desires, and by paying attention, a modification can be accomplished that makes a business that was moving toward failure become successful.

Deposit Banking

Deposit banking began as what would be called money warehouses, in that customers would deposit silver and gold coin/bullion and were given a warehouse receipt with which to claim these deposits. This receipt acted exactly as a demand deposit does today with inconvertible fiat paper money, so that coin or bullion were redeemable on demand. This is a bailment contract, as compared to a loan contract, because the bank was hired for the safekeeping of silver, gold, or anything else of value. By the end of the civil war, deposit banks began to loan out some of the silver and gold on which they had already issued a warehouse receipt. In a truly free society, where a commodity-backed standard persisted, depositors would in fact pay banks interest for "storage costs" of gold and silver redeemable on demand.

Fractional-Reserve Banking (w/o a Central Bank)

This practice became more prevalent (which is equivalent to fractional reserve banking today) over time and clearly was responsible for bank runs and failures, although the market made this practice rather scarce. The founding of the Federal Reserve in 1913 maintained the same practice of loaning more than the bank truly had on deposit.

Thus the corruption of the U.S. dollar, which Andrew Jackson fought so hard to prevent, began anew, as "the banker's bank" in the U.S. implemented an initial 40% reserve requirement but FDR then devalued the dollar vs. gold, followed by Bretton Woods post WW2 and finally Nixon closing the gold window. The 40% reserve requirement (gold backed) slowly transformed into a 10% reserve requirement backed by worthless pieces of paper. In 1913, fractional reserve banking was now a "legal" scheme implemented by the bankers.

DEPOSIT BANK XYZ ~ BALANCE SHEET

Assets	Equity & Liabilities
1)	
Silver or Gold coin and Bullion : $100,000	Warehouse Receipts for Silver/Gold: $100,000
Total Assets: $100,000	Reserve Ratio: 100%
2)	
Silver/Gold Coin: $100,000 IOU: $150,000	Warehouse Receipts for Silver/Gold: $250,000
Total Assets: $250,000	Total Liabilities: $250,000

1) Deposit Bank XYZ starts with $100k worth of silver and/or gold coins from Person 1 making a deposit of this size. The warehouse receipt circulates from person to person as Person 1 buys something from Person 2 and so on.
2) Bank XYZ then issues an additional $150,000 worth of warehouse receipts, although it does not actually have the $150,000 worth of gold/silver. Therefore the reserve ratio is $100,000/$250,000, or 40%. Warehouse receipts for gold and silver acted as money, as they were "redeemable on demand" and much more convenient for use in exchange. The bank has therefore inflated the money supply while engaging in fraud. The bank would remain solvent in so long as more than the $100,000 worth of silver/gold it had on demand was redeemed (net of interest payments).

The above example has been called counterfeiting by some of us in the "honest money camp"; regardless, it is the current system. A bank operating in such a way needs to have a time structure of its assets to be no longer than the time structure of its liabilities. We began with a commodity-backed money to illustrate two things: (1) Why the banking system based on fractional reserve banking results in problems; and (2) That a commodity-backed monetary system can only be inflationary if and only if fractional reserve banking is present. A strong argument can be made that fractional reserve banking is present but government does not have monopoly control of the mint, the market would put the necessary checks and balances on monetary inflation such as that during the free banking era.

Absent of fractional reserve banking, deflation would persist in such an environment. Again, deflation is often feared by those undereducated about finance/economics but in an honest money standard, prices generally become lower over time and the society at large enjoys a greater standard of living.

In a free banking system (such as that which existed during the latter part of the 19th century), there is no government or regulating system/agency. Banks are free to engage in fractional reserve banking, however, should the bank fail to meet the redemption of demand deposits, it would be forced to liquidate and go bankrupt[72].

While one may think this would lead to banking that is extremely reckless and unviable, there are numerous limits imposed on the monetary inflation that could otherwise exist. Banking in general is built on trust, in that customers expect they can withdraw all their demand deposits at once. It isn't just the ability to repatriate all demand deposits but of also doing this while not inflating the money supply. Augmenting this limit on credit expansion is free market forces, in this case competition between various banks. If one bank in particular should garner an unrivaled track record, it would set the standard in the industry, causing other banks to follow suit by implementing similar practices—for example, vetting loan applications to a very high standard so the failure rate is very low. Competition could also foster banks to redeem demand deposits

---

[72] Murray Rothbard, The Mystery of Banking, pg. 111

(in the form of warehouse receipts) at other banks, giving those who do so a comparative advantage. If a bank chooses not to do so and to hold off redemptions from other banks, it would lose business.

As discussed earlier, historically the market chooses a commodity money, notably silver and gold. Therefore, if this were the case, bank money or paper money redeemable in specie would put further limits on the probability of monetary inflation.

Thus far, we have been discussing local banks; now let us examine international trade. For ease of this discussion, we will assume there is only one bank per country. If Country A inflates its money supply via fractional reserve banking, Country A would see an artificial economic boom take place and a corresponding increase in consumption and savings/investment. This would reverse course, as the money unit would flow out of the country to roughly the same degree investment in other countries is made. This is because claims will eventually increase abroad to the point where banks in other countries would redeem these clams. Again, stressing the market tends toward equilibrium. This will cause silver/gold to flow out of Country A such that it is forced to contract both its deposits and loans, or in other words, it will cause a contraction in the overall money supply.

It is worth noting that along with the artificial boom and corresponding bust, there are other considerations to take into account. Country A's balance of payments enters a deficit because during the inflation process, one effect was the increase in the price of consumer goods, which causes a decrease in exports. Once the bust is underway, the contraction of credit leaves less monetary units available to purchase domestic and international goods. This results both in decreased imports and in an inflow of gold.

The decrease in consumer prices in Country A reinvigorates exports and causes imports to fall. This will cause a further inflow of silver and/or gold. This is known as Specie-flow-price mechanism. From this, we can deduce that monetary inflation in a world of free banking will cause an outflow of gold and a boom period, followed by a contraction and at certain times a bust. Furthermore, domestically, the ONLY way for widespread monetary inflation to occur in free banking is if banks form a cartel and all banks engage in monetary inflation. Bank Cartels could legally be formed under free banking, however, it could never last as the profit and economic incentives wouldn't permit this to happen.

"It is a mistake to associate with the notion of free banking the image of a state of affairs under which everybody is free to issue bank notes and to cheat the public ad libitum. People often refer to the dictum of an anonymous American quoted by Thomas Tooke: '"free trade in banking is free trade in swindling.' However, freedom in the issuance of banknotes would have narrowed down the use of banknotes considerably if it had not entirely suppressed it. It was this idea which Henri Cernuschi advanced in the hearing of the French Banking Inquiry on October 24th 1865: '"I believe that what is called freedom of banking would result

in a total suppression of banknotes in France. I want to give everybody the right to issue banknotes so that nobody should take any banknotes any longer[73]."

In short, free banking would lead to hard money, so once again market forces would demand a sound monetary policy. The institution of a central bank is a cartelization of the banking system. While the Fed proclaims to be independent, the truth is it is a "quasi" government entity. Regardless, because the Fed is given the monopoly control of the currency supply, it receives a monopoly privilege[74].

Fractional Reserve Banking in a Fiat Monetary System

Bank reserves are the amount of money a bank keeps on hand for instant redemption, also termed "required reserves." Example: A bank receives a $50,000 deposit, otherwise stated as a $50,000 increase in demand deposits (checking accounts). The demand deposits can be redeemed by the customer at any time (savings deposits technically are not considered demand deposits, as by law, immediate redemption upon demand isn't required, but for all intents and purposes are "demand deposits" as if these weren't immediately available on demand, bank runs would surely occur).

If the bank keeps all $50,000 in its vault, then the reserve ratio is 100%. However, if the bank lends out the $50,000 to another customer, then the bank now has $100,000 of demand deposits backed by only $50,000 of reserves. The reserve ratio in this case has fallen to 50%. This is called fractional reserve banking, because the bank only has a fraction of their deposits covered by reserves.

In the United States, the legal reserve ratio at commercial banks is 10%. So taking this example one step further, the bank can lend up to $500,000, only needing the $50,000 to create an additional $450,000 out of thin air[75].

When a bank makes a loan, they do so by simply creating a demand deposit for the amount of the loan. Since demand deposits are money, banks create money when they make loans. When a bank originates a loan, it deposits 10% (the minimum reserve requirement at the Fed and in exchange, the Fed creates 100% of the loan. Technically, "excess reserves" are already at the Fed, so it is only a matter of an accounting entry.

Maturity Mismatching

Fractional reserve banking is inherently unstable. Firms should arrange their affairs so the time structure of their assets is shorter than the time structure of their liabilities. Let us examine this by way of another example. Suppose Mr. Andrew owes Mr. Black $1,000. In addition, Mr. Cowen owes Mr. Andrew $1,000. Mr. Andrew should arrange his affairs so Mr. Cowen pays him before he must pay Mr. Black.

However, the time structure of a fractional reserve bank's assets (its loans) is always longer than the time structure of its liabilities (its demand deposits). This is

---

[73] Ludwig von Mises, *Human Action*, pg 443
[74] Murray N. Rothbard, *The Mystery of Banking*, pg. 125
[75] Eddie Fuller & Christopher Marchese, "A Program For Economic Recovery," http://www.financialsense.com

known as "borrowing short (term) and lending long. Demand deposits are due instantly, so it is impossible for a fractional reserve bank to arrange its affairs accordingly.

This is equivalent to Mr. Andrew owing Mr. Black $1,000 on demand, while Mr. Cowen owes Mr. Andrew $1,000 five years from now. Consequently, fractional reserve banks are technically in a state of inherent bankruptcy. A fractional reserve bank can never satisfy all its customers' redemption demands simultaneously. This is also called maturity mismatching.

While maturity mismatching can be extremely profitable, it is also fraught with risk. It is especially risky when those in charge of banking operations don't understand basic economic principles. Unfortunately this is the case with every commercial bank, at least in North America. The profit (in a static world) is very simple to calculate, that is a bank takes on (issue) short-term liabilities and invests in long-term assets. This is a basic interest rate arbitrage. For example, if a bank borrows short at 1.25% and lends long at 4.25%, the bank makes a profit on the spread (4.25% - 1.50% = 2.75%). It is this spread multiplied by the size of the loan (whether quarterly, semi-annually or annually) that determines total profit, assuming the bank is able to borrow at the same rate each time its liabilities are rolled over.

The problem here is that the bank or as in the case of Icelandic banks during the financial crisis is the need to continuously roll over its short term liabilities. Central banks are lenders of last resort and the inherent moral hazard which accompanies a central bank, all but guarantees excessive maturity mismatching.

This more sinister effect of excessive maturity mismatching is not directly seen. It leads to falsifications in the economy by distorting the capital structure, which will be discussed in depth in chapter 7.

Following the financial crisis of 2008, when the Fed created a huge moral hazard by bailing out almost every commercial bank, it set a dangerous precedent for the future, implicitly stating the larger money center banks won't be allowed to fail and reckless lending does not produce consequences. In short, fractional reserve banking systems are highly unstable and not only susceptible to collapse, but a collapse is inevitable on a fiat monetary system. The precedent set in 2008 was just a confirmation of what large commercial banks implicitly knew after the savings and loan crisis in the late 80's and long-term capital management in the late 90's.

The Federal Reserve System

It is possible for governments to control the money supply through a central bank. The Federal Reserve System is the central bank of the United States. The Fed acts as a lender of last resort to combat the instability inherent in the fractional reserve banking system. The Fed influences the financial markets and economic activity by not only controlling the money supply but at times also uses rhetoric to influence market expectations.

The Fed exercises considerable influence over the money supply by controlling the level of reserve requirements of member banks and setting the discount window, which is the interest rate at which these same banks can borrow currency from the Fed. The following equation simplifies the process by which the Fed increases the money supply through changes in the levels of reserves. Let us define terms:

D = Demand Deposits
r = Reserve ratio
R = Level of Reserves
Change in Demand Deposits = (**Change in D = 1/r x Change in R**)

The Fed can directly control the level of reserves, and hence indirectly control the money supply, by engaging in open market operations. Open market operations entail the purchase or sale of securities in the open market. It is important that the U.S. government does not technically "print" money that the U.S. government needs to borrow from the Fed.

How the Supply of Money and Credit Expands and Contracts

The Fed *purchases* securities when it wishes to *increase* the money supply. This operation increases the level of reserves. Before these new reserves are multiplied through the banking system and the level of demand deposits increases, these are termed "excess reserves". On the other hand, the Fed *sells* securities when they wish to *contract* the money supply. This pulls reserves out of the system and thereby reduces the level of demand deposits. The supply of money and credit can expand and contract absent a central bank, provided fractional reserve banking is legal (although we've seen free market forces prevents this to a large degree). If society's time preference decreases or it becomes more future-oriented and begins to save more, the increased demand deposits allow for increased credit expansion. If society, however, become more present-oriented and saves less, credit necessarily has to contract. Lastly, the central bank can decrease the reserve requirement to expand credit and vice versa.

Prior to the financial crisis, when the Fed began injecting the banking system with what is now amounts to roughly $2.4-$2.5 trillion of excess reserves, the banking system had always tried to keep the reserve ratio at or near the absolute minimum (10%). The 2008 financial crisis will be examined in detail in chapters 8 and 9, but it is worth noting here to get a basic idea just how insolvent the banking system became, the reserve ratio dropped below 0.06% (.0567% at one point), that is for every one hundred dollars of demand deposits, it had less than $0.60 of bank reserves!

Suppose the Fed wishes to increase the money supply by $1,000,000. The Fed will go into the open market and purchase $100,000 of securities. The Fed writes a check to the seller, which can now done electronically. Now the person or institution deposits this check at their bank. This bank now has excess reserves of $100,000. This bank does not expand its loans by 10:1. Instead, the bank expands by 1 minus the legal reserve requirement (10%) multiplied by amount of securities purchased plus the amount of securities purchased.

In this case, the bank will create $90,000, or [$100,000 x (1-10%) = $90,000] worth of new loans, thereby increasing the money supply by an additional $90,000, in addition to the $10,000 demand deposit at the Fed. Eventually, a second bank will receive this $90,000. This second bank will have $90,000 of excess reserves and expand their loans by [$90,000 x (1-10%)], or $81,000, for total money creation thus far of $271,000. This process will continue until the Fed's initial purchase of $100,000 results in the Fed's desired increase in the money supply of $1,000,000. Technically, it only needs to involve two banks, with one creating 90% of $81,000, with the debtor then depositing the $81,000 in a second bank. The second bank could then lend 90% x $81,000, or $72,900, to another debtor, who then deposits that back into the first bank, and so on.

In the following case 10 x $100,000 = $1,000,000, or the [reserve ratio 10% x 100] x [increase in excess reserves] = Total money created inclusive of the $100,000 in purchased government securities by the Fed.

In the explanation below, we walk through the accounting process of another example of this. We will show the entire process of fractional reserve banking in the following two charts:

We start from Bank A in the current position, which has a reserve ratio of 10% ($200k/$2bm) or (bank reserves/demand deposits).

❶ Assets		Liabilities	
IOU's	$1,800,000	Demand Deposits	$2,000,000
Bank Reserves	$200,000		
Total Assets	$2,000,000	Equity and Liabilities	$2,000,000
Reserve Ratio: $200k/$2B = 10%			

Bank A wants to originate another loan but has to wait until it receives additional bank deposits. Customer X then deposits $500,000 in Bank A and so it is able to originate a $200k loan, which causes its reserve ratio to decrease (but not as much as it would if it did not make another loan) to 25.92% (500k + 200k) or $700k/$2.7m = 25.92% or (bank reserves/demand deposits).

❷ Assets		Liabilities	
IOU's	$2,000,000	Demand Deposits	$2,700,000
Bank Reserves	$700,000		
Total Assets	$2,700,000	Equity & Liabilities	$2,700,000
Required Reserves = 10%			
Reserve Ratio: $700K/$2.70B = 25.93%			

A bank's goal (pre-2008) is to reduce its reserve ratio to 10.00%, so Bank A originates loans such that its reserve ratio is 10% (700k/7m). In the case of Bank A, loans outstanding increases $4.3m to $6.3m.

❸Assets		Liabilities	
IOU's	$6,300,000	Demand Deposits	$7,000,000
Bank Reserves	$700,000		
Total Assets	$7,000,000	Equity & Liabilities	$7,000,000
Required Reserves = 10%			
Reserve Ratio: $700K/$7B = 10%			

Now let us look at an example when the Fed has decided to lower the interest rate, which is done via open market operations. In this case of Bank A's excess reserves increase by $300,000, increasing its reserve ratio to 14.29%. Again, Bank A then makes $2,700,000 worth of loans in order to reduce its reserve requirement to 10.00%. (Total Bank Reserves/Demand Deposits) or ($1b/$7b).

❹Assets		Liabilities	
IOU's	$6,300,000	Demand Deposits	$7,000,000
Bank Reserves	$700,000		
Excess Reserves	$300,000		
Total Assets	$7,000,000	Equity & Liabilities	$7,000,000
Reserve Ratio Before Loan = 14.29%			

These excess reserves or then multiplied by (1-reserve ratio

❺Assets		Liabilities	
IOU's	$9,000,000	Demand Deposits	$10,000,000
Bank Reserves	$1,000,000		
Total Assets	$10,000,000	Equity & Liabilities	$10,000,000
Reserve Ratio After Loan: 10.00%			

Alternatively, suppose the Fed buys $1,000,000 in government securities. The money creation process would be as follows. The first two charts below are only the first twenty processes of the money multiplier in full effect. Through this process, $8,000,000 has been created.

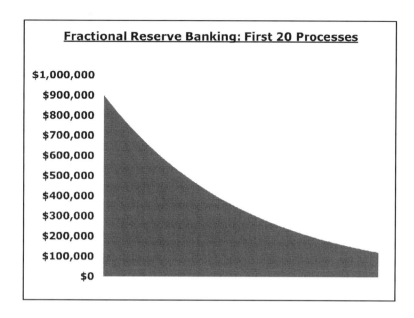

The cumulative money creation through the first twenty processes is depicted in the chart below, and the process all the way to completion is depicted in the chart below that.

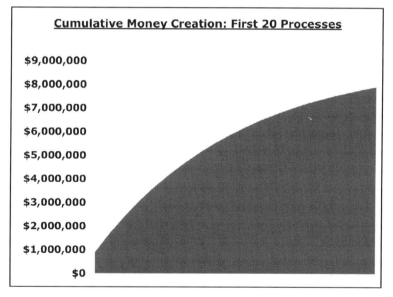

Amount Deposited	Reserve Requirement	Money Creation	Cum Money Creation
$1,000,000	$100,000	$900,000	$900,000
$900,000	$90,000	$810,000	$1,710,000
$810,000	$81,000	$729,000	$2,439,000
$729,000	$72,900	$656,100	$3,095,100
$656,100	$65,610	$590,490	$3,685,590
$590,490	$59,049	$531,441	$4,217,031
$531,441	$53,144	$478,297	$4,695,328
$478,297	$47,830	$430,467	$5,125,795
$430,467	$43,047	$387,420	$5,513,216
$387,420	$38,742	$348,678	$5,861,894
$348,678	$34,868	$313,811	$6,175,705
$313,811	$31,381	$282,430	$6,458,134
$282,430	$28,243	$254,187	$6,712,321
$254,187	$25,419	$228,768	$6,941,089
$228,768	$22,877	$205,891	$7,146,980
$205,891	$20,589	$185,302	$7,332,282
$185,302	$18,530	$166,772	$7,499,054
$166,772	$16,677	$150,095	$7,649,148
$150,095	$15,009	$135,085	$7,784,233
$135,085	$13,509	$121,577	$7,905,810

The chart immediately below shows this process in full or the money multiplier in full effect. As one can see, the increase in excess of $1,000,000 has caused money creation of an additional $9,000,000. In other words, total money creation of $10,000,000 has occurred, or a pyramiding of 10 to 1. The chart below depicts the money creation after the first $1,000,000.

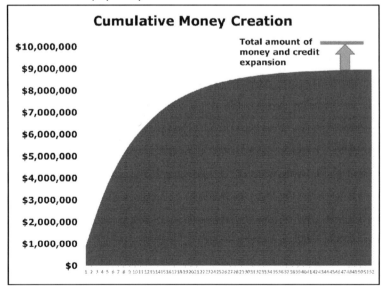

Prior to 2008 the banking system held very little excess reserves. Due to the over-investment in real estate, mortgages were near an all-time high. The massive wave of defaults had not effected the banking system prior to 2008 but it was only a matter of time before they would. Once they did, the Fed began to engage in periodic capital injections into the banking system, also known as adding liquidity, or simply injecting more capital into the system at large. This capital was then multiplied within the system using the fractional reserve system so that it was able to cover 10 times the amount injected for loan defaults.

Initially, the Fed did not realize the magnitude of the destruction its money policy caused but once it did it began to engage in quantitative easing programs, in which the Fed purchased mortgage-backed and Treasury securities. This was done to prop up the banking system, and is still not fully understood by many investors.

Banks have started lending this money, with some banks being better capitalized than others. It is worth noting that the Fed will eventually purchase most of the toxic assets that used to be held by the banks (mortgage companies). However, given the vast size of the derivatives held within the U.S. banking system (discussed in chapter 8), there is no telling the amount of toxic assets that have yet to be classified as such. The Fed can continue to buy these assets because it is still reinvesting maturing treasury bonds.

Furthermore, there has been a significant amount of credit expansion post 2008, which is manifesting problems. These include mortgage debt, commercial and industrial loans, auto loans and, more recently, student loans. Additional credit expansion could take place, likely at an increasing pace as time passes, because banks have excess reserves and the market will need to service the interest on all the new debt created since 2008. To what degree excess reserves are drawn down has yet to be determined, however, the following chart illustrates the potential money creation.

These principles are fundamental to understanding both the manipulation in the precious metals as discussed in the next chapter as well as fully grasping the incredibly fragile economic landscape.

Phases of Inflation

The current inflationary structure of the Federal Reserve and its member banks dictates three primary phases of inflation. In this case, we will start with society having deflationary expectations, such as was the case after the 2008 crisis. Note that many think that inflation's only ill effect is causing prices to rise but just as importantly is perhaps much more sinister in that it causes a redistribution of wealth. Those who get the newly created money first benefit but at the cost to those who receive it last. It is the banking system, select corporate entities and the political elites who receive this money first. In this way, slowly but surely ensured that the middle class is wiped out and the root cause of income inequality. This is the case today as will be further discussed in chapter 8, particularly with median household income currently at lows no seen since 1995.

Phase I - The government pumps a significant quantity of money into the system (in 2008 this was done via the countless bailouts) as well as the central bank increasing bank reserves at an unprecedented rate. This causes prices to rise far less, relative to the degree they would have risen if it weren't for the deflationary expectations. This only can only last so long as society's expectations of deflation persist[76].

Phase II - Deflationary expectations have been replaced by inflationary expectations. Prices begin to rise consistently every year until the aforementioned inflationary expectations take hold in full force with higher and higher prices. At some point, society begins to think prices will be higher the following year and then higher the year after that, and so on. At the end of this phase, expectations have caught up with reality and the populace at large. This change, however, cannot be predicted, as it varies quite widely from economy to economy. For example, trust in government, the central bank (notably with its ability to control the psychological aspect), culture, etc. Once this occurs, the economy enters dangerous territory[77]

Phase III - Inflationary expectations increase as prices begin to rise faster than the increase in the supply of money and credit. Historically, when this is realized, the public embraces the idea of the central bank increasing the money supply. If the government stops inflating, then these expectations will reverse. However, if the central bank/government continues to inflate (which is most often the case), the supply of money and credit increase along with prices of consumer goods until either runaway inflation takes hold and a hyperinflationary depression results or the majority lose confidence in paper money, resulting in a monetary reset or currency collapse[78].

Currently, the U.S. is near the end of Phase I of the inflationary process and arguably at the start of Phase II, with very marginal inflationary expectations beginning to set in. As we will discuss in the following two chapters, using a few very accurate indicators, the U.S. economy is turning down anew. When this happens, the FED has already exhausted all its tool's to "artificially stimulate" that are the least inflationary. It would be very reasonable to expect headline inflation of 5%+ in 2H 2016, if not 2017.

Additional Considerations

Once Federal Deposit Insurance Corporation (FDIC) insurance became prevalent, it started a long line of moral hazards that would be instituted over time. The very idea that there are no consequences for irrational behavior, financial or otherwise, has set a background for perhaps the greatest financial/monetary upheaval in recorded history. Although the 2008 financial crisis was a significant wake-up call, the banking cartels and the political will on a global basis continued onward as though the financial system was completely repaired.

The exception that has clearly moved away from this delusional thinking is the BRICS countries—Brazil, Russia, India, China, and South Africa. These countries (and

---

[76] Murray Rothbard, The Mystery of Banking, p. 69
[77] Ibid pp. 69-70
[78] Ibid pp. 71-72

others) have distanced themselves from the U.S. dollar to some extent, and will continue to move away from the U.S. dollar settlement in the future. Whether this will isolate them in the event of a dollar crisis remains to be determined, but obviously the effort continues.

Chapter 6: Intervention Induced Price Suppression in Silver and Gold

"Unlike farm crops, especially near the end of a crop season, private counterparties in oil contracts have virtually no ability to restrict the worldwide supply of this commodity. (Even OPEC has been less than successful over the years.) Nor can private counterparties restrict supplies of gold, another commodity whose derivatives are often traded over-the-counter, where central banks stand ready to lease gold in increasing quantities should the price rise." –Alan Greenspan, July 24, 1998

Thus far we have examined money and banking, emphasizing the practice of fractional reserve banking, which is necessary for us to fully appreciate how the same practice applies to silver and gold. We will examine the primary ways in which silver/gold market intervention[79] is accomplished. These include: fractional reserve bullion banking/gold (and silver) loans, intervention via the futures market, and outright government sales.

A 100% reserve bank is a safekeeping bank whose sole purpose is to protect the property deposited by its customers. One hundred percent reserve banking is "a situation in which banks' reserves equal 100 percent of their deposits" (Franklin and Bernanke, p. 652). Imagine that a depositor deposits $100 in a bank for safekeeping. In this case, the bank debits its cash account for $100 and credits its deposit account for $100.

Bank

Assets		Liabilities & Equity	
Cash	100	Deposit	100
Total	100	Total	100

The bank's $100 of deposits are backed by $100 of cash reserves. A bank's reserve-deposit ratio equals its cash reserves divided by its deposits, so in this example the bank's reserve ratio is 100%. Fractional reserve banking develops out of 100% reserve banking. A fractional reserve banking system is "a banking system in which bank reserves are less than deposits so that the reserve ratio is less than 100 percent" (Franklin and Bernanke, p. 653). To demonstrate, imagine that the bank makes a $100

---

[79] Dimitri Speck, *The Gold Cartel*, pg. 81

loan. The bank debits its loan account for $100 and credits its deposit account for $100.

	Bank		
Assets			Liabilities & Equity
Cash	100	Deposits	200
Loans	100		
Total	200	Total	200

The bank has $200 of deposits, but these deposits are backed by only $100 of cash reserves. In this case, the bank's reserve ratio is 50%. Only a fraction of the bank's deposits are covered by cash reserves[80].

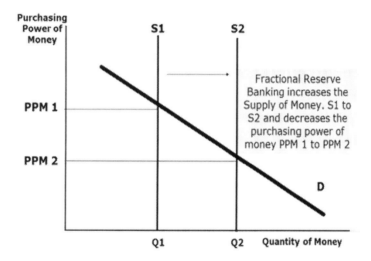

The supply and demand diagram *above* shows that fractional reserve banking is inflationary: "When an increase in the money supply makes dollars more plentiful, the result is an increase in the price level that makes each dollar less valuable" (Mankiw, p. 649). Fractional reserve banking increases the money supply and thereby reduces the purchasing power of money[81].

Fractional reserve banks also affect the interest rate. Like all prices, the interest rate is determined by supply and demand. "The interest rate is the price of a loan" (Mankiw, pg. 571), so the interest rate is determined by the supply and demand for

---

[80]See Mishkin for a textbook introduction to fractional reserve banking and see Rothbard for a critical introduction to fractional reserve banking. Some economists argue that fractional reserve banking is fraudulent and should therefore be illegal. See Huerta de Soto for more on the legal nature of fractional reserve banking.
[81]Mankiw (p. 647) and Rothbard (p. 29) use supply and demand analysis to show how an increase in the money supply reduces the purchasing power of money.

loans[82]. The left side of the bank's balance sheet above shows that fractional reserve banking increases the supply of loans. In the figure below, an increase in the supply of fractional reserve loans means the supply curve shifts to the right, from S1 to S2. An increase in the supply of loans by fractional reserve banks artificially reduces the interest rate.

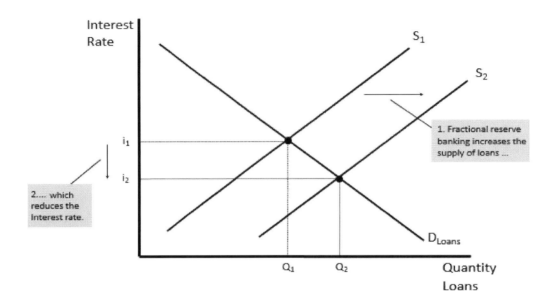

Fractional reserve banks can artificially reduce the interest rate when they make loans. However, does this constitute manipulation? It does, because the rate of interest signals society's time preference or its preference of present good to future goods.

Since the interest rate is determined by the supply and demand for loanable funds, central banks manipulate the interest rate by changing the supply of loans. Fractional reserve banks create money when they make loans, so fractional reserve banks also artificially reduce the purchasing power of money. It is impossible for a central bank to manipulate the interest rate without simultaneously manipulating the purchasing power of money.

Fractional reserve banking in fiat currencies is actually a corollary to fractional reserve banking in gold and silver: "The fractional reserve nature of [gold] bullion banking is analogous to the widely understood concepts of fractional reserve banking in currencies such as U.S. dollars" (Christian)[83].

---

[82]For more on the loanable funds theory of the interest rate, see Abel and Bernanke (p. 140), Bodie, Marcus, and Kane (p. 116), Franklin and Bernanke (p. 638), and Mankiw (p. 571).

[83]In fact, some economists teach money creation using gold: "In modern banking systems the money created by banks and reserves created by central banks are electronic. The lack of physical form makes money creation seem abstract and enhances the misconception that the process is arbitrary. In contrast, specie-based banking systems are rooted in a commodity—usually gold—whose physical aspects are well known. By simulating money creation in a gold-based banking system, students gain a more intuitive understanding of money creation" (Pearlman and Rebelein, pg. 1).

Again, a hypothetical example shows how fractional reserve bullion banking influences the price of silver and gold. Why would the central bank or bullion bank wish to engage in fractional reserve bullion banking, given that neither silver nor gold are accepted mediums of exchange? The answer lies in the fact that both metals arise as natural monies in a free market, as discussed in the first chapter. Another consideration is that currently the market only treats gold and silver at the same derivative level of currencies; this cannot be stated for any other commodity. Thus the market has once again said gold and silver are "money" even though they are not, in an official sense. By manipulating the price of silver and gold downward, neither poses as large a threat to the current monetary system. The following quotes by former Fed governor Wayne Angell and former Fed chairman Alan Greenspan, illustrate this.

"People can talk about gold's price being due to what the Chinese are buying; that's the silliest nonsense that ever was. The price of gold is largely determined by what people who do not trust in a fiat money system want to use for an escape out of any currency, and they want to gain security through owning gold. Now, if annual gold production and consumption amount of 2 percent of the world's stock, a change of 10 percent in the amount produced or consumed is not going to change the price very much. But attitudes about inflation will change it[84]."

"I have one other issue I'd like to throw on the table. I hesitate to do it, but let me tell you some of the issues that are involved here. If we are dealing with psychology, then the thermometers one uses to measure it have an effect. I was raising the question on the side with Governor Mullins of what would happen if the Treasury sold a little gold in this market. There's an interesting question here because if the gold price broke in that context, the thermometer would not be just a measuring tool. It would basically affect the underlying psychology[85]."

Imagine a depositor deposits 100 ounces of gold at the bank for safekeeping. The bank debits its gold account for 100 and credits its deposit account for 100.

Bank			
Assets			**Liabilities & Equity**
Gold	100	Deposit	100
Total	100	Total	100

Figure 1

---

[84] Wayne Angell, FOMC19930518meeting.pdf, pg. 32
[85] Alan Greenspan, FOMC19930518meeting.pdf, pg. 41

In this case the bank's reserve ratio is 100%. The reserve ratio equals gold reserves divided by gold deposits. The bank is operating with a 100% reserve because all gold deposits are covered by gold reserves.

Fractional Reserve Bullion Banking

Fractional reserve bullion banking emerges out of 100% reserve bullion banking. A fractional reserve bullion banking system is a bullion banking system in which silver and gold reserves are less than silver and gold deposits so that the reserve ratio is less than 100%. To demonstrate, imagine that the bank makes a 100-ounce fractional reserve gold loan. The bank debits the loan account for 100 and credits the deposit account for 100.

Bank

Assets			Liabilities & Equity
Gold	100	Deposit	200
Loans	100		
Total	200	Total	200

The bank's gold deposits of 200 are only backed by 100 ounces of gold reserves. In this case, the bank's reserve ratio is 50%: only a fraction of the bank's gold deposits are covered by gold reserves.

Fractional reserve bullion banking influences the price of both silver and gold. The gold supply equals silver and gold in circulation plus silver and gold deposits. If banks hold all silver and gold deposits in reserve, banks do not influence the supply. When banks hold only a fraction of gold deposits in reserve, banks create ("paper") gold.

Fractional reserve bullion banks create silver and/or gold out of thin air when they make precious metals loans. Using gold as an example again, the price of gold is determined by the supply and demand for gold. Since fractional reserve bullion banks increase the supply of gold, they influence the price of gold.

In the graphic below, the supply curve of gold shifts right, from S1 to S2, when fractional reserve gold banks create gold deposits out of thin air. An increase in the supply of gold by fractional reserve gold banks causes the price of gold to fall, from G1 to G2.

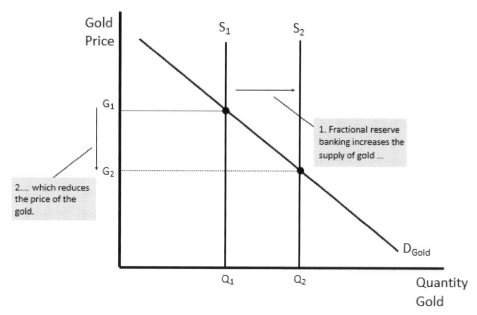

Bullion banks artificially increase the supply of silver and gold when they hold fractional reserves. Therefore, the price of gold is artificial in an economy with fractional reserve gold banking because the gold market is "pricing" gold and fractional gold as having the same value, when clearly only one is a physical reality and the other a derivative.

Precious Metal Leasing

Thus, the price of gold is manipulated in a fractional reserve gold banking system in the same sense that the interest rate and the value of the U.S. dollar are manipulated in a fractional reserve fiat money system. This is just part of the manipulation of the precious metals. One extension of fractional reserve bullion is the leasing of silver and gold. This includes both leasing metal by bullion banks and central banks. It has been rumored that some banks have "leased" their gold and/or silver for up to a term of 100 years. This of course is essentially selling, but technically is a lease. This is because on the bank's balance sheet, metal and metal receivable are one-line item. The former is fractional reserve bullion banking, and both the former and the latter cause market distortions such as creating the illusion of more supply than there actually is. In short, if the market thinks the supply of both metals is significantly higher than it actually is, lower prices result.

Sometime after gold was no longer a reserve asset, a business developed in which gold and/or silver was being leased. The idea began that gold was just lying around in central banks vaults and could be put to work to gain "interest" for the bank. In these "leasing transactions" the metal could be lent to mining companies and fabricators (jewelers) for hedging purposes. Like a normal loan, the banks simply function as a financial intermediary in such a transaction and have earned the name "bullion banks." In return, these banks receive a fee for selling gold on behalf of the mining company's gold and/or silver onto the market.

One example would be the following: A mine uses the proceeds of selling the gold on the market from the bullion bank to invest in new mining equipment. This in turn allows the mining companies to mine silver and gold. Once this is accomplished it repatriates the loan with silver and/or gold with the central bank. In short, this is just a form of financing but denominated in silver and/or gold instead of cash and has to be repatriated in kind. Note: There are exceptions to this at times, where settlement can take place in currency rather than metal.

Due to the lack of dependency on the silver or gold price and the risk of default if more predictable, it is easier to obtain these types of loans, at least in theory[86]. Where the gold and silver is lent is largely unknown because neither central banks nor bullion banks have to make that information public. The potential size of this market is very significant and not fully understood by many precious metals investors who actually are participating in this scheme without fully understanding what "investment" they actually hold.

Note: The gold that the mining company borrowed and subsequently sold into the market isn't repatriated using the same gold, rather with gold mined by the mining company[87]. This has the effect as any other type of sale that is increasing supply onto the market. Increasing the supply causes the supply curve to shift out and the price to necessarily fall. The odd thing in the case of gold or silver lending is the obscenely low interest rates, typically around 1% +/-. Furthermore, although there is no evidence of select ETFs such as the SLV, GLD, etc., it is very possible that the mining company also engages in leasing, as it does not allocate the metals; rather, they are unallocated.

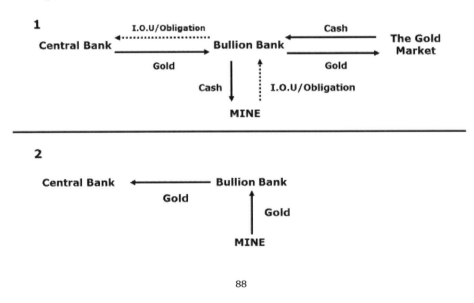

[88]

---

[86]Dimitri Speck, *The Gold Cartel*, pg. 44-45
[87]Ibid
[88] Ibid, p. 42

The Gold Carry Trade

A bullion bank borrows gold at a very low rate, perhaps 1%, then sells it into the market and invests the proceeds into a variety of assets that yield 4% per annum. Each year, the bullion bank makes the spread between the two assets or [4%-1% = 3%]. The bullion bank, or lending bank, is best served if the price of gold or falls in price. The following chart is how the gold carry trade functions[89].

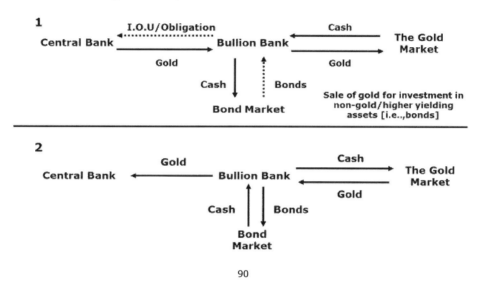

The quantity of central bank gold on lease is generally unknown. James Turk of Http://www.Goldmoney.com analyzed storage facilities, from which he concluded that at the change of the millennium, between 10-18,000 tons of gold were on loan, making up roughly half the central banks holding around the world[91].

Futures Markets

Intervention in the silver and gold market is also greatly influenced by the futures market. Every Friday a report is issued by the CFTC which shows the breakdown of the market in terms of the top four and eight commercial traders. These can be any entity that has a commercial interest, such as a mining company primarily, although this is extremely dominated by the banking industry. In fact many large mining concerns simply turn over their hedging activities to the banks, further yielding the power to influence the market to a select few.

They maintain a net short position in the precious metals at all times, varying from moderate to extreme. This is extremely correlated with large price movements in the precious metals.

---

[89] Dimitri Speck, *The Gold Cartel*, p. 45
[90] Ibid
[91] James Turk, "More Proof," 2003, http://www.org/node.4247

Another tool of intervening in the precious metals markets is central bank sales. While it could be argued that central banks collude in market interventions, it cannot be proven. However, the aforementioned tools play off one another because the same algorithms (math formulas run by computers) are nearly identical, thus the effect on the market is compounded. Simply stated, selling begets more selling and the algorithms are there for the benefit of the banking institutions and have nothing to do with determining the market price–although apologists for the establishment will state otherwise.

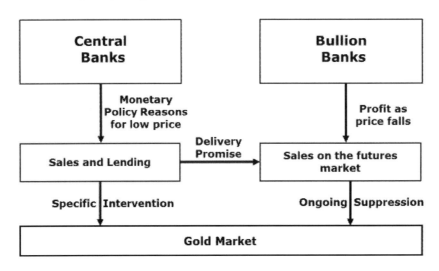

92

Commitment of Traders Report

The following graphic is an example of the Commitment of Traders Report released July 8, 2014. We have broken down the data sets to focus on those that shed the most light on the commercial traders, focusing on the four and eight largest:

---

[92] Dimitri Speck, The Gold Cartel, p. 47

Silver	7/8/2014	7/1/2014	6/24/2014	6/17/2014
Unadjusted Open Interest	162,879	156,698	158,093	164,576
Gross Long Position	51,053	52,495	58,728	66,461
Gross Short Position	109,071	104,450	101,625	89,299
Unadjusted Net Position	**(58,018)**	**(51,955)**	**(42,897)**	**(22,838)**
Number of Commercials Net Short	48			
Net Short Position of 4 Largest	**(42,674)**	**(40,115)**	**(39,049)**	**(37,359)**
Top 4 Net Short	26.20%	25.60%	24.70%	22.70%
Adjustment For Spreading				
Non-Commercial Spreads	21,539	19,883	19,306	25,775
Net Open Interest	141,340	136,815	138,787	138,801
New Percentage Held by 4 Largest	30.19%	29.32%	28.14%	26.92%
Net Percentage Held By 8 Largest	41.60%	41.20%	38.70%	35.90%
Net Position Held By 8 Largest	**(67,758)**	**(64,560)**	**(61,182)**	**(59,083)**

The first circled line item is the net position of commercial traders in aggregate. Keep in mind each contract is representative of 5,000 oz. of silver. Of the total (42,647) contracts held net short by just the four largest commercial banks/traders amount to 213.37m oz. (42,674 x 5,000). Per the bank participation reports, JP Morgan is always one of the four largest, which begs the question why would a commercial bank have such a vested interest in always being heavily net short silver, not matter the price environment? Suffice it to say JP Morgan is part of the cartel that intervenes in the silver market.

The forecast above-ground inventories of silver ranges from 800m to 1.6b oz. That being said, if the group on the other side of the contract all demanded delivery, it would send the price of silver skyrocketing, with each costing more than the last. Moving down to the last circled line item, the largest eight banks hold 338m oz. net short. We are not trying to make a case for manipulation solely by focusing on the paper market, rather it is meant to spark questions such as why in the world would commercial banks trade this much silver?

Forensic Studies

The late Adrian Douglas did several forensic studies in gold and silver price manipulation. Mr. Douglas studied trading gold and silver between the London AM Fix and the PM Fix and how it was unnaturally related in an inverse way to trading the PM Fix and the following AM Fix. Mr. Douglas calculated the probability of such an unnatural correlation existing, which came out to be an astounding 1-in-2.36×10^{31}! While this isn't depicted in any chart below, there is one of an extension of that study, covering Jan. 2, 2001, to Jan. 2, 2014, or 13 years of daily price data.

Mr. Douglas did several other studies but he also extended this by examining the correlation between the aforementioned trade in gold and silver. As you can see, there is an uncanny correlation between the two as seen through the R^2 of 95.72%. Keep in mind that during this time, silver did not receive the monetary premium that it did following the currency debasement that took place during and after 2008 financial crisis, yet the correlation is very high.

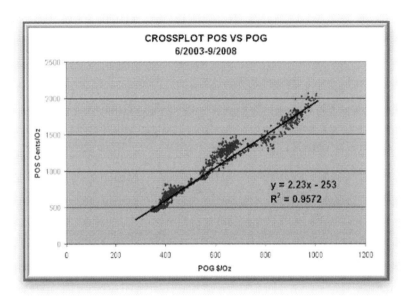

Following the 2008 crisis, Mr. Douglas did a study from September 2008 to September 2010, which is seen in the next chart. Again, a very high correlation continued to exist at 91.68%. This, in particular, is very odd because around the fourth quarter of 2008, assets across the board were being liquidated due to so much leverage in the financial system. Prior to the crisis, 10%-15% of silver was used for investment purposes while gold was 60%-80%.

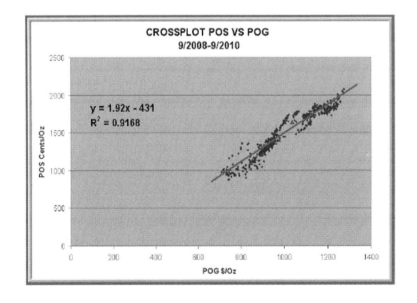

Mr. Douglas then overlays these two cross-plots in order to show that silver, along with gold, is heavily manipulated. The next two charts are extremely telling.

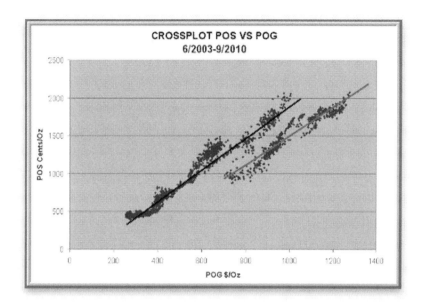

In the following chart, both equations have been used to generate a synthetic price of silver from June 2003 to September 2010. This is the red plot on the chart. This curve is only derived from the price of gold and the correlation equation. There is no input of the price of silver. The real price of silver is charted for comparison and is shown in blue.

What is significant is that one can generate almost a perfect reproduction of the price of silver by only knowing the price of gold. This "smoking gun" is forensic evidence that the price of silver is not only manipulated but is done so algorithmically. Such a perfect relationship with gold could not happen over a seven-year period by pure happenstance.

The silver price is determined in a manner that yields a price different than the fundamentals of silver alone[93]. It is impossible for such a correlation as seen below to exist, as the market is very dynamic; yet combining the equations: Y = 2.23x (Price of gold) – 253 & Y = 1.92x – 431, we arrive at the red line, which is almost exactly predictive of the price of silver. Y in the equations equates to the price of silver in cents, while X equates to the price of gold in cents.

For example, in the first equation, we will assume a gold price of $1,000 in mid-2008. Y = 2.23 x 1,000 – 253 = 2230 – 253 = 1977 = $19.77. The chart below yields a value just under 2000c, or $20.00. Coincidence? Highly doubtful!

Mr. Douglas's study, used only for the AM-PM Fix for gold:

---

[93] Adrian Douglas, "More Forensic Evidence of Gold and Silver Price Manipulation," September 21, 2010.

Edward Fuller, conducted an extension of Mr. Douglas' study, looking at the cumulative change in the price of gold intraday versus overnight and ran a regression.

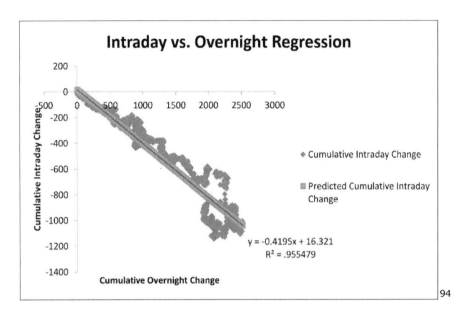

[94]

The chances of running a regression of 13 years, or roughly 4,000 +/- trading days, of the cumulative intraday price change and coming up with a 95.55% r-squared are astronomical! If this were stated in legal terms it would be well beyond a reasonable doubt. The next chart depicts the cumulative changes in the AM to PM Fix.

---

[94] Created by Edward Fuller.

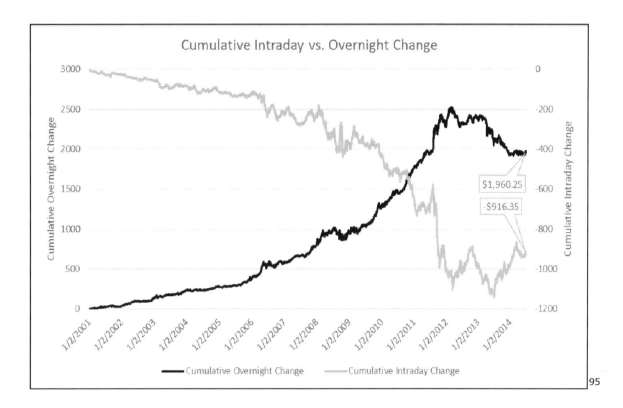

Advocates of returns-based analysis argue that it is easy to generate large gains and large losses with a high level of risk. Similarly, it is difficult to generate large gains and large losses with a low level of risk. One popular risk-adjusted return measure is the Sharpe Ratio, developed by the Nobel Prize winning economist William Sharpe.

The Sharpe ratio equals the average return divided by the standard deviation of returns. A high Sharpe ratio means that the average return is high, given the level of risk. **Frauds and manipulations** have high Sharpe ratios. For instance, Bernie Madoff's Sharpe ratio was 133%, while his benchmark's Sharpe ratio was only 19%. The table below shows gold's overnight and intraday Sharpe ratio over different time periods[96].

---

[95]Ibid.
[96]Created by Edward Fuller.

Annualized Sharpe Ratios

Period	Intraday	Overnight
1968-2014	-43.6%	72.6%
1970s	79.5%	92.7%
1980s	-114.1%	41.4%
1990s	-80.9%	19.7%
2000s	-95.3%	167.3%
2010-2014	-66.8%	73.0%

[97]

Gold has large negative intraday Sharpe ratios. This indicates that intraday gold traders have suffered large risk-adjusted losses. In contrast, gold has large positive overnight Sharpe ratios. This indicates that overnight gold traders have realized large risk-adjusted gains. Douglas would argue, "That cannot happen by chance."

---

[97] Ibid

Chapter 7: Austrian Business Cycle Theory

"True, governments can reduce the rate of interest in the short run. They can issue additional paper money. They can open the way to credit expansion by the banks. They can thus create and artificial boom and the appearance of prosperity. But such a boom is bound to collapse sooner or later and to bring about a depression." –Ludwig von Mises

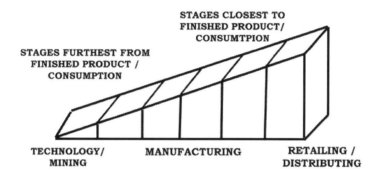

The modern day business cycle, otherwise referred to as the boom-bust cycle isn't commonplace even though the so called "expert economists" would like to make you think otherwise. Instead the central bank is the sole cause of economic booms and corresponding busts. This is because it is given monopoly control of the mint and because it is a government enterprise (despite the claims of being independent), those who are of FOMC (Federal Open Market Committee) do what is in the best interest of the Federal Government. While most people knew this all along, former Fed chairman Alan Greenspan confirmed this at the New Orleans Investment Conference in 2014.

On Capitalism vs. Socialism

Capitalism means personal property rights and sovereignty of the consumers in economic matters. Free enterprise, or the market economy, is a system or process in which individuals specialize in various occupations and where the factors of production are privately owned. Although everyone acts to satisfy his own needs, it is attained by satisfying the needs and wants of others. It can then be said those in charge of a market economy are the consumers. This system directs market participants toward areas where they can best serve the needs and wants of others. It is market prices that implicitly tell individuals how to adjust their behavior to best serve one another in the division of labor. It is these prices that make economic calculation possible. It is important to note that interest rates are the price of money. In a nutshell, the market is a profit-loss economy, in which the success of the capitalist is gauged by the profits or losses incurred.

While it is easy to come to conclusion that the market economy is that of survival of the fittest, it actually benefits all of society. This ensures the survival of those who are superior forecasters and weeding out of the inferior[98]. It takes the original factors of production from the incompetent and gives them to the competent. Regarding Income inequality, it is a good thing it is not equal because this allows some to take jobs which are needed by the economy (This, however is not the vast income inequality we see today, which is the sole result of inflation and wealth redistribution).

Socialism rejects capitalism, alleging that such a system is unjust and inherently inefficient. The supporters also suggest capitalism is the core cause of misery and poverty whereas it is in fact the opposite[99]. Since poverty exists and it is not solved by the redistribution of goods, but minimized as efficiently as possible by coordinating producers and consumers in the production of such goods, therefore it is socialism which is the core cause of misery and poverty.

Socialism is a system of violence, coercion, and government control of nearly every aspect of an individual's life. Private property rights, including <u>ownership of self</u>, don't exist under socialism. It is in direct opposition to the Founding Fathers' fundamental thinking, which dictates that human beings are born with natural rights of life, liberty, and the pursuit of happiness.

The socialist doctrine rests on three beliefs:
- Society is an all-powerful and all-knowing being
- As society advances, socialism is inevitable
- Continuous progress occurs under socialism

Origins of the Coming Currency Crisis

The origin of the coming currency crisis can be traced back at least one hundred years ago, with the founding of the Federal Reserve (1913). The coming currency crisis was inevitable and guaranteed to occur once Nixon closed the gold window (1971), with the average life of all inconvertible fiat monetary systems in history of roughly 35 years.

The U.S. dollar has had the advantage of being the world's reserve currency, however, this allowed the U.S. government to acquire the unsustainable debt load that it has now accumulated and continues unabated. The U.S. dollar still remains the world's reserve currency. However, this is beginning to change because trade between Russia and Iran, Russia and China, China and Brazil, etc. is taking place and continues to grow rapidly. In other words, the U.S. dollar is being bypassed for trade settlement.

It is important to go through a brief history of select economic events/policies enacted from the Fed's founding. History indicates and logic verifies that the course of

---

[98] Murray Rothbard, Economic Depressions: Their Causes and Cures, pp. 16-17
[99] Ludwig von Mises, Capitalism versus Socialism, p. 2 from The Intercollegiate Review 5, Spring 1969

fiscal and monetary policy taken in the past has provided the foundation for a currency crisis most likely before 2020. This currency crisis will, like all those before it, will take the form of hyperinflation or a monetary reset (the U.S. dollar will be revalued). We view the latter as the most likely scenario, although a "hyperinflation" type event could occur if the U.S. people lose complete faith in paper money, causing the rapidity of circulation or "velocity of money" to increase exponentially.

It bears repeating the fact that inconvertible paper fiat monetary systems have never worked. In fact, this type of monetary system became much more popular in the 20th century. Since the beginning of the 20th century, there have been well over fifty episodes of hyperinflation.[100]

1913-1971: Founding of the Federal Reserve, FDR and Nixon

The founding of the Federal Reserve in 1913 combined with fractional reserve banking meant business cycles would necessarily become more severe (having a bigger artificial boom and correspondingly larger bust) relative to the prior century, as a material portion of this period was without a central bank, although fractional reserve banking did persist. As discussed in chapter 2, if a country does have a central bank but fractional reserve banking is illegal or if a country has no central bank but does allow fractional reserve banking, there are predictable outcomes. The former means the central bank would be muted because it would have no power to inflate the supply of money and credit. The latter would find resistance, as the free market has always chosen a commodity money, that of silver and/or gold. (This has been human experience for 5,000 years prior to the 20th century). Further, as seen in the "Free Banking" era, the market puts necessary checks and balances on monetary inflation. Unfortunately, both a central bank and fractional reserve banking have persisted for over a century.

The advent of the Internet and the ability to do so much electronically only enhanced the danger of the central bank (in the U.S. this is the Federal Reserve) and all central banks around the world. Although the U.S. was technically on a "gold exchange standard," it is in the inherent nature of government that this minimal constraint would eventually be lifted. This inherent nature has to do with governments under political pressure to "provide" for their citizens more than production allows. The inherent nature of a government and politicians, especially in a democracy, is to achieve politically correct objectives without any regard for the cost of achieving that objective nor long-term ramifications.

In a Democracy, specifically the one in the U.S., politicians have shown they will do whatever it takes to get re-elected for another term. All of us have seen a politician's make promises they never planned on following through with. This is a result of having terms for congressmen and senators. Having these terms allow politicians to enact policies or the like, without having to bear the repercussions of such in the future. This is in contrast with Monarchical states (not to be confused all the other type of monarchies),

---

[100] The definition of hyperinflation most widely accepted is the doubling of consumer prices in one month or less.

in which the king does care a great deal regarding consequences of a given law, policy enacted or the like. This is because their empires are passed down to his heirs. Furthermore, as has been seen countless times in history, if a king does in fact enact policies which have medium or long-term consequences, his own family (queen, children, siblings, etc.) would actually kill them in order to preserve their reign over the empire. While wishing to remain politically neutral, it is difficult because being objective on a topic that has such differing views on what is "right" and what role, if any, government should play in the lives of its citizens is challenging and almost impossible to quantify.

To further clarify the idea of "natural rights"; that is, a human is born and because of that fact alone has the natural right to determine much of his own destiny. A clear example of this fundamental principle being usurped can be illustrated by Franklin D. Roosevelt's signing the Revenue Act into law in 1935, bringing this progressive tax's top tax rate to 75% in 1935, 79% in 1936, and 91% in 1939. It begs the question, what authority gives the government to levy taxes in the first place? It is often argued that this punishes the most productive aspects of society. As opposed to a market economy or capitalism, prices are manipulated because of government and central bank intervention. This distorts prices and therefore economic calculation becomes distorted under such a circumstance. It is important to reiterate here that an interest rate is nothing other than a price. We can therefore deduce that artificially suppressing interest rates distorts economic calculation.

The aforementioned signing of the Revenue Act into law is destructive because there are more resources to allocate toward investment projects if taxes did not exist. Furthermore, government make-work programs and other wasteful policies only increase the competition for scarce resources. Such a destructive tax policy vastly reduces the amount that could be invested into bettering people's lives. Abstaining from consumption brings about savings or capital formation. A high tax rate inhibits much of this capital formation from entering into the market, as it is diverted to government interests. Many still believe "government interests" serve the people, but this is rarely the case and at this point in history it is obvious the interests being served are for government power to remain and control more aspects of the citizens.

While often stated this tax only punishes the wealthy, in reality, it punishes everyone to a much greater degree, as less real viable wealth creation will occur when what would otherwise be investment capital is taxed to death first by the government. Additionally, in 1933, FDR prohibited the "hoarding" of gold and removed the U.S. domestic dollar from gold, in order to <u>inflate the supply of money and credit</u> by depreciating the dollar against gold.

"Economic progress is the work of the savers, who accumulate capital, and of the entrepreneurs, who turn capital to new uses. The other members of society, of course, enjoy the advantages of progress, but they not only do not contribute anything to it; they even place obstacles in its way." -Ludwig von Mises

It was during FDR's administration that the first attempt to enact a minimum wage law took place. They actually "signed it into law," but it was quickly declared unconstitutional by the Supreme Court. The Social Security system was also passed into law, which, however well intended, is based on an unrealistic assumption that never ending exponential growth in population will continue forever into the future. In short, the system boils down to a giant Ponzi scheme.

Also during the Roosevelt Administration, Fannie Mae (the Federal National Mortgage Association) was created to "help" with the financing of home purchases. Freddie Mac (Federal Home Loan Mortgage Corporation) was created in 1970, purportedly to create competition with Fannie Mae. It is important to keep in mind the definition of Socialism—any system of institutional aggression on the free exercise of human action or entrepreneurship[101]. We will come back to this later in the chapter but suffice it to say that aside from the founding of the Federal Reserve, FDR was the first overtly socialist president, with administrations since that time doing little to re-steer the federal government toward the founding principles. In other words, the U.S. had several characteristics of a market economy prior to 1913, becoming increasingly socialistic as time has passed, up until present day.

Time and Action

Economist Ludwig von Mises stressed the importance of action in his treatise "Human Action," regarding economic calculation[102], which is neither based on nor related to anything quantifiable, with ever-changing variables. Economic calculation is a result of the market's spontaneous order, which can also be look at as a self-organizing system or process. Man is always acting to improve his condition, that of dissatisfaction. Action is always directed toward the future and aimed at improving his circumstance or satisfaction. Action takes place in temporal sequences thereby making action and time inseparably linked together[103]. It is the concept of time why economics isn't a hard science, as is physics.

In free market economics, the supposition that human action can be accurately forecasted is outright ludicrous, deeming the use of econometrics not only impossible but also dangerous and outright reckless when employed in the real world. The most popular schools of economic thought (such as Keynesians, neo-cons, monetarists, etc.), however, disregard human action completely. This thinking is so static that it assumes market participants will act the same way every-time government spending is increased, interest rates are lowered, etc. No better example exists in modern times than when three brilliant economists, Fisher Black, Myron Scholes, and Robert Merton, came up with their mathematical formula to predict markets (human behavior). As their hedge fund, Long Term Capital Management, "proved" to work, more and more were anxious to

---

[101] Jesus Huerta de Soto, *Socialism, Economic Calculation and Entrepreneurship*, p. 49.
[102] "The quantitative treatment of economics problems must not be confused with the quantitative methods applied in dealing with the problems of the external universe of physical and chemical events. The distinctive mark of economic calculation is that it is neither based upon nor related to anything which could be characterized as measurement." –Ludwig von Mises, *Human Action*, p. 210.
[103] Ludwig von Mises, Human Action, p. 99

invest. However, their money machine reaped profits well above what was common in their era; their formula collided with reality and threatened to bring down the entire financial system. In simple summary, it can be stated that it is impossible to predict human behavior at all times. There are certain timeframes when "predictive" analysis will work, but people are not logical at ALL TIMES and circumstance is ever-changing, thus the best predictive models will be proven invalid.

By excluding the time element completely, modern economic theory (which dominates academia and monetary policy) is able to justify the use of static econometric models, in which everything is quantified[104]. One of the most popular and at the heart of current economic thought is the AS-AD model, which says if the central bank increases the supply of money (via open market operations/the purchase of government securities/artificially suppressing interest rates), it can "engineer" the economy to perform better than it would otherwise, meaning if left to the free market.

Such illogical models also think government spending can promote economic growth as opposed to allowing members of society to keep a greater portion of their total income. Removing the time element and therefore human action from economics as a soft science is analogous to removing the gravity element when discussing space. This is so because man is subject to the passage and economization of time, which has an unusual character because of the distinct and irreversibility of the temporal order.

Interest and Economic Calculation

Economic calculation makes it possible for business to adjust production to meet the needs and wants of the consumer. Interest rates reflect the time preferences of market participants and allocates of resources between current consumption and investment for the future. Market interest rates are therefore fundamental for economic calculation. This is also called "the natural rate of interest" where savings is used for expanding the economy's productive capacity in ways consistent with people's willingness to postpone consumption[105].

Every individual places a higher value on present goods relative to future goods. To what degree present goods are more valuable varies greatly from person to person as value is at all times, subjective. At any given time, some people have a higher time preference, valuing the present much more than the future. This group is more present-oriented, characterized as having a low savings-to-consumption preference. Those with a low time preference are willing to give up present goods in exchange for future goods valued only a bit higher.

---

[104]"A process of measurement consists in the establishment of the numerical relation of an object, viz, the unit of measurement. The ultimate source of measurement is that of spatial dimensions. With the aid of the unit defined in reference to the extension one measures energy and potentiality, the power of a thing to bring about changes in other things and relations, and passing of time. A pointer-reading is directly indicative of a spatial relation and only indirectly of other quantities. The assumption underlying measurement is the immutability of the unit. The unit of length is the rock upon which all measurement is based. It is assumed that man cannot help considering it immutable." – Ludwig von Mises, *Human Action*, pp. 210-211.

[105] Roger Garrison, Natural and Neutral Rates of Interest in Theory and Policy Formation, p. 58

Interest rates in a free market also signals the prevailing time preference of society (particularly between savers, consumers and capitalists) as a whole and when this rate is artificially manipulated downward, it causes proper economic calculation amongst market participants to become distorted. The rate of interest in a free market is society's valuation ratio of present goods versus future goods (otherwise viewed as the <u>price</u> premium society is willing to pay to "consume" a good immediately relative to the future), it reflects the time preference of all market participants, and just as importantly serves as a market-signaling mechanism to capitalists regarding society's savings/investment-to-consumption preference. This can otherwise being explained as society being present-oriented (higher interest rates) or more future-oriented (lower interest rates). This also helps capitalists in their forecasting abilities such that they best meet the needs and wants of consumers.

The interest rate is the <u>price of a loan</u>. Present goods are always preferable to future goods, the differential being the market rate of interest. In short, the interest rate can also be viewed as the <u>price of time</u>. This is because interest on a loan is both determined by the time preference of society as well as ones credit history.

Capital formation and accumulation

A falling time preference underlies economic growth; as a market participant's time preference declines, a growing portion of current income is saved. In other words, a greater portion of capital is accumulated due to abstaining from a portion of consumption and instead saving. This causes the rate of capital accumulation to increase and therefore capital formation occurs at a faster rate. This market rate of interest (not to be confused with the prevailing rate of interest set by the central bank) is referred to as the "natural rate of interest"—the rate of interest on loans that is neutral. This is the same as the rate of interest that would be determined by the intersection or equilibrium of the supply and demand for loans. It can be described as the current value of the natural rate of interest on capital, or, just the natural rate of interest[106]. Sustainable growth can also be set in motion by changes in inter-temporal preferences. These changes are gradual and largely has to do with cultural issues or demographics[107]. For example, many baby boomers are reaching retirement age and have to save a higher proportion of their pensions, social security etc. This is because it is becoming more obvious the Ponzi scheme that is the social security system is a farce but even more so is the fact that "cost of living adjustments" to retirees receiving social security is adjusted according to the C.P.I which couldn't be more disconnected from reality.

If it were the case that future goods were more valuable, man would never consume, only accumulate, capital into perpetuity. There are two aspects of interest when dealing with the capitalist and that of the consumer. In a free market, capitalists make investment decisions, in large part, based on the perceived needs and wants of the consumer, making these two aspects almost completely intertwined. In other words,

---

[106] Knut Wicksell, *Interest and Prices*, p. 102.
[107] Roger Garrison, *Time and Money*, p. 61

capitalists maximize accounting profits by best meeting the needs and wants of others. Furthermore, producers are also consumers, so they too make up a portion of the consumer.

To fully grasp this concept as well as the effect of intervention in the market via the Fed, we will first go through the effect of voluntary savings in a free market, meaning society's desire to increase its savings/investment-to-consumption ratio then go through the cause and effect of intervention and the impact to the production structure and, in turn, the economy. Discussing this will illustrate how the market process naturally coordinates people, such that the new product or idea is best able to meet the wants and needs of the consumer.

We will look at these effects from the capitalist point of view because savings is positively correlated with interest rates whereas investment isn't. For example, if the Fed Funds Rate or the rate one receives on bank deposits is 7.50% and there is the option of investing instead of saving money in the bank and the investment projected would generate a risk-adjusted rate of return of 6.0%, we know which option would be chosen. However, ceteris paribus, society's time preference falls, reflected in the market rate of interest falling to 5.00%, and the risk-adjusted rate of return increases to 7.30%. In other words, because the cost of capital has fallen, the option of saving or investing now means the capitalist is more likely to invest his money instead of saving it. This is because accounting profits are more valuable if discounted by a lower interest rate.

We will take a simple example to illustrate: a given investment will generate $200 annually for five years, it is worth more if the alternative ("putting the funds into a savings account") is lower. In this case, the prevailing rate of interest acts as a price in that it is a cost (opportunity cost) by which an investment project needs to be discounted, in addition to the subjective view of risk. The two graphics represent the time value differential when the Fed Funds rate is 7.50% and the time value of money when the Fed Funds Rate decreases to 5.50%. The lower the interest rate, the higher the value of cash flow. The cost of capital in the charts below is equal to the fed funds rate + risk premium or 7.50% + 1.50% = 9.00% and 5.50% + 1.50% = 7.00%. Note: The cost of capital compounds therefore the accounting profit is lower each year.

Year	Cash Flow	Interest Rate	Risk Premium	Cost of Capital	Accounting Profit
1	$200	7.50%	1.50%	9.00%	$183.49
2	$200	7.50%	1.50%	9.00%	$168.34
3	$200	7.50%	1.50%	9.00%	$154.44
4	$200	7.50%	1.50%	9.00%	$141.69
5	$200	7.50%	1.50%	9.00%	$129.99
Total	**$1,000**				**$777.93**

Year	Cash Flow	Interest Rate	Risk Premium	Cost of Capital	Accounting Profit
1	$200	5.50%	1.50%	7.00%	$186.92
2	$200	5.50%	1.50%	7.00%	$174.69
3	$200	5.50%	1.50%	7.00%	$163.26
4	$200	5.50%	1.50%	7.00%	$152.58
5	$200	5.50%	1.50%	7.00%	$142.60
Total	**$1,000**				**$820.04**

In the two examples above, the "accounting profit of the $200 received annually for five-years is worth more when the interest rate is lower.

Market Process

It is necessary to understand that in a socialist economy as a result of aggression and/or coercion, man acts differently that he would otherwise. In a market economy, social life is possible because an individual acts, at times without realizing it, in such a way that their behavior meets the needs of others. The learning process of such behavior is entrepreneurship. This constant interaction between individuals initiates a process of perpetual adjustment or coordination. Massive amounts of information are transmitted in an economy, which results in spontaneous market order and a cluster of successes by the capitalist. This information is tacit and therefore cannot be articulated. Market participants can make use of this dispersed tacit knowledge because of prices. While this includes market prices in general, the most important price from which implicit knowledge can be attained is from interest rates as this represents the loanable funds market. In other words, should this be manipulated in the case of socialism, it leads to a cluster of errors via the falsification of economic calculation/of accounting profits (otherwise known as the net present value of a series of cash flows).

Why Socialism (Central Banking) Can Never Work

Market price formation is vital in order for an economy to run smoothly. Market intervention by the central banks artificially lowering the interest rates prevents accurate market price formation. This leads to capital being misallocated.

Because of this, it is impossible for a governing body to consciously acquire this knowledge. This knowledge is only known by market participants implicitly and in a dispersed manner so information is transmitted by the activity of the marketplace itself. Thus, the market makes sense of all this information, as it is a self-organizing system. It is logically impossible for all this information to be obtained by a governing body, such as in socialism. But even if it were, it would be impossible to articulate, as it isn't explicitly said or transmitted[108]. However, even if this knowledge were known, the governing body

---
[108] Jesus Huerto de Soto, *Socialism, Economic calculation and Entrepreneurship*, p. 52-54.

would still be unable to engage in economic calculation because market prices are absent lack of a price system of the factors of production, a computation of profit and loss is not feasible[109].

In other words, the problem at the heart of socialism isn't knowledge, rather, economic calculation. In our case, for this chapter, the following are the effects of the central bank/government's manipulating the most important price and market signal, the Fed Funds Rate, and therefore all interest rates across the yield curve and the consequences of such actions. In other words, this governing body is manipulating the information that is being transmitted between market participants because it believes it can maximize coordination in the marketplace. However, the governing body, in this case the Federal Reserve, has shown through its extremely poor track record of economic forecasts, lacking control of and regarding knowledge of the business cycle induced by its own policies that modern monetary policy is a failure. Since its founding, the Fed has taken a more active role in monetary policy with each passing decade, yet the monetary catastrophe which results from such action has been getting increasingly worse. Coincidence?

The Federal Reserve, in fact, does not even try to articulate this information, instead relying the incredibly flawed modern economic theory. Modern economic theory tells them that an increase in the supply of money and credit (lowering interest rates) will stimulate economic growth and if the economy "overheats" it should contract the supply of money and credit (raise interest rates). In short, inflation created by the central bank is the primary cause of the modern day business cycle as it leads to distortions and dis-coordination amongst market participants. But note that the central bank does not directly create inflation, instead doing so indirectly, via purchasing government securities and therefore increasing excess reserves at its member banks. These member banks then engage in typical banking operations, notably loan origination via fractional reserve banking, from which inflation arises from new credit expansion.

The Fed and a Long History of Failure

It is astonishing that the Federal Reserve and, more importantly, the public at large have failed to realize that the more the Fed intervenes in the market, the more dire the consequences. It is quite clear that central bank was at the heart of the technology bubble, the housing bubble, and now the bond bubble, yet few have tried to hold them accountable. Even more remarkable is the fact that policies enacted by the central bank have never led to a positive outcome, rather only those that vary in the degree to which economic destruction results.

Has the Federal Reserve set society back? If so, how many years? The Fed is certainly responsible for wiping out the middle class as its inflationary policies have caused on-going wealth redistribution. One of the less talked about insidious effects of

---

[109] Yeager, Leland, Mises and Hayek on Calculation and Knowledge, *The Review of Austrian Economics Vol 7, No.2*, p. 94.

inflation is the wealth redistribution it has on society as a whole and the sole reason why the U.S. has such a small middle class.

It is worth noting that true median household income as of the most recent data (2013) hasn't been as low since 1995! This will be discussed further in chapter 8, however, the logical outcome of the technological revolution (the railroad, the automobile, and most recently the Internet and related technologies) is that because of the vast increases in productivity, either median household incomes should have increased or consumer prices should have decreased. Every economic contraction (having occurred far more frequently that reported in the mainstream headlines, and numerous mathematical gimmicks are used to calculate GDP and inflation) destroys the production structure to varying degrees.

Economic Growth and Increased Credit Expansion Backed By an Increase in Voluntary Savings (Capitalism)

The graphic above is a mere representation on the structure of production structure. We will focus on the structure of production and analyze how and why changes in the spatial dimensions occur and the significance thereof. The following graphic is the entire framework for understanding what causes the boom-bust or "business cycle," also known as Austrian Business Cycle Theory, which was developed over a long period of time. The group who developed the primary economic principles of this theory and free market economics in general were the following: Aristotle, Richard Cantillon, Anne-Robert-Jacques Turgot, and Jean-Baptiste Say.

The founders of the Austrian School of Economics put the aforementioned economic principles into a temporal sequence beginning with Carl Menger and Eugen Bohm-Bawerk, being fully put together by Ludwig von Mises. There have been further insights into this theory as well as in developing in-depth analysis after Mises passed, with Roger Garrison having completed arguably the most in-depth analysis, including such things as impacts of deficit spending, among other considerations. Other notable modern day economists specializing in Austrian Business Cycle Theory include Jesus Huerta De Soto and Philipp Bagus.

In the bottom right quadrant, the interest rate (on a specific duration loan) is determined at the equilibrium (towards the equilibrium as the market is never in perfect equilibrium) between the supply and demand for loans. As discussed above, this is merely a reflection on society's time preference.

Note: the prime rate is what those with a good credit history typically pay on a loan and is usually 300-350 basis points (3.00%-4.00%) more than the Federal Funds Rate.

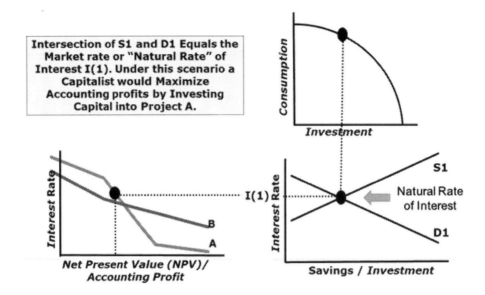

The diagrams below may help some to better understand how changes in the interest rate effects the structure of production. The two diagrams below incorporate the production structure (upper left quadrant) as well as depicting how interest rates determine investment project rankings.

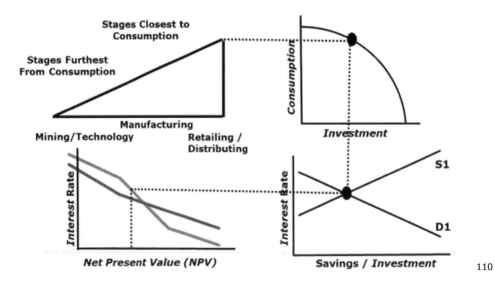

---

[110] Roger Garrison, Time and Money, p. 50

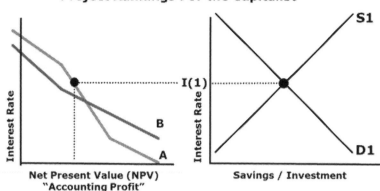

The Natural Rate of Interest

Using the equilibrium market rate of interest in the bottom right quadrant, at the "natural rate of interest," we follow that line left and see that Project A has the highest accounting profit or net present value. Then, going back to the bottom right quadrant, following the natural rate of interest up to the top right quadrant, we see that the savings/investment-to-consumption proportion is relatively low. Using these three graphs, it can be deduced that interest rates are relatively high.

First, between the two investment projects we will examine, Project B generates significantly higher accounting profits at lower interest rates and at the current natural rate of interest, it is project A which maximizes profit. We can also deduce that project is near finished product/consumption.

We also see in the top right quadrant that relatively low savings/investment-to-consumption proportion cannot be reduced significantly, meaning society is currently more present-oriented and less future-oriented. Society is more present-oriented, preferring more to consume rather than save. This is an example of the market clearing and making economic calculation relatively easy for capitalists. This is not to say all capitalists will be successful in their investment endeavors, however, misallocated capital will solely be the result of entrepreneurial error, not market intervention. Looking back on the production structure, when interest rates are relatively high, capitalists maximize accounting profits by investing in projects closest to consumption such as retail or the like.

The chart below is how the capitalist views the environment of relatively high interest rates (the Fed Funds Rate is 6.00% for this example, with the prime rate 300 basis points, or 3.00%, higher than the Fed Funds Rate, or 9.0%). Keep this chart in mind; we will use it several more times. Project A would clearly be chosen, as it yields a positive accounting profit.

Net Present Value (NPV) or Accounting Profit

Economic Calculation In a Market Economy

Project A √		Project B	
Interest Rate	9.00%	Interest Rate	9.00%
Risk Premium	1.50%	Risk Premium	2.50%
Cost of Capital	**10.50%**	**Cost of Capital**	**11.50%**
Nominal Profit	Accounting Profit	Nominal Profit	Accounting Profit
$245,000	**$21,654**	**$525,000**	**($6,452)**
($250,000)	($226,244)	($550,000)	($493,274)
($130,000)	($106,468)	($300,000)	($241,308)
$62,500	$46,323	$137,500	$99,192
$62,500	$41,921	$137,500	$88,962
$62,500	$37,937	$137,500	$79,786
$62,500	$34,333	$137,500	$71,557
$62,500	$31,070	$137,500	$64,177
$62,500	$28,118	$137,500	$57,558
$62,500	$25,446	$137,500	$51,621
$62,500	$23,028	$137,500	$46,297
$62,500	$20,840	$137,500	$41,522
$62,500	$18,860	$137,500	$37,240
$62,500	$17,068	$137,500	$33,399
$62,500	$15,446	$137,500	$29,954
$62,500	$13,978	$137,500	$26,865

Supposing the time preference of society as a whole decreases, this results in the savings/investment-to-consumption ratio increasing and a concurrent decrease in the market rate of interest. We will use the loanable funds market for a graphical example, which is depicted below.

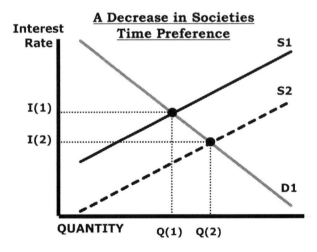

Prior to the decrease in society's time preference, the natural rate of interest of 9.0% is depicted above at I(1) and determined by the equilibrium of the supply and demand for loans. Once society starts to become more future-oriented, it begins to save a higher portion of total income, which gradually increases the supply of loanable funds. Once this change has taken place, the supply of loans has increased from S1 to S2 and the new interest rate is seen at I(2). Again, we want to look at this in full, both with the change in the (savings)/investment-to-consumption proportion and the change in the accounting profits of both projects A and B.

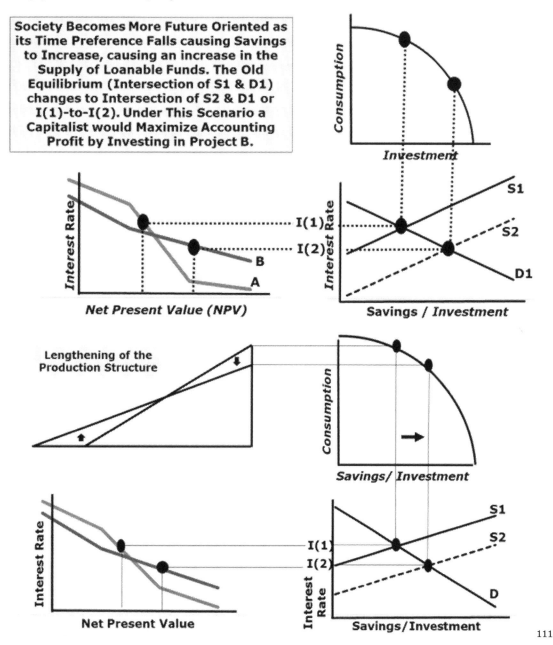

[111]

---
[111] Ibid, p. 62

Any of the following could and would happen in a market economy[112]: Capitalists who have investments operating at different stages of the production structure may choose to reinvest more of the income saved from consuming less and/or acquire capital goods such as original means of production, natural resource, and labor. Those who have existing investments in stages closer to final consumption will witness a temporary decrease in accounting profits, as less is spent on consumer goods in the near-term and as society is more future-oriented and begins saving a larger portion of their income. We use the term "accounting profit" as the nominal profit discounted by the prime rate (risk-free interest rate received on bank deposits + 300-400 basis points 3.0-4.0%) plus the capitalist's subjective view of opportunity cost or cost of capital. A capitalist has no problem with this if they are allocating capital in one or more investment projects further away from finished goods/final consumption because the accounting profits in the future will more than offset this temporary decrease.

Alternatively the owners of the original means of production may decide to take on the role of a capitalist and adjust their savings/investments-consumption ratio and invest capital into various stages in the production structure. The lower the interest rate, the more capital investment is directed to the stages further away from consumption precisely because consumer's time preference has decreased, making investments further from consumption appear to have a far higher rate of return than the cost of capital (required return by the individual) or the previous forecast of gross profit resulting in higher forecast accounting profit due to this gross profit being discounted at a lower rate. In other words, the interest rate allows for the inter-temporal allocation of resources, or coordination of the actions of the capitalists with that of the consumer. The rate of interest reflects the time preference of society which is absolutely necessary and crucial in economic calculation. Next, we will analyze how and why the production structure changes, due to a decrease in the time preference of society.

In the graphic below, the decrease in society's time preference causes the supply of loans to increase from S1 to S2 (bottom right quadrant). This is reflected in top right quadrant as the savings/investment-to-consumption ratio falls.

We then see that capitalists operating nearest consumption decrease, while those operating further from production rise, by looking at the bottom left quadrant where projects that are more profitable and therefore more capital intensive and further from consumption maximize the net present value of profits from investment projects. Furthermore, the production structure has lengthened (vertically) and widened.

We can also view this in another way: starting back at the new equilibrium of the supply and demand for loans, we move to the quadrant to the left. At a higher interest rate the net present value (accounting profit) of the investment project is higher at B relative to A. In other words, the investment project the capitalist would choose (as his goal is to maximize profit) at the higher interest rate necessarily operates in a stage of production closer to consumption than the alternative project, as the time preference of

---

[112] Jesus Huerta De Soto, *Money, Bank Credit & Economic Cycles*, pp. 313-314.

society is higher or more present-oriented. For that reason, we see the net present value isn't particularly high. When the rate of interest does reflect the decrease in society's time preference, we see that the other, more capital intensive and thus more profitable project would be undertaken.

Net Present Value (NPV) or Accounting Profit
Economic Calculation In a Market Economy

Project A		Project B √	
Interest Rate	7.00%	Interest Rate	7.00%
Risk Premium	1.50%	Risk Premium	2.50%
Cost of Capital	**8.50%**	**Cost of Capital**	**9.50%**
Nominal Profit	**Accounting Profit**	**Nominal Profit**	**Accounting Profit**
$215,000	**$44,449**	**$525,000**	**$83,640**
($250,000)	($230,415)	($550,000)	($502,283)
($130,000)	($110,429)	($300,000)	($250,203)
$40,000	$31,316	$137,500	$104,727
$55,000	$39,687	$137,500	$95,641
$62,500	$41,565	$137,500	$87,344
$62,500	$38,309	$137,500	$79,766
$62,500	$35,308	$137,500	$72,846
$62,500	$32,542	$137,500	$66,526
$62,500	$29,992	$137,500	$60,754
$62,500	$27,643	$137,500	$55,483
$62,500	$25,477	$137,500	$50,670
$62,500	$23,481	$137,500	$46,274
$62,500	$21,642	$137,500	$42,259
$62,500	$19,946	$137,500	$38,593
$62,500	$18,384	$137,500	$35,244

Note: *Economic Calculation is only possible because we are using the market rate of interest and NOT that where the Fed manipulates interest rates such as that which has persisted since 1913.*

It is the change in society's time preference that underlies economic growth (this includes the whole cycle of being both more present-oriented at certain points in time as well as more future-oriented at other points in time). Even in the rare case of technological revolutions (invention of railroads, automobiles, and most recently the Internet and related technologies), increased capital accumulation and therefore capital formation allow for these revolutions to take place in the first place.

So called "expert economists" such as Alan Greenspan, Ben Bernanke, and Janet Yellen have never tried to understand how an economy could go right, focusing on how and why it goes wrong. Are they misguided? Do they have no understanding of a market economy?

Note: *Only the Austrian School predicted and wrote hundreds of articles forecasting the bursting of the tech bubble and the housing bubble. Furthermore, since the Publication of*

"The Theory of Money and Credit" by Ludwig von Mises in 1913, Austrian Economists have forecasted ever boom-bust cycle or "bubbles."

As the interest rates fall, capital goods such as an airplane, real estate, or a producing copper mine increase in value. This is because when an investor allocates capital, he/she has a required rate of return for an asset based both on a risk premium specific to each investment project and the prevailing rate of interest (what he/she could earn in a bank or "opportunity cost.)"

We just illustrated how the capitalist's forecast of accounting profits changes along with society's time preference and therefore the interest rate. Initially at a 6.00% Fed Funds Rate (which means the prime rate is more or less at 9.00%), Project A yielded a positive net present value while Project B did not. However, when society's time preference changed, reflected by a decrease in the Key interest rate/overnight borrowing rate by 2.00% to 4.00% (therefore the borrowing rate or prime rate fell from 9.0% to 7.0%], Project B overwhelmingly would be chosen by the capitalist. Projects B has a higher risk premium because it is further away from final consumption.

Those who think more in financial terms are likely to prefer the charts representing the capitalist's thinking, such as the most recent one. Either way, understanding the importance of interest rates should be clear.

Just to recap, before the change in interest rates, Project A generated a Net Present Value of $11,600 (cash outflows in year 1 and 2 of $250,000 and $130,000 and 13-years of cash inflows of $62,500). While the paper profits show a total inflow of $432,500 over the life of the investment project, these have to be discounted by 9.0% each year, from which we come to an accounting profit, or net present value mentioned above. The same goes for Project B, which actually generates a total cash inflow of $937,500 over the life of the project, the higher initial cash outflows in year 1 and 2, and a slightly higher cost of capital yields an accounting profit (NPV) of negative **($-6,452).** Project A requires significant less capital investment and generated a much smaller nominal profit annually, which told us society is more present-oriented and therefore interest rates are relatively high.

Once the time preference of society falls, meaning it becomes more future-oriented, interest rates fall. In this case the prime rate falls from 9.0% to 7.0%. The capitalist economic calculation changes, as seen above. The nominal profits of Project A actually sees its profit fall slightly because less consumption in the short- term persists. This short period of decreased nominal profits actually decreases the accounting profits of the project over its life disproportionally as near-term cash flow/profits are always worth more, courtesy of the time value of money. Project B not only becomes profitable but over $50k more profitable, relative to Project A.

Capital goods arise from the combination of natural resources, labor, and time. Keep in mind every capital goods contains various commodities which are derived from natural resources, so it does not mean it has to come directly from natural resources, rather, indirectly in the case of parts needed for investment in equipment. The production process is complicated, as there are many stages in the productive structure every good must go through. Each additional stage a product goes through is deemed more profitable (said differently, is value added) by the capitalist, otherwise there would be no incentive to invest in projects furthest or even further away from consumption/finished goods. Projects further from consumption are necessarily more capital intensive than those that begin closer to consumption.

Stages Away From Final Consumption/Finished Good

Stages	104-84	83-63	62-42	41-21	20-1	Finished Good
Profit /(Value Added)	$80.00	$82.50	$87.50	$95.00	$105.00	
Cumulative Profit	$80.00	$162.50	$250.00	$345.00	$450.00	**$450.00**

In an unhampered free market, the modern day boom-bust cycle would no longer be present. There would be periods when the economy was growing faster than the average rate. There would also be occasional periods of slight economic contraction, but unnoticeable, relative to modern day recessions. These would be far less prevalent and would likely be called the natural ebb and flow of an economy. Furthermore, periods of higher economic growth wouldn't necessarily be followed by a bust or economic contraction, as is the case today. In short, economic growth would be far less volatile.

The bust or liquidation of mal-investments and other imbalances is actually the healthy part of the modern day central bank induced business cycle with the boom period being relatively unhealthy. Human beings are in effect voting with their purchasing power as to what they want/need, and it is the most efficient and immediate feedback mechanism necessary for the best overall economic outcome for the population at large, whether a town, state, nation or the world.

This is contrary to modern economic thought, which views these events differently, considering the boom as the healthy part of the business cycle and the bust as unhealthy. The production structure, like everything else in economics, is ever-changing and tends to expand both horizontally and vertically, meaning the production structure lengthens (vertically) as new projects are taken on that are the furthest away from consumption, as well as new stages of the production process added, which are the same length away from consumption as other projects that have been taken on in the past (widening of the production structure). The widening and lengthening would be slight but essentially continuous, which is far different than the boom-bust cycle the Federal Reserve has cursed us with today. During the boom, the production structure lengthens and widens (temporarily) more than it should, until the liquidation of economic imbalances, which make the economy less productive than if we adopted a market economy.

There could still be periods of economic contraction or liquidation of unsound investments; however, these would be much milder and in some cases unnoticed by many, relative to the violent bust periods we witness today. The periods of economic prosperity, or "booms" as they would be called today, would also be absent, at least to the degree these we have become accustomed to today. Instead longer periods of robust economic growth would be seen instead of short periods of abnormally high economic growth, such as those seen prior to the bursting of the tech and housing bubbles.

The Central Bank Induced Business Cycle (Socialism)

When the central bank decides to lower interest rates, the increase in the supply of money, credit origination is augmented by fractional reserve banking and causes a distortion in the inter-temporal allocation of resources. Capitalists feel they can expand the production structure without having to make any sacrifices (increasing their savings/investment-to-consumption ratio). In other words, the capitalist views this as society's time preference falling and become more future-oriented. The capitalist makes investment decisions accordingly. This dis-coordination is obvious to Austrian trained economists. Current thinking acts as though it is possible to expand the production processes without having capital formation. Economic calculation is impossible under such circumstances, yet most individuals interpret market signals as though there were no intervention.

Capitalists respond to the credit expansion as if savings had increased and prompts process of dis-coordination with other entrepreneurs and consumers. The aforementioned impossibility of economic calculation eventually results in mal-investments. This initially causes an artificial economic boom but the inter-temporal misallocation of resources begins to build on itself though not yet recognized. The artificial boom created through government/central bank intervention can last quite a while with the inevitable bust forestalled. When capitalists make economic calculations, the primary motive is concerning the chance of profitability on the investment project considered. This includes the prices of material factors of production, wage rates, and the anticipated future price of products, and interest rates are items that enter into the planning of a capitalist's calculation.

The day of reckoning can be postponed but at the expense of the society at large; however, the bust will inevitably take place and the longer it's been postponed, the more severe the impending bust will be. This postponement and "current solution" is that the central bank increases reserves and its member banks have to lend out additional credit and an ever-increasing rate in order for the postponement of the bust, making full use of the money multiplier.

From Boom to Bust

The following processes take place once the boom starts to go bust[113]: The rise in the price of the original means of production, as capitalists show a greater demand for the original means of production further from finished goods/consumption.

---

[113] Jesus Huerta de Soto, *Money, Bank Credit & Economic Cycles,* pp. 366-377.

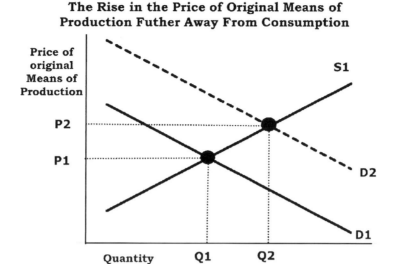

The Rise in the Price of Original Means of Production Futher Away From Consumption

The price of consumer goods begins to rise both because of the growth in income of the owners of the original factors of production and consumer goods being in relative short supply due to no increase in supply in the original factors of production nearest to consumption.

The relative short supply of consumer goods combined with the fact the new projects taken on further from finished goods/consumption takes time to be completed. There is also a slowdown in the production of new consumer goods in the short and medium-term due to increased demand for the original means of production.

There is also an increase in demand prompted by the artificial entrepreneurial/capitalists profits. In other words, the prices of consumer goods begin to rise due to both a decrease in supply, increase in demand, and inflation causing the prices of consumer goods to rise.

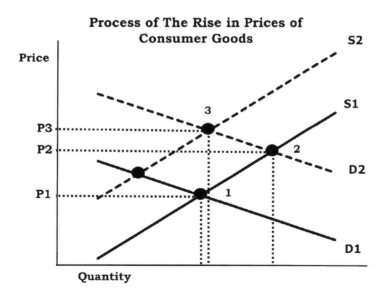

Process of The Rise in Prices of Consumer Goods

The accounting profits of the companies operating closer to finished goods/consumption see a significant rise relative to those operating further from consumption. Costs also rise, but not as fast as the price of goods and services. Those companies operating furthest from finished goods/final consumption don't see a material increase in price, while the costs at each stage between where it operates and final consumption rise. Through each passing stage, the costs mount, generating less profit and soon begin to incur significant losses, revealing the effect of not being able to engage in proper economic calculation and causing the liquidation of unsound investments and reallocation of resources from stages furthest from consumption to those closest to consumption.

In the chart above, the monetary inflation, courtesy of the central bank and its member banks, pushes up prices causing the demand to increase, as seen from D1 shifting to D2, and therefore causing the price to move up from P1 to P2. Supply of consumer goods closest to consumption decreases due to capitalists' desiring the higher accounting profits by allocating capital into investment projects further from consumption/finished goods. But this is an illusion and distortion of market signals caused by the central bank (Federal Reserve). This decrease in supply is illustrated through the shift of the supply curve from S1-to-S2, causing the price of consumer goods to increase from P2-to-P3.

"Like the repeated doping of a horse, the boom is kept on its way and ahead of its inevitable comeuppance by repeated and accelerating doses of the stimulant of bank credit. It is only when bank credit expansion must finally stop or sharply slow down, either because the banks are getting shaky or because the public is getting restive at the continuing inflation, that retribution finally catches up with the boom. As soon as credit expansion stops, the piper must be paid, and the inevitable readjustments must liquidate the unsound over-investment of the boom." –Murray Rothbard, *For a New Liberty*, p. 237

The opposite of the Ricardo effect begins to set in, meaning the real wages necessarily fall due to the companies operating further from consumption being less profitable or even unprofitable concurrently with the aforementioned monetary inflation resulting in rising consumer prices. Interest rates begin to increase once the rate of credit expansion stops accelerating. The interest rate is driven up by creditors seeking to generate the same real rate of return (rate of return net of inflation) as that seen before the increase in the supply of money and credit, which drove up commodity prices/consumer goods. Some capitalists/entrepreneurs will be willing to pay higher and higher interest on new loans, seeking to complete their projects, further driving up the interest rate to levels higher than that prevailing prior to the onset of the artificial boom[114].

At some point those companies operating furthest from consumption at a relative loss (not necessarily nominal losses) to those operating nearest consumption begin to recognize the vast entrepreneurial errors (cluster of errors) made in these investments,

---

[114] Jesus Huerta de Soto, *Money, Bank Credit, and Economic Cycles*, pp. 375-377.

and quickly liquidate what has turned out be mal-investments and they reallocate these resources to a stage close to consumption in the production structure[115].

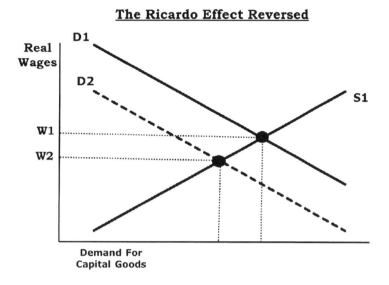

While the boom and the corresponding bust are not all that damaging one by one, this occurring consecutively causes massive structural issues that damage other parts of the economy (i.e. the state and federal government increase spending while bringing in less government revenue from tax receipts, which results in having to resort to issuing debt) and at some point cannot be reversed. Such is the case of the U.S., which will be discussed in the next chapter.

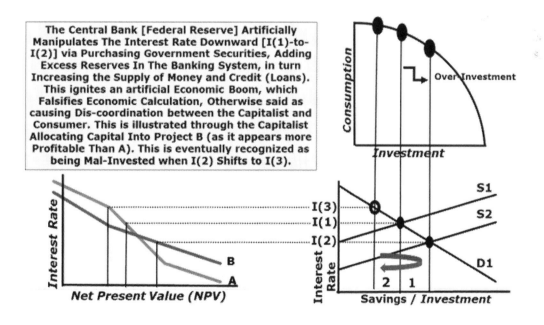

---

[115] "Precisely for this reason we have argued elsewhere that business cycles are a practical example of the errors in economic calculation that result from state interventionism in the economy (in this case in the monetary and credit field)." – Jesus Huerta de Soto, *Socialism, Economic Calculation and Entrepreneurship*, p. 111.

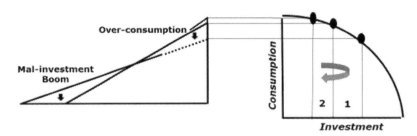

The Production Structure initially lengthens and widens, however after investment projects are revealed for what they are, misallocated capital, the production structure shortens and narrows.

[116]

The central bank ignites an artificial boom by purchasing government securities on the open market, increasing its member banks' excess reserves. This is represented in the graphic above in the bottom right quadrant. Initially, the supply of loans is at S1 at interest rate I(1). Capitalists view Project A as maximizing profits. Once the Fed buys government securities, thereby increasing the supply of loans at S2 at an interest rate of I(2), the capitalist now views Project B as maximizing profits. As previously mentioned, this artificial economic boom can only go on as long as the supply of money and credit grow at an ever-accelerating rate. The bust can be depicted in the bottom right quadrant by 1 reverting to 2. At this point, the supply of money and credit contracts, increasing the interest rate past the point it was to start out with. The liquidation of unsound investments is revealed and liquidated. As long as the central bank allows the corrective bust to take place, it will be short lived. This is contrary to what the central bank and federal government typically do, most recently in 2008 and 2009, which is why the economy has yet to recover. And as will be discussed in chapter 8, the vast structural damage inflicted on the economy and production structure combined with an even more dangerous debt bomb waiting to explode has made the chances of some type of currency crisis inevitable.

Maturity-Mismatching and Business Cycles

Banks also engage in maturity mismatching as briefly mentioned in Chapter 5. Maturity-mismatched loans also cause falsification of economic calculation via distortion of interest rates along the entire yield curve. When banks expand credit, they create demand deposits and invest in long-term loans. To be specific, borrowing short can be in the form of customer demand deposits, interbank loans, repurchase agreements, etc. Lending long is typically in the form of commercial loans or residential mortgages. Borrowing short and lending long reduces long-term interest rates, causing dis-

---

[116] Roger Garrison, Time and Money, p. 69

coordination between capitalists and consumers. Ceteris Paribus, it is a simple interest rate arbitrage. But as we discussed back in Chapter 5, this practice is fraught with risk.

There is a term structure of savings and a subsequent term structure of investing that align, optimally, with consumer' plans. Once again, re-iterating the importance of the time element in economics, Savings therefore, should not be looked upon as being homogenous as it does have a time dimension[117]. So far in this chapter we have simplified or aggregated savings and the loanable funds market, which was necessary to get the basic idea of cause and effect of intervention in the market or *Austrian Business Cycle Theory.* We won't expand on the disaggregation of the loanable funds for varying maturities which yield different interest rates, hence the yield curve[118]. Note: All commercial banks engages in maturity mismatching because fractional reserve banking involves borrowing short (demand deposits) to originate loans.

Examining the Central Bank Induced Business Cycle from a Capitalist's Point of View: Ranking Investment Projects

Briefly returning to the previous example where we examined the accounting profit of two different projects at two different rates in the cost of capital, one having a costs of capital of 9.0%, Project A returned a positive accounting profit while Project B did not. However, when the interest rate fell to 4.0% (and the prime rate to 7.0%) as savings increased, Project B generated a present value over $39k higher than Project A. So if the rate of interest was artificially manipulated to 4.0%, the capitalist would choose to invest in Project B, but this would result in a loss or mal-investment. Not until later and after a significant amount of capital has been spent would it become apparent to the capitalist. The distortion in economic calculation is seen through the accounting profit which capitalist views because of central bank intervention, with the real accounting profits are seen in the second circle. The interest rate exceeds that which previously existed in the market, therefore instead of reverting back to 6.0%, it goes to 6.50%. Project A actually yields a NPV of $11,660, while Project B yields a more significant loss at **($26,118)**, relative to **($6,452)** when the interest rate was at 6.0% (with the prime rate at 9.0%).

---

[117] Phillip Bagus and David Howden, *The Term Structure of Savings, The Yield Curve, and Maturity Mismatching*, p.65, The Quarterly Journal of Austrian Economics Vol. 13 Fall 2010
[118] Ibid, pp. 66-67

Net Present Value (NPV) or Accounting Profit

Economic Falsification In a Socialist Economy			
Project A		**Project B**	
Interest Rate	7.00%	Interest Rate	7.00%
Risk Premium	1.50%	Risk Premium	2.50%
Cost of Capital	**8.50%**	**Cost of Capital**	**9.50%**
Nominal Profit	Accounting Profit	Nominal Profit	Accounting Profit
$245,000	$67,476	$525,000	$83,640
($250,000)	($230,415)	($550,000)	($502,283)
($130,000)	($110,429)	($300,000)	($250,203)
$62,500	$48,932	$137,500	$104,727
$62,500	$45,098	$137,500	$95,641
$62,500	$41,565	$137,500	$87,344
$62,500	$38,309	$137,500	$79,766
$62,500	$35,308	$137,500	$72,846
$62,500	$32,542	$137,500	$66,526
$62,500	$29,992	$137,500	$60,754
$62,500	$27,643	$137,500	$55,483
$62,500	$25,477	$137,500	$50,670
$62,500	$23,481	$137,500	$46,274
$62,500	$21,642	$137,500	$42,259
$62,500	$19,946	$137,500	$38,593
$62,500	$18,384	$137,500	$35,244
Interest Rate	9.50%	Interest Rate	9.50%
Risk Premium	1.50%	Risk Premium	2.50%
Real Cost of Capital	**11.00%**	**Real Cost of Capital**	**12.00%**
Real Accounting Profit	**$11,660**	**Real Accounting Profit**	**($26,118)**

Looking back into the economic landscape in which an artificial boom began in 1996 or so, with the first quasi bust occurring in 2000-2001, in which the process started all over again in the housing bubble and the corresponding financial crisis in 2008. The central bank tried and is still trying to re-inflate asset bubbles, seen through the non-existent Fed Funds Rate and artificially suppressed interest rates across the entire yield curve. It is not just the easy credit that now ensures a currency crisis but fiscal policy as well.

In summation, the lowering of the interest rate stimulates economic activity by deeming projects profitable that otherwise wouldn't be if it weren't for the artificial suppression of interest rates. Business activity picks up and causes an increased demand for production materials and for labor. Monetary inflation initially gives the illusion of prosperity, but over the medium-term the view of widespread economic prosperity is revealed for what it truly is, an illusion. When the artificial boom goes to bust, a healthy period of cleansing of the imbalances from the economy.

This model or in fact application of the general Fed policy has "worked" to move the U.S. economy (and others) out of recessions, but opening the money spigots and inflating another bubble only causes the boom-bust to repeat. However, from the time of the 2008 financial crisis all the "stimulus" that has poured into the financial markets has in reality had a very minimal effect. This has the Fed and many policymakers concerned, although this is never stated openly and is only occasionally hinted at or voiced directly, with little to no mainstream coverage of this vitally important fact about where the economic well-being may be heading, both in the next few years to perhaps the next generation.

The price of the means of production rise, and usually wages, but this has not been the case with more of a globalized economy where wage pressure is downward while prices of goods and services continue to increase generally far more than the official statistics indicate.

The banks so far have done very little credit expansion, the new credit has been sent back to the central bank, and a "risk-free" interest return is realized. This of course is distorting the economy. And some new ideas/projects/expansions are not taking place because banks prefer not to take the risk and use the leverage in the derivatives market to boost their yields, while closing off credit to many people who would be inclined to use credit for entrepreneurial purposes. While there was a period of deleveraging in 2008 and 2009, by late 2012 total debt (which is the same of credit) increased back to the peak levels in 2008. The next two chapters will illustrate that credit expansion has reached record levels for the past three-years.

In the present economic environment, the banks continue to expand credit on a larger and larger scale by the use of financial instruments. This cannot continue indefinitely because all of that has the ability to increase the quantity of currency. The increase in currency, or the perception of a "coming" increase in currency, can result in consumer price inflation, and the public becomes aware that price inflation will continue as political policies are questioned for their merit.

If this credit expansion does not subside at some point a, panic or more likely a tipping point sets in as individuals don't want to hold money due to the prevailing inflation and more importantly the expectation that this inflation is moving or perceived to move out of control. Consumers rush to spend money in exchange for goods, as holding goods is preferable to holding cash. Commodity prices rise and if this belief/thinking continues, it leads to a complete collapse of the currency, as has been the case more than fifty times in the last 114 years[119].

"The boom can last only as the credit expansion progresses at an ever-accelerating pace. The boom comes to an end as soon as additional quantities of fiduciary media are no longer thrown upon the loan market. But it could not last forever even if inflation and credit expansion were to go on endlessly. It would then encounter the barriers which prevent the boundless expansion of circulating

---

[119]Ludwig von Mises, *The Austrian Theory of the Trade Cycle and Other Essays*, p. 76-78.

credit. It would lead to the crack up boom and breakdown of the whole monetary system." –Ludwig von Mises, *Human Action*, p. 555

This is necessary to comprehend not only in order to illustrate why the tech and housing boom and bust occurred but also to demonstrate the fact that it isn't possible for the U.S. economy to undergo a real viable recovery. The longer the policy of ZIRP or NIRP (zero-interest rate policy, negative real interest rate policy) persists, the greater the distortions become.

This, combined with the current financial position of the U.S., allows for an undetermined outcome. This outcome will most likely manifest itself in either a (hyper) inflationary great depression or monetary reset accompanied by a depression. To be consistent, it would be arrogant to suggest that human behavior can be predicted and these are the only outcomes. To be objective, the possibility exists at some level that human ingenuity could pull the economy from the current course and move into a more vibrant future.

However, based upon historical review this is not a likely outcome. It is generally considered that a reset is much preferable because the capital markets can be reformed as bad debt is "washed" from the system. Whereas in a true currency destruction the currency is not trusted and a new system needs to emerge with the participants agreeing to trust the new order, in the past this has usually been a return to a gold standard or a quasi-gold standard.

Additional Considerations

It is argued by many, albeit naively, that debasing a country's currency, or "inflating the money unit," helps increase exports. This has caused all fiat paper currencies to depreciate in value as every major country in the world is in the "race to debase"—otherwise stated to be a worldwide currency war. We will use basic deductive reasoning to illustrate why this mainstream thinking is invalid.

If Country A inflates its currency, in part to increase exports, what are the repercussions? First, every country has a trade balance, in that it is either a net importer or net exporter. By inflating its currency unit, while making it cheaper for other countries to purchase its goods, Country A also increases the cost of the goods it imports.

Inflation makes its way to commodities, as they are essential for production of capital goods, and these price increases at the very least cause the price of commodities and capital goods to rise as fast as consumer non-durables and services. As discussed earlier in this chapter, wages tend to rise after commodities and/or consumer prices in general, so while the cost of importing goods increases, the purchasing power of consumers lags the price increase. This misdirected thinking causes other countries to do the same and hence we come to the phrase, "the race to debase."

Putting everything together, the Fed's artificially manipulating interest rates well below the market rate not only causes vast misallocations of capital due to the dis-coordination amongst capitalists and consumers but also creates inflation while doing so.

The economic woes facing the world are more prevalent than ever. Many of the riots reported upon as being done by dissatisfied populations are really about food prices, although not reported by much of the mainstream press. There is perhaps a global awakening taking place where people from many different backgrounds are questioning the authorities at many levels, with the banking system being questioned most of all.

Chapter 8: Monetary Malfeasance

We can look back at Austrian Business Cycle Theory and put it into practice. Looking back at the tech and housing bubbles and more importantly what they say about the current and future state of the U.S. economy gives us tremendous insight into what to expect in the future. It is this insight coupled with "The Debt Bomb" (the next chapter) that we can extrapolate crucial information concerning our economic future and our personal financial future.

Before analyzing the current state of economic affairs, it is first worth taking a look back at the last two bubbles and elaborating exactly how and why they formed. Is it odd the Fed Funds Rate was more or less unchanged at the peak of the central bank induced boom relative to five years prior ending in the year 2000? Remember, an interest rate is nothing more than a reflection of society's time preference.

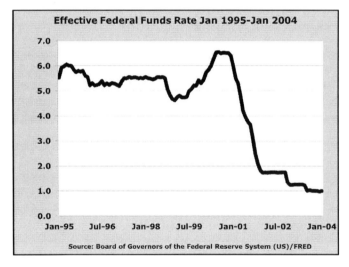

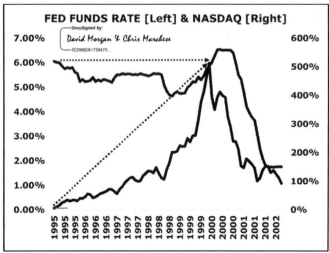

In the above chart, the key interest rate (the overnight borrowing rate), referred to as the Fed Funds Rate, is more or less at the same levels in 1995 and the year 2000 after seeing a greater than 500% increase in the NASDAQ. This fact coupled with a general increase in the major stock market indices, slightly higher housing prices and commodities flat for all intents and purposes, is alarming. This caused a significant increase in the supply of money and credit that would have otherwise been kept in check by the market.

<u>"Tech Boom and Bust"</u>

During the 1980's vast innovations were made in technology, during the 90's, these innovations began to change the way the world communicated using the internet. A technological revolution is the recipe for a natural economic boom, however, in a market economy this major event would have been seen through more moderate albeit robust economic growth (not abnormal growth) but over a longer period of time and a much more moderate increase in select asset prices. Absent inflation, it is common for some prices to rise and others to fall. People generally would see a significant reduction in the cost of living due to this powerful technology making efficiencies greater than any other time.

Instead of allowing the free market to run its course, allowing the interest rates to be reflective of people's time preference and bid up to market clearing levels, the Federal Reserve was convinced it could "engineer the economy" and do a better job than that of the free market. During the Greenspan era rates were held artificially low during and following this technological revolution. This resulted in a natural economic boom to become much greater than it would have otherwise been and therefore a corresponding bust. The economy was doing well in the early 1990's ('92-'95) as it had fully recovered from the previous recession in 1990-91'. Innovations in technology were paying off, with increasing productivity. The NASDAQ Composite Index started 1995 at 755 then continued upward. The Fed signaled interest rate hikes were coming to an end. By the middle of the year interest rates peaked at 6.0% yet the NASDAQ still appreciated 23.57%.

The Fed then began lowering the Fed Funds Rate to 5.25% by early 1996, to prolong the technology boom rather than allow market to determine when it would occur. The IPO boom began in late 1995 however, the Fed continued with its loose monetary policy[120] while this was taking place and employment was considered to be at "full employment."

Moving forward to mid-1998, the Fed Funds Rate was still only 5.50% with the NASDAQ Composite at 1,894, an increase of another 103% from mid-1996 to mid-1998. The NASDAQ Composite peaked in March 2000 at 5,048 or another 166.53% and 569%

---

[120] Any policy in which the prevailing interest rate was below the natural rate of interest as dictated by the market forces of supply and demand.

over early 1995 or a five-year compound annual growth rate of 46.22%, which is very abnormal and as we saw later, very unhealthy.

By this time the Fed began to raise rates, but it was far too late, bursting the bubble in mid-2000 as seen by all the mal-investments or companies that were forced into bankruptcy due to economic falsification. In order to clear the imbalances from the economy, further liquidations needed to take place by letting the market rate of interest prevail but Alan Greenspan and the Fed cut interest rates 11 times!

If the Fed Funds Rate were allowed to float (determined by the supply and demand for loanable funds) interest rates would have gone up, not down. This is because the demand for loanable funds would have been driven up by capitalists who had misallocated capital and would have been willing to pay higher and higher interest rates in hopes of either completing projects that were incomplete or keeping those investment projects afloat that needed restructuring in hopes of becoming profitable in the future. Capital that was either mal-invested (and liquidated during this time and reallocated elsewhere in the economy's inter-temporal capital structure) or in some cases, mal-invested but not recognized as such until The Fed blew up another bubble via a further distortion in society's time preference, was spared in large degree but at the expense of larger bust in the future.

The spectacular period of mal-investment and illusory wealth creation was only possible (as least to the degree that persisted near the top of the bubble) due to the Fed suppressing rates for so long. In the loanable funds market, the optimism in the market was absolutely phenomenal though unwarranted as the valuations for each component of the Index did not support the price. This meant the demand for money (loanable/investment funds) was high yet the Fed's suppression of interest rates distorted this reality, causing dis-coordination between society's time preference (consumers) and capitalists.

The housing bubble really started in the late '90s but because the aforementioned liquidation was only allowed to happen to a small degree, stalling the boom a bit during 2000-2002 and then resuming in 2003. The Fed Funds Rate was manipulated downward because the Fed purchased government securities, increasing bank reserves. In other words, the Fed through its member banks needed to constantly inflate the supply of money and credit.

Following the bust, the Fed slashed rates to a then historic low of 1.0%, which led to another much larger and as we will see, an exponentially more dangerous bubble. The mainstream financial press was praising this, but they would not have been so optimistic if they understood the ramifications in the future. Prior to President Bush's taking office, Bill Clinton had already built the foundation to exacerbate the housing bubble. In 1995, he changed the community reinvestment act, pressuring banks to lend to low-income neighborhoods (subprime).President Clinton and his appointee Andrew Cuomo are both responsible for a variety of reckless policies enacted and for pushing Fannie and Freddie into making high-risk loans, including the first with no money down. The following quote by Clinton makes it pretty clear:

"Over the past few years, I have emphasized three basic ideas – community, opportunity and responsibility – that I believe are at the heart of a more dynamic and prosperous America. The priorities of the Department of Housing and Urban Development, from making sure that hardworking American realize the dream of home ownership to addressing the tragedy of homelessness, are outstanding example of how our government can empower people and institutions." – President Clinton

While the idea of everyone owning their own house may sound just, it is also unrealistic. The irony here cannot be more obvious. For example President Clinton says he emphasized "responsibility" but he was as irresponsible as you can get when it came to housing as he not only pushed Fannie and Freddie to make subprime loans but also enacted countless other initiatives and policies, for example:

- Overhauled the Federal Housing Authority (FHA) to "meet the needs of today's consumers," streamlining services and "providing loans for low-income and minority homebuyers at twice the rate of conventional home loan insurers."
- Launched an "innovative" public-private partnership initiative to encourage pension funds to invest in producing and rehabilitating affordable multi-family housing.
- Tore down 30,000 units of the worst public housing and replacing them with townhome-style development to "help renew our neighborhoods."
- Department of Housing and Urban Development (HUD) was awarded $1.44 billion to spur economic development and "change the shape of 85 public housing developments nationwide."

Objectively it is necessary to look at the effects of an insurmountable number of initiatives and policies enacted during any political reign to determine the longer-term consequences of such actions. Both parties have provided ample evidence that their perhaps well-meaning intent has unintended consequences.

The 2008 Financial Crisis

Interest rates would have been higher, likely significantly (seen through the expansive issuance of credit, meaning the demand for loans was high) without Fed intervention that took interest rates to 1.75% for most of 2002, and 1.0% by July 2003 through June 2004; the only question is how high? There is no way to provide evidence, just logic, that interest rates would have been significantly higher than they were.

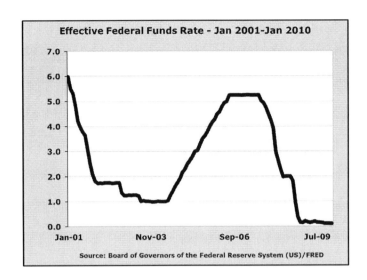

The demand for money (loans) at the start of 2008 should have bid up interest rates but instead they were artificially suppressed and cut to zero! This was an unprecedented move in American history as the overnight borrowing rate/Fed Funds Rate had never been this low. The severity of the housing bubble and the leverage in the banking system would have caused interest rates to absolutely skyrocket. All those companies that were given government bailouts would have been more than willing to pay higher and higher interest rates and eventually a healthy liquidation of these companies would and should have occurred. It very well could have made the interest rates in the late 1970's and early 80's look low. But as we saw, asset price inflation took hold with a vengeance as nearly all asset classes went up in lockstep with either other. We saw the Case Schiller Index, the CRB (Commodity Index) and all the major stock market indices rise together over a very prolonged period of time, which was a clear warning sign. Numerous commodities hit a record high, oil and gas prices hit record highs along with gold as well as a few other key commodities.

When a central bank induced bubble eventually pops, the solution, as dictated by the market is to bid up the interest rates as capitalists try to salvage investment projects in the works and those which are complete become unprofitable and capitalists are willing to pay higher and higher borrowing costs in hopes these investments can be restructured. We've said this already but it is important to understand why the market rate of interest would be high without central bank intervention during the bust. That aside, the bust necessarily means the savings/investment-to-consumption ratio will decrease for obvious reasons. This is driven by a more present-oriented time preference at least throughout part of the economic contraction. When the Fed-induced housing bubble began to form, the foundation had already been laid by Bill Clinton prior to the bursting of the tech bubble, which his successor, President Bush further championed:

"You see we want everybody in America to own their own home. That's what we want. This is a homeownership-compassionate society. More and more people own their homes in America today. Two-thirds of all Americans own their homes, yet we have a problem here in America because a fewer than half of the Hispanics and half the African

Americans own their home. That's a homeownership gap. It's a gap that we've got to work together to close for the good of our country, for the sake of a more hopeful future. We've got to work to knock down the barriers that have created a homeownership gap."
– President George Bush

Like President Clinton, President Bush also pushed numerous housing policies and various initiatives to "close the gap." One of these was the American Dream Down Payment Assistance Act which was aimed at helping (financially) 40,000 families a year with the down payment on a house. Once the housing bubble burst, countless houses were foreclosed upon. , The common theme was to blame corporate America, however commercials banks really are not corporate America. Banks can only originate loans through the Fed via fractional reserve banking.

It was not the private sector that allowed these financial institutions to obtain obscene amounts of leverage. It was because of the Federal Reserve and Federal Government which not only allowed this to occur but actually promoted this circumstance. The Fed, whether anyone tries to claim otherwise, is a government entity.

While the foundation laid by President Clinton and President Bush was terrible, the true destruction of the financial system was only allowed because the Federal Reserve encouraged recklessness through extremely loose "easy money" monetary policy. Chairman of the Fed Alan Greenspan in his well-publicized manner had "justification" for the bursting of the tech bubble such as the following:

"The retrenchment in capital spending over the past year and a half was central to the sharp slowing we experienced in overall activity." He continues "Businesses require that new investments pay off more rapidly than they had in the past…. The economic slowdown which followed the bursting of the bubble was because of the falloff in demand courtesy of the overcapacity that had developed."

He accounted for everything but what brought about the bubble that resulted in overcapacity and the misallocation of capital, keeping interest rates artificially suppressed. This related signals to capitalists to investments because they were deemed profitable but due to falsification of economic calculation, were in fact not. Market interest rates would have prevented this misallocation if not for central bank intervention[121].

The real estate bubble was more dangerous than the tech bubble because the entire banking system was so severely over-levered due to a combination of, artificially low interest rates, the encouragement of subprime lending by the Federal Government, new financing instruments such as new types of derivatives, structured products, asset backed securities, mortgaged-backed securities and collateralized loan obligations among others!

Greenspan had mentioned the recession following the bursting of the tech bubble, that the recession wasn't as severe as "the long history of business cycles would

---

[121] Note: The "Fed Funds" rate influences all other rates across the yield the curve, therefore manipulated the prime rate and all interest rates.

suggest." Surely it can be suggested that Greenspan knew exactly why this wasn't the case as the housing bubble took off and he stated:

"The attractive mortgage rates have bolstered the sales of existing homes and the extraction of capital gains embedded in home equity that those sales produce. Low rates encouraged households to take on larger mortgages when refinancing their homes. Drawing on home equity in this manner is a significant source of funding for consumption and home modernization."

Total Mortgage debt outstanding stood at just $4.6T in 1995, increasing to $6.3T in 2000. From there, the acceleration of growth in total mortgage debt outstanding skyrocketed, reaching a peak in Q2 2008 of $14.8T! It then dipped in 2008 and 2009, until mid-late 2012 at which time it began to turn up again to present day.

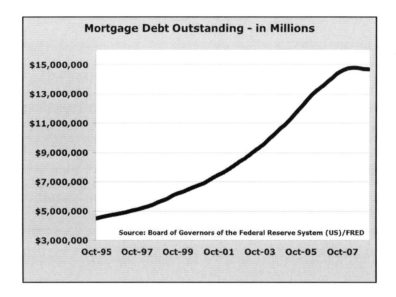

Housing prices began to increase at an accelerating rate from 2000-through-mid 2006 due to easy monetary policy, stock prices going up seemingly every day, with the wealth effect taking hold or society as a whole feeling wealthier than it actually was.

Securitization of mortgages and other assets had begun and this added to the availability of currency coming into the housing market as now new financial products "backed" by real estate only fueled the enthusiasm. Fannie and Freddie began to expand loan origination at a furious pace.

Alan Greenspan said the following in April 2002: *"The on-going strength in the housing market has raised concerns about the possible emergence of a bubble in housing prices."* By mid-2002, real estate speculation began to really pick up, Greenspan kept on cutting interest rates, reaching a low of 1.0% in July 2003 and keeping it at this level through June 2004. By the end of 2003, the housing market was on fire. Individuals began to finance their homes in very creative ways. Lending standards became nearly nonexistent and the securitization process drove down lending standards further. Home equity lines of credit became commonplace to the point where homeowners could borrow up to 125% of the value of their home. A great deal of people did just that, borrow against their home.

Subprime borrowing accounted for more than 20% percent of total mortgage lending in 2005-2006. From 2003-2005, mortgage debt grew by a whopping $3.7 trillion! At the time it seemed almost everyone thought real estate could "only go up in price." We and others stated firmly this was a bubble but were ignored by the mainstream financial press. The Community Reinvestment Act (CRA), was a Carter-era measure that was strengthened in 1995 and used to pressure banks and thrifts that enjoyed deposit insurance into lending in all neighborhoods where they accepted deposits, including low-income, weak-credit areas. The government also released the paper "Closing the Gap" suggesting to banks they needed to originate more sub-prime loans in an attempt to "Close the Gap" between the majority and the minority. The Working Group on Financial Markets—also known as the "plunge protection team"—which was established in response to the 1987 stock market crash.

The financial crisis of 2008 was largely the result of institutions failing to protect themselves from (what seemed to be) improbable but catastrophic scenarios, even though writers such as Nassim Taleb have been famously warning about "black swan" events. Modern Portfolio Theory (MPT) is used almost universally by money and fund managers alike. The fiscal and monetary conditions were the perfect storm to precipitate a financial crisis of this size.

MPT says the best portfolio is built using some positively correlated assets with negatively correlated assets. The problem is almost all asset classes are correlated to each other. Even though gold is the most negatively correlated asset to the stock market, it too was sold off during the crisis.

Credit Default Swaps

These contracts are traded OTC, which does not require any reporting by banks. Estimates place the worldwide notional (Face Value) value of all CDSs in the neighborhood of $50 trillion at the end of 2007. It was largely because of its issuance of CDSs that the giant insurance company AIG needed a government bailout. The AIG episode showed that the financial mistakes weren't not limited to firms that overinvested in mortgage-backed securities but also could spread to those companies that had issued credit default swaps on the bonds of these now at-risk firms. It wasn't the mortgaged-back securities, credit default swaps or anything else that caused the 2008 financial crisis, as some believe: it was the Federal Reserve. In fact, Blythe Masters, who first came up with and created credit default swaps was considered a visionary as these should play a very important role. It's nothing more than insurance on debt obligations.

Although in practice CDSs can be complex, the idea behind them is simple. The seller of a CDS agrees to compensate the buyer in the event of a "credit event," which was nearly every investment bank, mortgage origination companies and some retail companies such as General Motors (financing arm). In return, the buyer makes periodic payments to the seller. At its core it is simply buying insurance on any company's debt obligations. It can be viewed as the buying insurance on your neighbor's house, in that the buyer does not need to actually own a company's debt to buy insurance against default. The buyer of a credit default swap is either betting against the solvency of an indebted company or as a hedge in the case of the buyer also owning that debt it bought insurance on of a credit default swaps

One reason these contracts are structured as "swaps," rather than standard insurance, is to <u>evade the regulations</u> governing traditional insurance products. This, however, is in the process of changing, so that it will be traded on an exchange in order to make sure the seller can pay the buyer in the event of a credit event. If the seller cannot it will fall; on the exchange, in other words, counterparty risk will be eliminated.

The problem was that companies such as AIG we unable to cover their losses, meaning the counterparties became insolvent. In the case of AIG the government provided a bailout. The government on its own, along with the Federal Reserve bailed out many but not all investment banks, mortgage origination companies (such as Countrywide), and most importantly the commercial banks. The commercial banks were "bailed out" indirectly, through the increase in banks reserves the Federal Reserve masked, by "trying to spur economic growth" and under the guise of "Quantitative Easing" (discussed later) In order to get perspective on the magnitude of the issue dealing just with CDSs, in 2007, the size of the market was $62.2 trillion[122]. In 2011, the size of the derivatives market OTC and market traded was $783 trillion[123]. The Derivatives market started to heat up in the early 2000's and garnered increasing momentum as the years passed, first peaking in late 2007, then again in 2013 and 2014.

The case of AIG also reinforces an earlier point, propping up some institutions inhibits the marketplace's making the decision. In a free market, the risk of counterparties defaulting would be a risk in buying these securities; however, these would most likely be exchange-traded and therefore have two counterparties, greatly reducing the risk. Futures markets at the onset were of benefit. Contracts on oil, for example, allow producers and major consumers such as airlines to lock in guaranteed prices and confidently engage in long-term projects that would otherwise be too risky. That being said CDS contracts had merit, but due to unreasonable leverage they became a moral hazard.

Even the widely criticized credit default swap allows the transfer of risk in mutually beneficial trades. Especially in an uncertain financial environment, CDS contracts allow certain firms to raise cash because those lending them money can buy CDSs on their bonds—and the price of a particular CDS contract itself communicates information about the market's view of the firm being insured. The idea that some of this "insurance" was being bought on triple AAA rated securities was fraud of the highest order! Purported "private rating agencies" such as Moody's, S&P and Fitch are greatly influenced by

---

[122] ISDA, Notional Amounts outstanding at year end, all surveyed contracts 1987-2009
[123] The Economist, Clear and Present Danger, Centrally cleared derivatives, April 2012

political parties and the federal government. The U.S., the biggest debtor nation in the history of the world has investment grade debt based on all three assessments, despite the CBO (Congressional Budget Office) forecasting that the budget deficit will bottom in 2015, remaining higher at least through 2024.

Asset Price Inflation During the Housing Bubble

Below is a graphic of the Fed Funds Rate from the start of 2000 through May 2006. Housing prices continuously increased, although this increase actually started prior to 2001. The DJC or Dow Jones Commodity Index also increased significantly. The major market indices hit new highs in the later years (2007 through early 2008).

The S&P Case Schiller Index peaked first, followed by commodity indices peaking in early-mid 2008 as well as the major market indices, particularly the Dow Jones, which peaked more or less around 14,200.

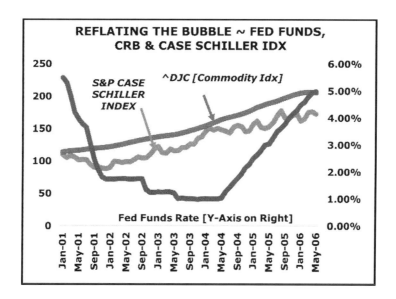

The next chart is very telling, with the Fed Funds Rate overlaying the interest rate on the 10-year Treasury. Even Modern Economic Theory interprets an inverted yield curve as very alarming and a leading indicator of a coming economic contraction. In fact, it has accurately predicted the last seven recessions, dating back to the 1940s. In the case of both central bank induced booms and busts in the last 15 years, inverted yield curves were present before the recession or "bust" set in (at the same time in 2007 as the recession officially started at that time). An argument can be made that the Fed knew this in both cases.

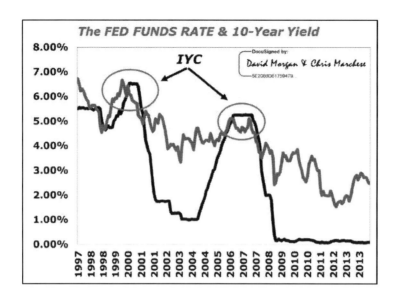

GDP growth during this period was again abnormally high, Starting when the "recovery began" (2003), the compound annual growth rate of GDP was very abnormal for such a large economy over the five-year span beginning in 2003 and ending in 2007. The 2008 financial crisis and the housing bubble were one and the same. Derivatives of all classes became increasingly popular post 1999, when the Glass-Steagall Act was repealed (allowing commercial banks to operate as investment banks).

Papering Over the 2008 Financial Meltdown

In 2008, the Fed needed to make several capital injections in order to keep nearly all major money center banks/large commercial banks afloat because they were all so leveraged, primarily due to such large exposure to such things as toxic mortgage-backed securities and other new derivatives. Prior to 2007 and 2008, the Fed held $880 billion in Treasury holdings on its balance sheet. The Fed began to purchase Treasuries and mortgage-backed securities prior to QE^1, amounting to roughly $850-$925 billion from July 2008-March 2009 (bringing the total to roughly $1.73-1.8T.

In March, however, the Fed announced QE^1, in which it would purchase $350m worth of mortgage-backed securities and Treasuries, which caused the Fed's balance sheet to balloon in size and reach over two trillion dollars. At the time, maturing securities weren't being reinvested and the Fed's balance sheet and correspondingly bank reserves began to fall but the FED decided to keep its balance sheet at a minimum of $2.05 trillion. QE^2 was announced in November 2010, this time buying Treasury securities amounting to $600B by July 2011. It should be noted that at the time QE2 was announced silver took off from roughly the $26 level and moved to test the nominal high of nearly $50. Our explanation for this is that silver more than any other asset is the MOST INFLATION sensitive of any investment. This is borne out by Silver the Restless Metal by Professor Roy Jastram.

However, silver failed to hold onto the spectacular gains for a variety of reasons, but one significant reason is that much of the expectation that inflation would be realized in the marketplace had not arrived yet! This is because most of the excess liquidity is being held in the banking system to keep it solvent and not moving into an area available to the public at large.

The Fed's balance sheet stood at around $2.62 trillion, before announcing operation twist September 21st 2011. The objective of this wasn't to increase the size of its balance sheet and reserves in the system, but rather to change the term structure of its holdings, such that it would put downward pressure across the yield curve. Basically, the Fed sold $400 billion worth of short-term securities that were less than 3 years from maturity and bought $400 billion worth of longer-term securities 6-30 years from maturity. The initial capital injections, QE^1 and QE^2 focused on buying short-term Treasury securities (1m-3yrs) and mortgage-backed securities. At first thought, the swapping of short-term for long-term maturities has little impact one way or another but the opposite is true. When the overnight rate is essentially zero, the slope of the yield curve should not only be upward sloping but a relative steep upward slope (which doesn't necessarily mean high interest rates). Operation Twist focused on keeping the medium and longer term Treasury yields lower, which causes distortions especially encouraging capitalists to invest capital further away from finished production/consumption.

Operation twist was followed by QE^3 announced in September 2012 and QE^4 in December 2012. QE^3 $40 billion/month and QE^4 $45 billion/month were part of the same program and from here on, we will refer to this as QE^3. Starting in January 2013 through January 2014, the Fed purchased $85 billion/month of both mortgage- backed securities and Treasury securities. This was also accompanied by the reinvestment of maturing securities. From the outside and listening to the Fed, it seemed as if these programs were aimed at spurring economic growth, but this isn't the case. First and foremost, it was aimed at keeping the banking system and now the Federal Government afloat, including the current Negative (Real) Interest Rate Policy (NIRP).

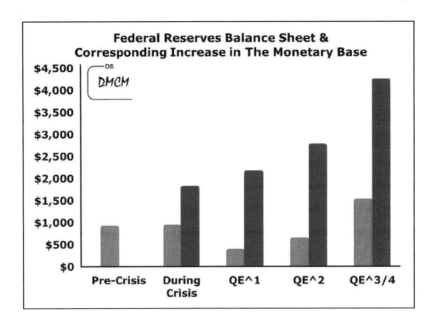

While most don't consider the size of the Federal Reserve's balance sheet to be dangerous, it is of no great significance in and of itself but is very telling about the health of the financial system. This is to say, the banking system hasn't fixed any of the underlying issues that caused the financial crisis in 2008: rather it is just papered them over.

From 2008-Present day, the most destructive policy of them all remains, ZIRP or NIRP. Coming back to Austrian Business Cycle Theory, we know there is an unfathomable amount of mal-investment in the economy, which will be revealed once the market forces up interest rates on the longer end of the yield curve. Note that the market always wins out in the end and therefore it is only a matter of time until we see significantly higher interest rates.

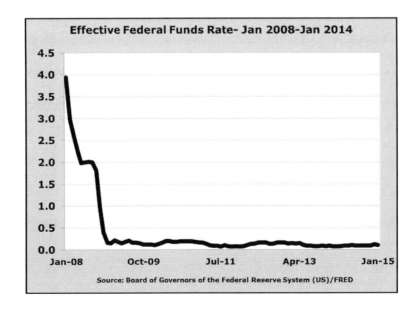

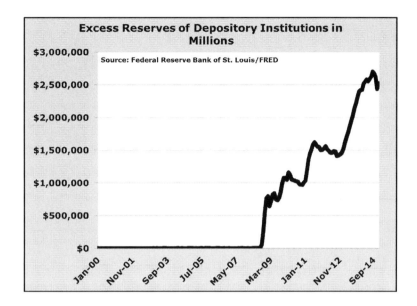

If the excess reserves in the banking system were to be loaned out to the max per the money multiplier, well over $21T +/- can be created out of thin air!

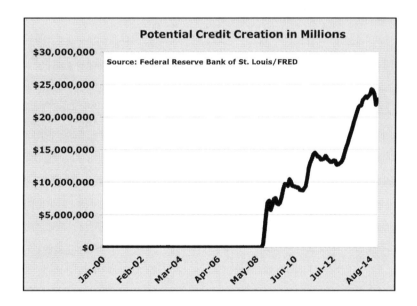

This incredibly destructive monetary policy isn't confined to just the U.S., Rather it is a worldwide problem, notably in the Western world. The Bank of England, Bank of Japan and Bank of Canada all have their overnight or "key interest rate" at or near zero. In other words, all of these have negative real interest rates. The European Central Bank has a negative overnight rate, which promotes banks to originate loans. Furthermore, the BOJ, BOE and ECB have undertaken quantitative easing, although the ECB has only done a variation thereof until now. Quantitative Easing has not and will not work. It was an utter failure in the U.S., failure in England, failure in Japan and is soon to failure in the EU.

Real Median Household Income

Inflation has persisted, despite claims of the opposite. We are using the classical definition of inflation, which is an increase in the supply of money and credit. Inflation is also a redistribution of wealth and as depicted in the chart below, median household income hasn't been this low for nearly twenty years! The destruction caused by the FED has been so insidious that all the benefits of the technological revolution have been wiped out. This is portrayed in the next chart. Initially there was a benefit, from 1995-2010. This is using nominal median household income deflated by the C.P.I, which makes this picture look a lot better relative to reality. In terms of purchasing power, it is very likely that Real Median Household Income is anywhere from 10% to 25%+ lower relative to 1995. This is using John William's calculation of inflation which was used in 1990.

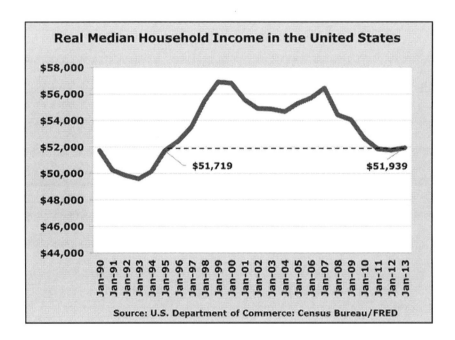

The issue with the economy being in an "official recession" is the way GDP is accounted for and more importantly the real rate of inflation. For the economy to show real growth, it has to be positive net of inflation. A strong argument can be made that the U.S. economy never ended the recession that began in 2007, based on the real rate of inflation.

The True Money Supply and GDP Growth

Note: Real GDP growth = nominal GDP growth – inflation. A great indicator or tool illustrating the U.S has entered or will soon be entering "official recession" territory is the growth of the TMS (True Money Supply) and how it has forecast economic growth or lack thereof once Nixon closed the gold window. As one can see immediately below, the growth in the TMS has been decelerating since 2011. In the two charts below that, the decelerating growth rate in the TMS has been a precursor to booms and busts since

1978. Additionally, there has been a significant amount of seasonal adjustments that have skewed the economic data since Q2 2014. In Q1 2014, the 2.9% economic contraction was blamed on the weather but there was no uptick is real gross investment nor personal savings rate. More recently, the economic data released has been nothing short of horrific. Retail sales during the holidays in 2014 set a low not seen since 2008. Real wages fell and although the headline unemployment rate declined to 5.60%, the labor participation rate is again flirting with 40-year lows.

A Look at Real GDP (Y/Y%) v. True Money Supply (Y/Y%)

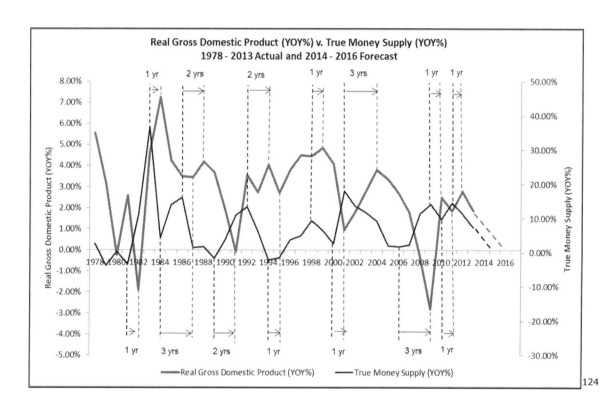

---

[124] Thornton, Mark, GDP Forecast Based on TMS, March 5th 2014

TMS Growth and Forecasting GDP growth: 1977-1991

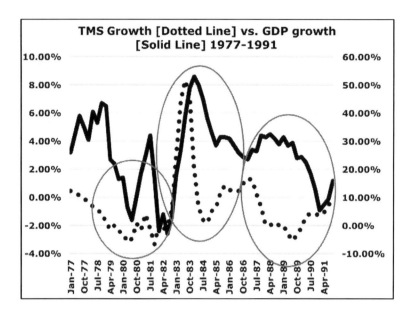

Under a fiat monetary system an economy "grows" if the supply of money and credit grows at an accelerating rate. The TMS is positively correlated with credit expansion. Under a fiat monetary system the economy "grows" if the rate of growth of the TMS is increasing and vice versa, therefore it is a remarkably accurate forecasting of what the economy will do, albeit a one-four year lag. In the graph above, it forecasts a recession in 1977, which began in 1980. The accuracy of looking at this is depicted in the circles. The rate of growth of the TMS began pre-Volcker as inflation was beginning to become an issue and as seen in the chart above, a deceleration in the TMS growth rate preceded a recession in mid-1980 and again in 1982. It also began to increase significantly prior to mid-1983, when GDP growth reached 8.00%. Towards the end of the chart above (1987-1988), it forecasts a recession, which came to fruition beginning in 1990.

The next two charts further validate that the TMS has a very high correlation to GDP growth. The first chart forecasts the bursting of the tech bubble and in conjunction with the second chart illustrates why it was so mild and short lived. That is because the rate of growth in the TMS increases substantially. The second chart again accurately forecasts the recession that officially began in 2007.

Resuming from the chart above, the recession ends in the second half of 1991, which the TMS forecasts yet again at the growth rate accelerated in late 1989.

TMS Growth and Forecasting GDP growth: 1991-2001

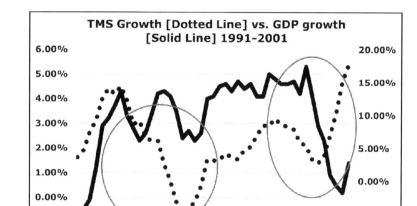

Following the recovery in 1992, the rate of growth in the TMS turns down anew in late 1993, which causes GDP to grow a bit slower and by 1995, one would forecast that the TMS growth would signal an impending recession. The explanations for why this didn't occur was the technological revolution that took place prevented this from happening. Later in 1998, when the growth rate in the TMS decelerated, it did forecast the 2000 crash.

TMS Growth and Forecasting GDP growth: 2002-2001

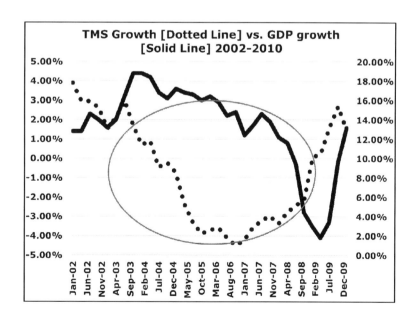

The growth rate in the TMS decelerated beginning in 2003, which forecast the financial crisis of 2008 (although it really began in 2007). The chart below illustrates the TMS growth peaking in late 2011 through present, December 2014 (at the time of this writing). It peaked August 2011 at 15.83% and with the growth rate decelerating to present day. We should have entered or should be (in the very near future) entering a recession based on the TMS. Based on recent economic data, this could very well be the case right now. Retail sales were the lowest since 2008 during the holiday season, the labor participation rate is trending downward, real wages are falling, and median household income has fallen to levels not seen since 1995. The retail sales are meaningful because 70% of our GDP is composed of consumption.

What the Growth Rate in the TMS is telling us now

The labor market does not paint a rosy picture in the least. While the headline unemployment rate is currently just 5.70%, the labor participation is 62.70% but this includes seasonal hires and is likely to fall in the near future. According to John Williams of http://www.ShadowStats.com, the current unemployment rate adjusted for the qualitative deterioration is 23.00% as of December 2014. His methodology is very simple and extrapolated from government statistics. This too may understate the labor market's qualitative aspects and is very difficult if not impossible to access (i.e. someone who is overqualified for their job, someone forced to take a part-time job instead of a full time job and those who see their work hours cut). This is inclusive of seasonal hiring, therefore the February 2015 jobs report should be more indicative of reality. The U-6 unemployment remains elevated at 11.20%.

But we should rely on logic to try to determine how it is possible the real unemployment rate could contract. Economic growth and therefore job true job creation is fueled by savings. The personal savings rate remains right around 3.0% +/- 1% (the personal savings rate needs to be measured net of household debt. If this were measured, the adjusted savings rate would be zero or below), but why should it be significantly higher? Savers are punished through a loss in purchasing power, by saving. The market is also signaling to capitalists to allocate capital furthest away from final consumption as the projected cash flows of investment projects could not be higher by looking at the yield curve. In other words investments are being misallocated, spelling trouble in the near future as it has now been seven years of significant distortions of society's time preference.

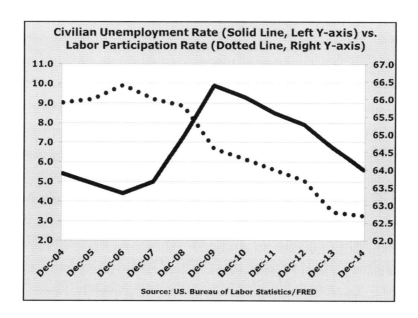

"*What is less well understood is that cheap-money cannot be continued indefinitely. It sets in motion, forces that eventually drive interest rates higher than if a cheap-money policy had never been followed. The expansion of money and credit that is necessary to hold interest rates down also raises commodity prices and wages. Higher commodity prices and wages make it necessary for businessmen to borrow correspondingly more in order to do the same volume of business. Therefore the demand for credit soon increases as fast as the supply. Later on, still another factor comes in. When both borrowers and lenders begin to fear that inflation is going to continue, prices and wages begin to go up more than the increase in the supply of money and credit. Borrowers want to borrow still more to take advantage of the expected further rise in prices, and lenders insist on higher interest rates as an insurance premium against expected depreciation in the purchasing power of the money they lend.*[125]"

While the monetary recklessness has led to severe business cycles, especially the housing bubble, the earmark of nearly if not all currency crisis' in an economy throughout history is characterized by debt. Debt based economies, which is really all those which have a fiat monetary systems are doomed to fail from the start. The U.S. is

---

[125] Hans Herman Hoppe, The Ethics and Economics of Personal Property Rights.

the biggest debtor nation in the history of the world! Moreover, all the major economies in the world are laden with debt, setting the stage for the first worldwide currency crisis.

Chapter 9: The Debt Bomb

"The West cannot solve its problems, hardly properly described as a financial crisis anymore, under the current framework bound to the fiat paper currencies. The global monetary war is heating up notably. The heavy liquidity has caused unfixable distortions in every conceivable bond market niche. The new and better debt devices have been exposed for their shams. The leading central bankers lost their credibility long ago. The weakness is as broad as it is deep, a reliance upon paper wealth and paper structures and paper contracts, during a time of zero bound interest rates and unfettered hyper monetary inflation to cover the debts. Almost no foreign US Treasury Bond buyers exist anymore. The US has become Weimar Amerika, a fascist enclave." – Jim Willie

The U.S. was more or less a structurally sound economy in the 1970's and most of the '80s. Even in the '90s, the technological revolution that was the Internet and related technologies was not enough to halt the transformation of the United States into a structurally unsound economy. It was during the '2000s and the 2008 financial crisis which put the U.S. past the point of no return. The inflationary monetary policy combined with fiscal recklessness is what caused such severe structural changes. The next bubble to pop will most certainly be the debt bubble. It is not just the U.S. that has accumulated a remarkable debt burden, but the whole world. Total worldwide government debt outstanding is well in excess of $70T and total worldwide private debt outstanding is several times the size of total government debt. There is also the "derivatives bomb", of which the total size is unknown due to being traded OTC but estimated to be between $800 billion and $1.4 quadrillion.

Total Debt of Major World Economics

While it is impossible to determine total worldwide private and public debt, given the difficulty of finding state, city/provincial debt, debt held by all the very small countries, those who don't report the real numbers and shadow banking, notably that in China. Based on the information we were able to gather, total world debt is anywhere from $200-to-$300 trillion. The following table depicts those countries which have the highest debt-to-GDP ratios. But this isn't complete because GDP needs to be adjusted for deficit spending, personal savings rate and how each economy calculates GDP. For example a miniscule personal savings rate of 4.60% ($601b for Q4 2014) especially when compared to household debt ($16.77t) or just 3.58%. Household debt alone (mortgage debt, credit card debt, auto loans and student loans) accounts for over 90% of GDP! Government spending is included in GDP, however, the amount deficit spending needs to be deducted from GDP. Lastly, the way U.S. GDP is calculated is absolutely preposterous and is far and away the most manipulated or "massaged number" reported by the government. This is in contrast with China, which has a personal savings rate well over seven times that of the U.S. China is also a big creditor nation and does not engage in deficit spending. Notice U.S. household debt (mortgage debt + personal loans + credit card debt + student loan debt + auto loans) is more than twice the Household debt in China. The U.S. is a debtor nation and China a creditor nation, in other words, The U.S. Total Debt/GDP is actually higher than reported and that of China is actually lower.

Note: for the U.S. Non-Financial, Non-Corporate Debt is included with Household Debt. U.S. government debt is gross federal debt + state debt + municipal debt or over $21t.

Country	Total Debt/GDP	Government Debt	Corporate Debt	Household Debt	Fin Sector Debt
Japan	517%	234%	101%	65%	117%
Ireland	390%	115%	189%	85%	291%
Greece	321%	183%	68%	65%	5%
U.S.	316%	122%	69%	88%	37%
U.K	435%	92%	74%	86%	183%
China	283%	55%	125%	38%	65%
Chile	177%	15%	86%	36%	40%
Brazil	160%	65%	38%	25%	32%
India	135%	66%	45%	9%	15%
Mexico	93%	44%	22%	7%	20%
Russia	88%	9%	40%	16%	23%

[126]

Prior to start of the Tech bubble, gross federal debt stood at $4.9 trillion, which is a large but manageable debt burden. What is so interesting in the chart below is how much debt the U.S accumulated during what was a "supposed economic boom." Over the course of the tech boom, gross federal debt grew very mostly, increasing roughly 14.50% from 1995-to-2000. During the Housing bubble, gross federal debt increased another 42.63%.

The U.S. reached the point of no return when the housing bubble burst, with gross federal debt increasing an astonishing 82.37% to $18.1 trillion today and over $21 trillion inclusive of state and municipal debt. We then need to add total private debt, which is upwards of $39 trillion, bringing total public and private debts to roughly $60T. The size of the next two components are almost unthinkable with net present value of unfunded liabilities being anywhere between $60 and $100 trillion, depending on which

---

[126] Mckinsey Global Institute, *"Debt and (not much) deleveraging"*, p. 105 – All data taken therefrom except U.S. data, which we updated.

discount rate is being used. Lastly, the exposure to derivative the largest five commercial banks in the U.S. alone is $289 trillion!

The Derivatives Bomb

Bank/Holding Company	Assets	Derivatives	Assets/Derivatives
JP Morgan Chase	$2,527,005	$65,504,143	3.86%
Citigroup	$1,882,849	$64,810,159	2.91%
Goldman Sachs	$868,995	$58,204,853	1.49%
Bank of America	$2,126,138	$56,950,418	3.73%
Morgan Stanley	$1,636,855	$43,910,113	3.73%
Total	**$9,041,842**	**$289,379,686**	**3.12%**

[127]

    If we take a conservative figure and use $60T for both private and public debts as well as unfunded liabilities and add 2% loss on the derivatives portfolio as a whole, total U.S. debt would total nearly $126 trillion. Continued debt accumulation will continue unabated, even according to the CBO. Deficit spending is forecast to bottom in 2015, although the economy will grow nowhere near that projected by the CBO at 3.40%, having a higher probability of contracting, barring additional monetary stimulus.

    These forecasts by the CBO should be taken with a grain of salt, if that. The Congressional Budget Office holds a long history of woefully inaccurate forecasts. It has a record of underestimating spending and over-estimating tax revenue. This is a direct result of being overly optimistic regarding economic growth, as is currently the case.

---

[127] Officer of The Comptroller of The Currency, Quarterly Report on Bank Trading and Derivatives Activities Third Quarter 2014.

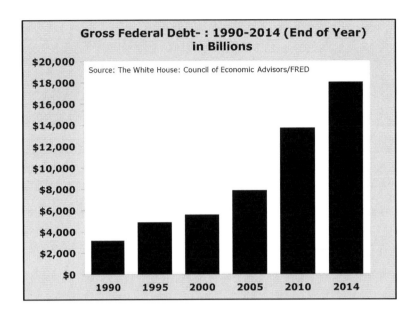

Following the 2008 financial meltdown, the U.S. became a full-fledged debt- based and more importantly debt-reliant economy. Many Americans believe everything is right whereas in reality most everything is a privilege. Presently, the U.S needs constant debt financing to operate and due to the accumulated debt and the government, programs and liabilities, it also needs constant deficit spending. As we will show, even using the one-sided CBO projections, nothing improves in the coming years. This is the earmarking of countries that experience currency crises.

The following is an abbreviated list of where significant government spending occurs according to the Congressional Budget Office: The first chart is just the mandatory government spending for the Military Industrial Complex, health insurance and social security. Of the three primary categories below, spending will increase from $2.845 trillion in 2013 to $3.495T in 2018 and $4.62T by 2024.

Mandatory Government Spending on Defense, Healthcare & Insurance Programs

Military Industrial Complex

Year	2013A	2014	2015	2016	2018	2020	2024
Defense	$600	$606	$608	$611	$641	$672	$742
Federal Civilian & Military Retirement	$153	$157	$160	$169	$170	$187	$205
Veterans Programs	$80	$86	$88	$98	$91	$104	$104
Total	**$833**	**$849**	**$856**	**$878**	**$902**	**$963**	**$1,051**

Healthcare Spending

Year	2013A	2014	2015	2016	2018	2020	2024
Medicare	$585	$612	$627	$672	$706	$831	$1,051
Medicaid	$265	$299	$330	$368	$418	$464	$576
Healthcare Subsidies	$1	$15	$50	$84	$103	$116	$137
Total	**$851**	**$926**	**$1,007**	**$1,124**	**$1,227**	**$1,411**	**$1,764**
Total Healthcare Spending Net of Receipts	**$768**	**$837**	**$916**	**$1,024**	**$1,106**	**$1,272**	**$1,577**

Retirement/Income - SS, DI, Income Security

Year	2013A	2014	2015	2016	2018	2020	2024
*OASI	$668	$702	$736	$778	$884	$1,009	$1,291
**DI (Disability Insurance)	$140	$143	$147	$152	$164	$177	$217
Income Security Programs	$340	$316	$315	$323	$322	$323	$346
Other	$96	$88	$98	$106	$115	$121	$140
Total	**$1,244**	**$1,249**	**$1,296**	**$1,359**	**$1,485**	**$1,630**	**$1,994**

* Trust Fund to be fully depleted in 2013
**Trust Fund to be fully depleted in or before 2017

The U.S. is now stuck between a rock and a hard place. On the one hand, in order to foster real economic growth and create real viable sustainable jobs, the U.S. needs to let interest rates float (let the market determine interest rates), cut spending and pay down debt. On the other hand is the consequence of allowing the market rate of interest to prevail, which would certainly send the economy into a complete tailspin, potentially much worse than that witnessed in 2008. The financial system has not been fixed in the least, rather the problems have been greatly exacerbated.

Even if the Fed were willing to hike interest rates to any meaningful degree, the cost of servicing the interest on our debt would become insurmountable. The U.S. has to service the existing debt load but just as importantly, the vast structural changes undertaken have made it reliant on constant debt financing, therefore the newly issued debt would have a significantly higher interest rate. The CBO listed mandatory government spending in the above chart through 2024; however, its estimates have proved to be overly conservative. Regardless, it is precisely the unfunded liabilities, massive debt burden, structural problems in the economy, and lack of political will that make generating a government surplus impossible. The U.S. has become so bureaucratic that for all practical intents and purposes, it can't cut spending in any way that makes a difference.

It is both the mandatory and discretionary spending that make it so difficult to cut spending. Mandatory spending includes healthcare and insurance costs, notably social security. For the dollar to have any chance of surviving, one place in which spending needs to be cut is its social security obligations. Another is the massive Military Industrial Complex. There is absolutely no need to spend even one-tenth the amount the U.S. does on defense. Further, because the inflationary policies of the Fed have caused the middle class to become extremely meager, promoting what amounts to a two-class system, upper and lower, the government can't stop (realistically speaking) giving handouts or cut spending on programs or eliminating detrimental policies because it alienates at least one group of voters. The U.S. has been, for some time now, one of the largest welfare states (if not the largest).

While the two primary political parties love to put on a show, intentionally trying to make disagreements overly dramatic, these differences have to do with minor things. Both parties want to spend money, think government entities and policy can solve problems, primarily care about satisfying the political interests of parties they really represent, and doing whatever is necessary to get re-elected. Can you think of a single government program that has added anything of value to society? Sure, what is now a welfare state gives government handouts but has it really added anything beneficial? Each and every time, the end result, no matter which party has control over the presidency, house, and senate, is spending going up. This spending is nothing more than waste and more often than not, is permanent, not temporary.

Due to the fragility of the economy and the unwillingness of the federal government and the Federal Reserve (who serves to accommodate the wishes of those in office) to undergo a large but healthy deflationary process concurrently with a severe recession as interest rates need to be increased significantly, there is no realistic chance of this occurring. There is no assurance that even this would save the dollar, making our current circumstance nothing but a pipe dream.

The chart below is the financial position of the Federal Government. If it were a stock, its book value would be NEGATIVE $17 trillion! Its liabilities are 6.70x greater than its assets. In 2013, it generated a new loss of $805 billion. While the CBO projects deficit spending to bottom this year, 2015, this will likely prove incorrect given the early signs that the economy is turning down anew.

Financial Position of The Federal Government

Table 1
The Federal Government's Financial Position and Condition

Dollars in Billions	2013	2012	Increase / (Decrease) $	%
FINANCIAL MEASURES				
Gross Cost	$ (3,940.9)	$ (3,844.9)	$ 96.0	2.5%
Less: Earned Revenue	$ 415.5	$ 350.8	$ 64.7	18.4%
Gain/(Loss) from Changes in Assumptions	$ (131.2)	$ (320.2)	$ (189.0)	(59%)
Net Cost[1]	$ (3,656.6)	$ (3,814.3)	$ (157.7)	(4.1%)
Less: Taxes and Other Revenue:	$ 2,842.5	$ 2,518.2	$ 324.3	12.9%
Unmatched Transactions & Balances	$ 9.0	$ (20.2)	$ (29.2)	(144.6%)
Net Operating Cost[2]	$ (805.1)	$ (1,316.3)	$ (511.2)	(38.8%)
Assets[3]:				
Cash & Other Monetary Assets	$ 206.3	$ 206.2	$ 0.1	0.0%
Loans Receivable, Net	$ 1,022.3	$ 859.6	$ 162.7	18.9%
Inventories & Related Property, Net	$ 311.1	$ 299.0	$ 12.1	4.0%
Property, Plant & Equipment, Net	$ 896.7	$ 855.0	$ 41.7	4.9%
Other	$ 531.9	$ 528.5	$ 3.4	0.6%
Total Assets	$ 2,968.3	$ 2,748.3	$ 220.0	8.0%
Liabilities[3]:				
Federal Debt Held by the Public & Accrued Interest	$ (12,028.4)	$ (11,332.3)	$ 696.1	6.1%
Federal Employee & Veterans Benefits	$ (6,538.3)	$ (6,274.0)	$ 264.3	4.2%
Other	$ (1,310.9)	$ (1,243.0)	$ 67.9	5.5%
Total Liabilities	$ (19,877.6)	$ (18,849.3)	$ 1,028.3	5.5%
Net Position (Assets minus Liabilities)	$ (16,909.3)	$ (16,101.0)	$ (808.3)	(5.0%)

Is the CBO is overly optimistic regarding GDP growth, job growth and government revenue? We will start with GDP in which the CBO forecasts real GDP growth in 2014 to be 3.10%, 3.40%, 3.40% and 2.70% in 2017. This won't happen or even come close. Even in 2014, the final print of Q4 GDP growth will more than likely prove to be well below consensus estimates and when combined with a contraction in Q1, achieving annual growth of 3.10% is extremely unlikely.

The first print of Q4 GDP growth came in far below consensus estimates 2.60% vs. 3.20%. John Williams of Shadowstats.com has gone through the preliminary estimates and came to the conclusion the Affordable Healthcare Act (Obama Care) added a minimum of 0.8% to GDP. It is highly likely that by the final print, the economy will show no growth and possibly an economic contraction. This is because of horrendous economic data including the worst December (holiday season) 2014 retail sales number since 2008! Retail sales is so telling of the U.S. economy because roughly 70% of GDP is consumption.

The issue with the economy being in an "official recession" is the way GDP is accounted for and more importantly the real rate of inflation. For the economy to show real growth, it has to be positive net of inflation. A strong argument can be made that the U.S. economy never ended the recession that began in 2007, based on the real rate of inflation.

We could argue QE1 may have prevented a worsening of the financial crisis, but even if that were the case, from that point onward (QE2 until present) the stimulus is not working! Regardless, if QE1 did prevent a worsening of the financial crisis, longer term it will result in exacerbating the next crisis, which could rear its head at any time. This gives us pause as it is crystal clear proof that the entire economic policy tools of the Fed and Federal Government are FAILING!

The Fed is unlikely to reverse course, keeping the Fed Funds Rate essentially nonexistent and at some point in the near future will be forced to pursue another type of inflationary policy. This is discussed is more detail at the end of the chapter. Although the Quantitative Easing programs are claimed not to have caused any material inflation, as we discussed in a previous chapter, monetary inflation has been in place for quite some time (see True Money Supply).

The Fed still has policy tools that could be implemented, but this doesn't have to be done explicitly, and for example, it could direct commercial banks to be more lax on their lending standards. This would most likely be done along with various government officials, as monetary and fiscal policy are now completely intertwined. This would keep credit expanding and the illusion of a recovery will remain in place, but this wouldn't last long, as once the downturn intensifies it will become increasingly difficult to prolong this illusion. In fact, some investors state that this is already the case. In short, the U.S. has no other option than defaulting on its obligations, whether through an outright default, hyperinflation, or monetary reset.

The CBO forecasts government revenues (via tax receipts) will increase at a faster rate than GDP this year and next, followed by growing as fast as GDP thereafter The CBO forecast is for government revenue to increase to 17.50% of GDP this year from 16.70% in 2013, followed by a further increase in 2015 to 18.20% of GDP. In 2016 onwards, revenue is forecast to average 18.00%-18.40%.

The CBO projections, forecast of gross federal debt and correspondingly cost of servicing this debt are both very underestimated, especially the cost of servicing newly acquired debt in the future. We are focusing on this because this variable alone is the most worrisome and will definitely be one of several factors that will eventually break the back of the USD.

The chart below shows the CBO projections of debt-to-revenue growth through 2024, accompanied by a sensitivity analysis directly following the chart. Then the following pair of charts depict the interest-to-revenue multiple as well as accompanying sensitivity analyses. The CBO also shows four alternative scenarios.

Currently the gross federal debt stands at roughly $18.1T, which alone is unsustainable. The Fed can continue to monetize a significant portion, but that will lead to a loss of confidence in the USD, which has been taking place the past few years. The primary evidence of this is the BRICS nations moving to monetary settlement processes circumventing the U.S. dollar altogether, and this trend continues.

Congressional Budget Office (CBO) Baseline Projections of Revenue and Spending

As seen in the 2014 CBO baseline numbers, Government Revenue, Government Outlays, Deficit Spending, Gross Federal Debt, and Debt Held by the Public are all unrealistically conservative, which means at some point the market forces themselves will manifest.

CBO Basline Projections	2014	2015	2016	2017	2018	2019	2020
Government Revenue	$3,032	$3,305	$3,475	$3,621	$3,764	$3,927	$4,099
Government Spending	$3,523	$3,774	$4,011	$4,197	$4,391	$4,649	$4,903
Budget Deficit	($491)	($469)	($536)	($576)	($627)	($722)	($804)
Gross Federal Debt	$17,677	$18,354	$19,087	$19,896	$20,786	$21,739	$22,742
Debt Held By The Public	$12,717	$13,263	$13,861	$14,507	$15,218	$16,028	$16,925

Having the already astoundingly high debt-to-revenue is bad in and of itself. Under an unrealistic assumption that this multiple drops to and stays at 5, this does nothing except make the financial position of the U.S. Government worse, just at a slower pace, and in turn putting the U.S. dollar at risk anyway.

Debt-to-Revenue Sensitivity Analysis

Debt-to-Revenue Multiple CBO Adjustment for Overestimation of Revenue (Vertical) & Underestimation of Spending (Horizontal) in 2021

7.77	0.5%	1.0%	1.5%	2.0%	2.5%	3.0%	3.5%	4.0%
-0.5%	5.8	5.9	6.1	6.2	6.4	6.6	6.7	6.9
-1.0%	**6.1**	**6.3**	**6.4**	**6.6**	6.7	6.9	7.1	7.2
-1.5%	**6.4**	**6.6**	**6.7**	**6.9**	7.1	7.2	7.4	7.6
-2.0%	**6.7**	**6.9**	**7.1**	**7.2**	**7.4**	7.6	7.8	7.9
-2.5%	7.1	7.3	7.4	**7.6**	7.8	8.0	8.1	8.3
-3.0%	7.4	7.6	7.8	8.0	8.1	8.3	8.5	8.7
-3.5%	7.8	8.0	8.2	8.4	8.5	8.7	8.9	9.1
-4.0%	8.2	8.4	8.6	8.7	8.9	9.1	9.3	9.5

If one looks back at nearly all CBO projections from previous years, government revenues fall short, while spending comes in higher than projected. We will use the CBO baseline projections and adjust for higher outlays (+1.50% annually) and less government revenue (-1.50% annually).

Historically these are conservative. However, given the destructive policies in place, these are extremely conservative. While we doubt our adjustments will prove aggressive regarding the revenue/spending, these adjustments may slightly overestimate government spending and underestimate government revenue in 2015, but from 2016 and beyond, it will at some point prove conservative.

Deficit Spending Sensitivity Analysis

Additional Accumulated Deficit Spending in 2021 For Changes in CBO's Government Revenue & Outlays Forecast

-1,708	0.5%	1.0%	1.5%	2.0%	2.5%	3.0%	3.5%	4.0%
-0.5%	($569)	($879)	($1,194)	($1,513)	($1,836)	($2,163)	($2,494)	($2,829)
-1.0%	($827)	($1,138)	($1,453)	($1,771)	($2,094)	($2,421)	($2,752)	($3,088)
-1.5%	($1,083)	($1,393)	($1,708)	($2,027)	($2,349)	($2,676)	($3,008)	($3,343)
-2.0%	($1,335)	($1,645)	($1,960)	($2,279)	($2,601)	($2,928)	($3,260)	($3,595)
-2.5%	($1,583)	($1,894)	($2,208)	($2,527)	($2,850)	($3,177)	($3,508)	($3,844)
-3.0%	($1,829)	($2,139)	($2,454)	($2,773)	($3,096)	($3,423)	($3,754)	($4,089)
-3.5%	($2,071)	($2,381)	($2,696)	($3,015)	($3,338)	($3,665)	($3,996)	($4,331)
-4.0%	($2,310)	($2,621)	($2,935)	($3,254)	($3,577)	($3,904)	($4,235)	($4,571)

The following chart (Scenario A ~ CBO Baseline) is directly out of the 2014 CBO Budget Outlook... As you can see, the debt-to-revenue multiple steadily declines in 2015-2017, then flattens out by 2019-2020 to 5.55x. Anything over 4 is considered unhealthy and unsustainable, yet even with the CBO's overly optimistic projections, it only managed to get it down to 5.55x.

CBO Scenario A Projections

Scenario A ~ CBO Baseline Projections

Year	2015	2016	2017	2018	2019	2020	2021
Government Revenue	$3,305	$3,475	$3,621	$3,764	$3,927	$4,099	$4,284
Government Spending	$3,774	$4,011	$4,197	$4,391	$4,649	$4,903	$5,162
Budget Deficit	($469)	($536)	($576)	($627)	($722)	($804)	($878)
Gross Federal Debt	$18,354	$19,087	$19,896	$20,786	$21,739	$22,742	$23,786
Debt Held By The Public	$13,263	$13,861	$14,507	$15,218	$16,028	$16,925	$17,899
Implied Interest On Debt	1.45%	1.69%	2.01%	2.36%	2.61%	2.79%	2.92%
Interest Expense	$266	$323	$400	$491	$567	$635	$695
Debt-To-Revenue Multiple	5.55	5.49	5.49	5.52	5.54	5.55	5.55

We went ahead to see just how much this would change if government overestimated revenue and underestimated outlays, which is typically the case. Note that implied interest rate remains abnormally low in Scenario B and C, using the CBO baseline.

CBO Scenario B Projections

Scenario B ~ 1.50% Overestimate of Annual Revenue & Underestimate of Spending							
Adjusted CBO Baseline	2015	2016	2017	2018	2019	2020	2021
Government Revenue	$3,255	$3,374	$3,467	$3,556	$3,663	$3,778	$3,903
Government Spending	$3,831	$4,129	$4,379	$4,642	$4,973	$5,306	$5,648
Budget Deficit	($575)	($755)	($912)	($1,086)	($1,310)	($1,528)	($1,745)
Gross Federal Debt	$18,460	$19,277	$20,259	$21,429	$22,827	$24,448	$26,252
Debt Held By The Public	$13,369	$14,186	$15,168	$16,338	$17,736	$19,357	$21,161
Debt-To-Revenue Multiple	5.67	5.71	5.84	6.03	6.23	6.47	6.73
Interest Rate (CBO Baseline)	1.45%	1.69%	2.01%	2.36%	2.61%	2.79%	2.92%
Interest Expense	$268	$326	$407	$506	$595	$683	$767

CBO Scenario C Projections

Scenario C ~ 2.50% Overestimate of Annual Revenue & Underestimate of Spending							
Adjusted CBO Baseline	2015	2016	2017	2018	2019	2020	2021
Government Revenue	$3,222	$3,308	$3,367	$3,422	$3,496	$3,576	$3,667
Government Spending	$3,868	$4,208	$4,504	$4,815	$5,200	$5,590	$5,996
Budget Deficit	($646)	($900)	($1,137)	($1,393)	($1,704)	($2,014)	($2,329)
Gross Federal Debt	$18,531	$19,493	$20,700	$22,177	$23,969	$26,076	$29,022
Debt Held By The Public	$13,440	$14,402	$15,609	$17,086	$18,878	$20,985	$23,931
Debt-To-Revenue Multiple	5.75	5.89	6.15	6.48	6.86	7.29	7.91
Interest Rate (CBO Baseline)	1.45%	1.69%	2.01%	2.36%	2.61%	2.79%	2.92%
Interest Expense	$269	$330	$416	$524	$625	$728	$847

The compounding effect of just a 1.5% variance each year in both categories would make the U.S. extremely fragile, as can be seen in the charts above. The chart below depicts the change in the debt-to-revenue multiple each year under both scenario B and C.

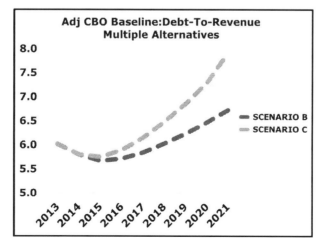

Alternatively, the following is another sensitivity analysis but this time regarding different rates of revenue and debt growth.

Projected 2024 Debt-to-Revenue Multiple

Debt Growth

Revenue Growth	0%	1%	2%	3%	4%	5%	6%	7%	8%	9%	10%
0%	6.0	6.7	7.5	8.4	9.4	10.4	11.7	13.0	14.5	16.2	18.1
1%	5.4	6.0	6.7	7.5	8.4	9.4	10.4	11.7	13.0	14.5	16.2
2%	4.8	5.4	6.0	6.7	7.5	8.4	9.4	10.4	11.7	13.0	14.5
3%	4.3	4.8	5.4	6.0	6.7	7.5	8.4	9.4	10.4	11.7	13.0
4%	3.9	4.3	4.8	5.4	6.0	6.7	7.5	8.4	9.4	10.4	11.7
5%	3.5	3.9	4.3	4.8	5.4	6.0	6.7	7.5	8.4	9.4	10.4
6%	3.1	3.5	3.9	4.3	4.8	5.4	6.0	6.7	7.5	8.4	9.4
7%	2.8	3.1	3.5	3.8	4.3	4.8	5.4	6.0	6.7	7.5	8.4
8%	2.5	2.8	3.1	3.5	3.9	4.3	4.8	5.4	6.0	6.7	7.5
9%	2.2	2.5	2.8	3.1	3.5	3.9	4.3	4.8	5.4	6.0	6.7
10%	2.0	2.2	2.5	2.8	3.1	3.5	3.9	4.3	4.8	5.4	6.0

Interest-to-Revenue Ratio w/ 4 Alternative Scenarios

CBO forecasts that the interest-to-revenue multiple will be 17.8% in 2024. The CBO also provides four alternatives illustrated in below. Given the historic inaccuracies, the first two alternatives are extremely unlikely and even the third alternative provided is unlikely for several reasons—the first being that government revenues don't grow at the same rate of GDP unless it is very marginal real GDP growth using the heavily manipulated CPI. Ironically, the alternative numbers we use from above have the same interest-to-revenue ratio as alternative 4. This comes out to roughly 52% in 2021, that just the cost to service the interest on the federal debt would be more than half of total government revenue.

Baseline Interest-to-Revenue Ratio

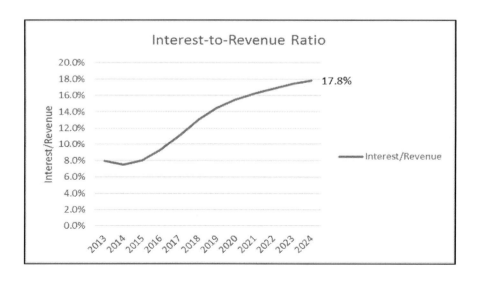

	Revenue Growth Rate	Interest Rate
Alternative 1	GDP	CBO
Alternative 2	Historical	CBO
Alternative 3	GDP	Historical
Alternative 4	Historical	Historical

Alternatives 1 and 2 Interest-to-Revenue Ratio

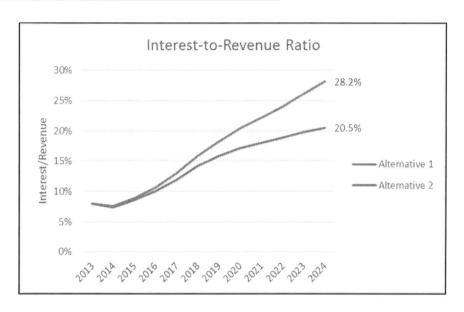

Alternatives 3 and 4 Interest-to-Revenue Ratio

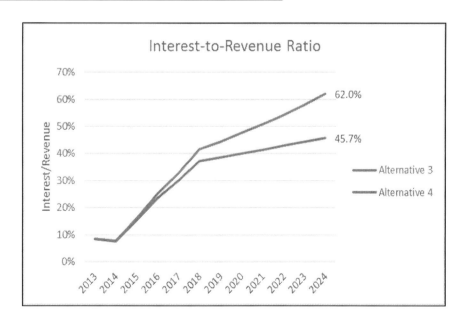

Deficit spending under a gold/silver standard is severely limited. The abandonment of the gold standard made it possible for the central bank to use the banking system as a means to an unlimited expansion of credit. As the supply of money and credit increases relative to the supply of tangible assets in the economy, prices must eventually rise and rise substantially.

During this timeframe, mortgage-backed securities became all too popular, along with literally hundreds of trillions' worth of derivatives. One would think that all the "deleveraging" that the media said was taking place would have reduced a lot of derivative exposure but that wasn't the case. As of the end of the third quarter 2014, the U.S. banking system (holding companies) held $304 trillion in derivatives and (banks, saving associations, and trusts) held $238.90 trillion.

According to the CBO (Congressional Budget Office)[128], those reaching retirement will far outpace those paying into the system indefinitely. Those eligible to receive social security payments will increase by 37% between now and 2023 and 85% between now and 2038.

Those who will pay into the system will increase 5% and 11% based on the CBO's forecast. In other words, 57 million people currently receive social security, increasing to 76 million by 2023 and 101 million in 2038. Social security outlays have exceeded annual revenues paid into the system since 2010 and will continue to do so by an increasing amount. Over the next ten years, this discrepancy will increase to 13% and increase through 2038 to over 33% annually[129]. Furthermore, the three trusts that hold social security funds that have been paid into the system—DI (disability insurance), OASI (old age and survivors insurance), and HI (hospital insurance)—will become depleted in 2017 and 2031 and the latter is already depleted. After 2031, the Social Security Administration will no longer be able to pay full benefits[130]. Beyond that, payment will be constrained to annual revenue. This is a major issue over the medium term as much of the U.S. society plans their retirements based on social security to some extent and in many cases it is the sole or major portion of their retirement.

According to the CBO, funds will run out in 2031. Funds are transferred between the trust accounts if one falls short or is depleted. This forecast is also based on the assumption that the labor market suddenly reverses and the unemployment rate decreases. This, however, won't occur unless steps are taken to allow the free market to solve some of the structural issues in the economy. This is important because receipts from those forecast to pay into the system will fall short, to what degree remains to be seen. Realistically speaking, it is likely the OASI trust fund will be depleted much earlier than forecast. While there are many estimations of the net present value of all future unfunded liabilities, using a more conservative estimate of $60T is incredibly alarming.

---

[128] CBO report 2014, p. 51.
[129] CBO report 2014, p. 52.
[130] CBO report 2014, p. 54.

Conclusion

The coming currency crisis is due to numerous individuals following a policy dating back more than 100 years. If these individuals had never existed, the same circumstance the U.S. is in today would still persist, maybe earlier, maybe later. As long as the government is given monopoly control of the mint (the monetary unit), it has ALWAYS been the cause of monetary catastrophe and fiscal reckless, in turn resulting in currency crisis. Could it be different this time? Yes, the possibility cannot be ruled out entirely.

History has proven the best "way out" is for the market to be allowed to work within moral boundaries. It is because the monetary system is the backbone of any economy, and having a stable measurement that can be trusted by all involved provides for the basic idea that money is to be of service to all citizens at large.

The U.S. dollar will experience a currency crisis in the future, which will result because of a few key factors. First, the massive debt burden that the U.S. has acquired and the continuing debt accumulation that cannot be paid off without a debt default or continued depreciation of the currency.

We have gone through why this is the case with regard to federal, state, and local debt. The largest component is private debt, which continues to grow, keeping the illusory "economic recovery" intact. The chart below illustrates the growth in government debt and private debt from January 1992 to January 2015.

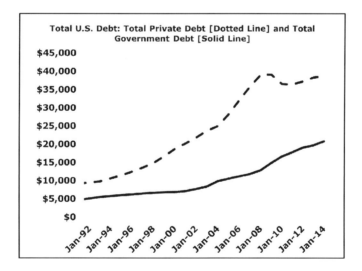

The Federal Reserve could get a grip on the situation. This is because commercial banks will essentially do what the central bank instructs them to do with loan policy, interest rates, etc. However, today more than ever the larger banks know they will be bailed out if they once again over-extend themselves. This is called a moral hazard, and when the Fed assumes responsibility for errant behavior it is society at large that will pay a very high price. While the Fed could do the right thing and let the market allow the monetary system to run efficiently, it may be too late, for reasons already discussed in this chapter.

The artificially low Fed Funds Rate, and all interest rates for that matter, will eventually succumb to market forces and rise, despite the Fed doing everything it can. Reiterating the focus of this chapter, it is the debt bomb that will break the dollar, at least in its current form. It may be able to be pushed further into the future, but at what cost? The only way to prevent interest rates from rising is to print more and more money, which, if not stopped could lead to inflation to hyperinflation. While we view a monetary reset as the most likely resolution to this debt bomb, nothing can be ruled out entirely.

One way this crisis could play out is the onset of a "crack up boom" whereby market participants realize that inflation is a policy that will never stop. This in turn causes a complete collapse in confidence, causing a mass exit from the U.S. dollar and a collapse in the financial markets. A monetary reset in the U.S. or even on a global scale could occur overnight. This list goes on, with one common theme—the purchasing power of the dollar and numerous currencies throughout the world

The need for constant financing is driven by the spending by the government, which continues to borrow more money. Most recently, the Affordable Healthcare Act has required further borrowing by the U.S. Federal Government. Will this spending ever end? Politicians don't have the will and something such as changing social security alienates groups of people whom these politicians rely on for votes. The same goes for almost every large spending program, that is, if stopped, it hurts a group of people who benefit from it, and most politicians are not really aware of what is being discussed here and the future impact.

Increasing taxes, while that has increased government revenue in 2013 and could continue another year or two, will eventually drive those whom it hurts most to another country where there are more favorable tax structures.

The Federal Reserve may talk tough at times, such as Janet Yellen and the FOMC indicating a rate hike in 2015, but if all the tomfoolery in the economic data released by the government or related agencies is accounted for and adjusted properly, the reality is that a rate hike will not be seen in 2015. The Fed faces numerous hurdles if it even wants to increase the Fed Funds Rate to a higher but still lower rate than would otherwise persist if determined by the market. It would both send the economy downward and increase the budget deficit beyond what is projected, as less government revenue is received in an economy contracting.

We aren't too far away from seeing turmoil in the bond market, primarily when looking at sovereign debt. The U.S. may see the first bond bubble to burst; if not, Japan, the U.K., or the like. On top of the debt bomb waiting to explode, there is also the derivatives bomb, from which another financial crisis could arise in the event of a credit event. Furthermore, monetary and fiscal policy are completely intertwined.

The Fed is stuck between a rock and a hard place. If it raised the Fed Funds Rate just one or two hundred basis points (1%-2%), it would cause turmoil in the bond markets. If this were to occur, the Fed might be forced politically to cut rates again.

While there are many predictions on how this will play out, there is one policy we can count on regardless of how things transpire—that is inflation. It is doubtful that a true hyperinflation would occur, as the bond markets are watched carefully by the big money interests. Regardless, at some point comes a complete loss in confidence in the dollar, which means enough people, nations, funds, governments, exchanges, et al., trying to leave the U.S. dollar will occur. That is the beginning of the end of the U.S. dollar, perhaps NOT to absolute zero, but once this amount of confidence is lost in the marketplace, a huge wealth transfer will have occurred.

Most if not all of the financial problems the U.S. faces today were brought upon by government and the central bank. But this isn't a problem solely confined to the U.S.; it is a problem plaguing the world.

While the central bank caused vast misallocations of capital and allowed the banking system to become as fragile as it is today, a currency crisis would be avoidable if it weren't for the Federal Government. The mass debt accumulation and the transition into a debt-based and debt-reliant economy is due to the inability for the government to spend within its means.

Ironically, some can think of it as the people wanting things they cannot afford, and getting them. The irony is that is it the people who have to pay the bill; the government does not pay it, the people do! This one fact alone is probably understood by less than one percent of the population because these "government services" do exist but few if any ask how they are paid for, and more importantly who is doing the paying.

Reiterating the debt issue from earlier in the chapter: Total government debt (federal, municipal, state) together with total U.S. private debt is arguably the fact that will guarantee the demise of the U.S. dollar. Remember, however, that the accumulation of private debt (currently $38 trillion-$39 trillion) was only possible due to the easy money policies enacted by the Fed and its member banks. Private debt includes mortgage debt, commercial and industrial loans, student loans, car loans, margin debt, consumer loans (inclusive of credit card debt), etc. Together with public debt and gross federal debt, the debt bubble is roughly $60 trillion in the U.S.

At this point, we are dealing with a remarkable amount of debt. This debt bubble continues to grow as the days, weeks, months, and years pass. Ultimately, a crack up boom, hyperinflation, or one of the various ways currency crises can play out, results not solely through reckless monetary policy, but through reckless monetary and fiscal policy for a prolonged period of time.

The U.S. is already getting close to a major debt crisis, seen through the unwillingness of both the public and foreigners alike in choosing to avoid purchasing U.S. Government debt. In the first six months of 2014, the Federal Reserve has been forced to purchase 91.20% of all debt issued by the Treasury Department. Furthermore, since the onset of the expanded QE3, essentially starting in January 2013, the Fed has monetized almost 50% of government debt issued (47.70%). The Chinese, Japanese, and Russians have not bought U.S. debt for years now, instead letting existing debt mature.

This continues to be problematic, and according to the CBO, the U.S. will issue an additional $5+ trillion of debt by the end of decade. This projection is under unrealistic assumptions about government spending, revenue, interest rates, and economic growth, and in all likelihood the debt will be far greater. We have already witnessed foreign debt holder unwillingness to buy additional U.S. Treasuries, instead letting current securities mature and not reinvesting them. Additionally, there is absolutely no logical reason for U.S. citizens to purchase U.S. Treasuries at ANY maturity because the real (nominal yield less inflation) rate of return is negative. If interest rates rise, the price of bonds goes down and bond prices and interest rates are inversely related. The chart below is provided as a reminder of where we were in 2000 and where we are now.

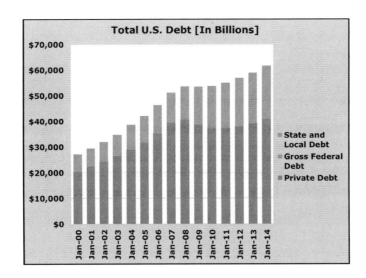

Almost all discussions about the U.S. debt problem are confined to total federal debt, which is just one part of the debt bomb waiting to explode. For the past several years, politicians made a performance of the situation—a debate regarding whether to raise the debt ceiling.

While politicians for the most part are self-serving, there have been a valiant few, who have actually tried to change some of the damage caused by the government as a whole. Those, however, are dwarfed by the amount of "career politicians" in office, who for the most part, aren't guided by ethics or morals, rather by power.

In aggregate, the debt bomb waiting to explode, just in the U.S., is composed of $21+ trillion of government debt and almost $39 trillion of private debt, $300+ trillion of derivatives and $60-to-$100 in unfunded liabilities!

The Western world will suffer the brunt of effects of a currency crisis; however, the Eastern world will not go unscathed. The Eastern world meaning the BRICS countries (South America, Africa, Russia, India, China and countless smaller countries) have been reckless and have abused paper money just like all governments throughout history have done, although these countries have been the largest buyers of precious metals and natural resources since the turn of the century.

There is another bubble that will dwarf all other bubbles that have preceded it, this being the debt bubble. Debt is the problem, and the solution globally has been to add to the debt. The international bankers have printed currency and loaned it to governments that rely on "the people" to pay it back. Once this legal fiction becomes so great that even the interest on the debt cannot be paid, the bubble will burst. The consequences will go into the financial record books, putting all others to shame. The tulip mania, John Law, the housing crisis, tech wreck, and even the precursor of the financial crisis of 2008 will be dwarfed by comparison.

Chapter 10: Building a Precious Metals Portfolio

Anyone familiar with our philosophy will know that we have advocated that the ONLY way to build a precious metals portfolio is with real physical metal first! This is critical to understand for many reasons, but the primary reason is that physical precious metals are totally removed from the banking and financial system. As trite as this may sound, it is imperative to realize that there have been times in monetary history where the ownership of gold (silver) meant the difference between starting over or not after a financial calamity. In other words, it can be looked upon as insurance on paper financial assets.

Most investors will scoff at such thinking and protest that it borders on conspiracy thinking, yet the bold and unaltered truth is that it has happened in the past and will take place in the future because it is impossible for the present structure to continue as it currently exists. Consider yourself to be one of the few who understand this fact, as only one percent of investors ever bothers to invest in physical metal. This is astounding when considering that all the monetary systems throughout recorded history have used as their basis precious metals, which, although not perfect, were the most stable.

One of the most often asked questions is, "Who is the 'best' dealer to buy from?" and let us state, "It depends." It depends upon the investor and what they desire, which means for some, having holdings offshore is critical, while some prefer government-minted coins only, some prefer bars, others only want gold, and a few only want silver. Thus, there is not a set answer, but some basic investigation on the Internet will serve most investors well with choices of where to buy their precious metals.

How to Buy Physical Precious Metals

Let us caution the reader about a few areas to be considered, one of which is the confiscation issue. Some dealers will tell the potential buyer that rare coins will protect them, but this simply is not the case. The past treatment does not guarantee the future treatment. Secondly, these same dealers will fail to mention that for U.S. citizens U.S.-minted coins have legal tender status and at law are exempt from confiscation. Generally speaking, investing in bullion or common coins such as the American Eagle or Canadian Maple Leaf is a smart way to go. There are many online dealers with a proven track record. These include all dealers who can be found when using the site http://www.goldprice.com, which will find the lowest price for you, depending on the type and the quantity of coin or bar you want to buy. Don't always look for the lowest price, at least if you are going to buy in mass quantity as this may be a red flag.

Holding some precious metals offshore is recommended for those with significant assets, but this is not advisable for everyone. It is up to each individual whether he/she wants to hold silver and/or gold offshore. This is increasingly looking like a good option for many and helps diversify one's assets. Two recommended offshore storage facilities are Anglo-Far East in Switzerland and http://www.Goldmoney.com, which was founded by and is currently run by James Turk. This allows you store allocated metal at various depositories around the world.

We are often asked how much should be invested into this sector. Again this can only truly be answered by the individual, but we typically suggest ten percent as a minimum for most people, however, given the fragile global economy and that of the U.S. which is built upon a mounting of debt in addition to the current low metal price environment, it would be prudent to hold <u>20% as an absolute minimum</u>. Further, for those who wish to keep it extremely simple, a ten percent allocation to the physicall metals acquired over time in a dollar cost averaging basis is a sound, practical goal that would fall within the purview of one of the best and most recent studies on portfolio analysis, performed by Ibbotson and Associates[131]. Note, this study ends in 2004 but is a non-issue as it does include over thirty-years of data. Note that in the next graphic the precious metal component (which is weighted 1/3 each silver, gold and platinum).

Precious Metals Optimize Every Portfolio:

	U.S. Large Cap Stocks	U.S. Small Cap Stocks	Int'l Equity	SPMI	U.S. LT Government Bonds	U.S. Intermediate Government Bonds	Cash (90-Day Treasury Bills)	U.S. Inflation
U.S. Large Cap Stocks	1.00	0.79	0.59	-0.10	0.28	0.22	0.04	-0.22
U.S. Small Cap Stocks	0.79	1.00	0.47	0.05	0.13	0.10	-0.01	-0.06
Int'l Equity	0.59	0.47	1.00	0.04	0.08	-0.02	-0.10	-0.19
SPMI	-0.10	0.05	0.04	1.00	-0.18	-0.19	-0.03	0.43
U.S. LT Government Bonds	0.28	0.13	0.08	-0.18	1.00	0.93	0.04	-0.39
U.S. Intermediate Term Bonds	0.22	0.10	-0.02	-0.19	0.93	1.00	0.29	-0.22
Cash (90-day Treasury Bills)	0.04	-0.01	-0.10	-0.03	0.04	0.29	1.00	0.63
U.S. Inflation	-0.22	-0.06	-0.19	0.43	-0.39	-0.22	0.63	1.00
Average Correlation	0.26	0.22	0.15	-0.06	0.18	0.19	0.03	-0.15

[132]

---

[131] Ibbotson and Associates, Thomas M. Idzorek CFA, "Portfolio Diversification with Gold, Silver and Platinum," June 1, 2005.
[132] Ibid

Asset Class	Compound Annual Return High Inflation 1972-1981	Compound Annual Return Low Inflation 1982-2004
U.S. Large Cap Stocks	6.47%	13.65%
U.S. Small Cap Stocks	13.06%	14.06%
International Equity	10.62%	11.53%
SPMI	20.83%	1.68%
U.S. Long Term Government Bonds	2.81%	11.69%
U.S. Intermediate Term Bonds	5.80%	9.33%
Cash (90 day T-Bills)	8.16%	5.63%
U.S. Inflation	8.63%	3.12%

[133]

This study concludes that an investment consisting of one-third gold, one-third silver, and one-third platinum maximized (referred to from here on out as SPMI) the efficient frontier of a portfolio (the highest risk adjusted rate of return for the conservative, average and aggressive investor). Having diversification (according to what most asset management firms in the U.S. define it to be) include domestic stock, international stocks, larger,mid and small cap, various term debt and cash. Real diversification includes these as well as hard assets such as monetary metals (silver and gold), other precious metals (platinum and palladium), real estate (domestic and international) and numerous other alternative asset classes. The inclusion of the SPMI illustrates precious metals are the only asset class which has a negative correlation to all other asset classes (those classes which are considered investment worthy asset classes in the U.S.).

This study further concluded that for a conservative investor, a 7.1% exposure to precious metals maximized a portfolio's performance (adjusted for risk). For the average investor, a 12.50% exposure to precious metals maximized performance (adjusted for risk). And lastly, for the aggressive investor, a 15.70% weighting in precious metals maximized performance (adjusted for risk). Of course there are countless errors in modern portfolio theory, however, even using this flawed theory (which is practiced by countless money managers, brokers and the like), the risk adjusted rate of return for all portfolios are maximized with the inclusion of precious metals.

The remainder of this chapter will focus on those who wish to invest or speculate in the precious metals in ways other than physical holdings. These include royalty companies, mining operators, silver and gold miner ETFs, select mutual funds, options, futures, future options, convertible debt, silver and gold linked notes, preferred stock,

---

[133] Ibid

and warrants. The reason we suggest these other areas is simply as leverage to the increase in the silver and/or gold price. In fact, having some exposure to mining equities can generate significant returns if done correctly. In the previous precious metals bull market, the mining equities outperformed the actual metal conservatively by a factor of 3, meaning 3 times as much money was made in paper gold choosing a good, balanced portfolio of mining shares than was made in the metal itself.

However, so far in this new bull market, the results have been spotty, with the shares underperforming in many cases. This is largely due to the advent of the Exchange Traded Funds, where fund managers can now purchase equities that follow the metals prices without having all the risk associated with a mining company. At time of this writing as well as publication, investing it high quality, low cost producers will prove to generate absolutely remarkable returns as they are trading with extreme under-valuations.

This of course means that a great deal of capital that could have been placed into the mining sector has not been and will not be placed into mining shares. Investing in mining stock is an inherently risky proposition, which will be addressed first by going through some elements that our work has determined a mining company must possess. Our process uses a checklist from which you will be able to access the riskier companies and focus on companies that have a lower risk.

Our work aims at all types of investors except the very aggressive type, who would focus on the exploration companies that can generate returns unlike any other category (junior producers, mid-tier and top-tier) but come with far more risk. It is our belief, even for the fairly aggressive investor, investing in one or multiple royalty/streaming companies lays the best foundation for generating outsized returns. For the ultra-conservative investor, investing in just royalty/streaming companies is enough.

These types of companies mitigate risk and in our view will be the first to pay very large dividends. First, we examine four major royalty companies; then we outline a step-by-step process using two popular valuation models that are the best suited for application in the mining industry.

It may surprise some who are not familiar with the mining industry, but royalty companies don't do any mining whatsoever. They are widely considered a staple in all portfolios amongst the most successful investors and money managers. One of the easiest ways to think of a royalty company is to think of it as a bank. The twist here is that "interest" is in the form of silver, gold, oil, platinum, palladium, or most any commodity.

There can be tremendous upside to both royalty and streaming agreements, which we will go through but first we will give a generic streaming agreement as there can be additional clauses in the agreement that change the agreement once something is met (delivered metal, certain metal price, amount of time etc.):

Royalty Company A gives Mining Company B a payment of $450m in exchange for the right to purchase 25% of Company B's silver production for the life of mine at an agreed-upon small fixed price. In the initial contract, Company A purchases 25% of the 20m oz. of silver produced for $4/oz.

Suppose that at the time the contract was signed, annual silver production was forecast to be 16m oz. a year for 16 years but by the time the mine was constructed and reached production, Mining Company B increased both the production capacity (to 20m oz.) and life of mine from 16 years to 28 years. Royalty Company A does not need to pay anything for the extra production or anything for the additional 12 years of mine life. Pretty sweet deal in our view.

Higher production and mine life, thereby higher attributable production over a much long time period is a common occurrence with only four major players dominating this facet of the mining market; the top four companies at this time are Franco-Nevada, Silver Wheaton, Sandstorm Gold, and Royal Gold. We have seen this happen to every company in this niche except one—Royal Gold. There is a fifth company (Osisko Gold Royalties) in this niche which has two large high quality cash flowing royalties but we excluded it because it is a royalty and exploration company having slightly different characteristics, notably spending a certain amount on exploration of currently owned properties. Regardless, it is worth looking into for any investor who is interested in this niche.

Royalties
Net Smelter Return (NSR)

There are over a dozen types of royalties, however, two primary types of royalties account for over 95% of the industry NSR (Net Smelter Return). The most popular type of royalty and typically rages from 1% to 5%. An NSR is a royalty based on the revenue derived from a mine's operation. This royalty can apply to a particular commodity, several commodities the mine produces, or all the commodities the mine produces.

NSR Royalty Example	
Gold Price	$1,300
Zinc Price	$1.00
Royalty	3.0% NSR
Average Annual Production	
Gold	260K oz.
Zinc	185m lbs.
Attributable To Royalty Company A	
Gold	7,800 oz.
Zinc	5,550,00 lbs.
Attributable Revenue	
Gold	$10,140,000
Zinc	$5,550,000
Total	**$15,690,000**

Net Profit Interest (NPI)

This is the second most popular royalty, though it has become less prevalent over recent years due to rising operating costs, which not only include cash costs but general and administration expenses, finance costs, exploration, royalties and taxes. NPIs don't begin generating revenue until the percentage of the capital costs incurred during development is paid back. Typically, DD&A (depletion, depreciation & amortization—a non-cash charge) is added back to net income to come up with operating profit. On average these tend to range from 5% to 20%.

NPI Royalty Example	
Gold Price	$1,300
Zinc Price	$1
Royalty	20% NPI
Average Annual Production	
Gold Price	260k oz.
Zinc Price	185m lbs.
Operating Costs (Net of Zinc Credits)	
Gold	$920/oz.
Attributable Revenue	
From NPI	$19,760,000

Net Royalty Interest (NRI)

This is a slight variant of the Net Profit Interest except it is calculated as operating profit less capital costs. NRIs kick in immediately because royalty paid by the operator is net of both operating and sustaining capital costs. These royalties can vary but typically are in the neighborhood of 5%-15%.

NRI Royalty	
Oil Price	$104
Royalty	8.65%
Average Barrels of Oil Produced per Day	
Oil Production	25,000 bpd
Operating Costs	
Per Unit	$34
Capital Costs	
Per Unit	$22
Attributable Revenue	
From NRI	$36,330,000

Streaming

Streaming has grown in popularity since the pioneering of this model by Silver Wheaton in 2004. These are typically much larger than all other types of royalties. A streaming agreement can be for one or more assets that may already be in production.

Silver and gold metal streams is usually an agreement for a given mine's secondary metal; for example, a 100% silver stream may apply to a primary lead-zinc, copper, or gold mine. This is not always so, as in the case with Sandstorm Gold, which is known for buying gold streams on primary gold mines ranging from 8% to 20%. In other words, streaming deals need to be structured as to not make an otherwise economic mine, economical in the face of the lower revenue and profits it will generate with the inclusion of a stream.

One of the most noteworthy streaming agreements was made in early 2013 between Silver Wheaton and mining giant Vale. In this multi-stream deal, Silver Wheaton paid an astounding $1.9B in exchange for a 70% gold stream on Vale's Sudbury Mines, but the primary stream was a 25% gold stream on the Salobo Mine in Brazil.

Salobo is Brazil's largest copper mine and one of Vale's cornerstone assets as well as one of its primary growth drivers over the next several years. In 2015, Silver Wheaton will buy each ounce of gold at both mines for $400/oz. and amount to 35k-45k oz. from Sudbury and 45k-50k oz. from Salobo.

By 2016, attributable production from Sudbury will increase to 50k-55k oz. and to 65k-75k oz. from Salobo. Salobo will undergo several more expansions, one of which will likely be completed before the end of the decade. Regardless of what metal price volatility, given the financial position of this mining giant, a further expansion will lower operating costs per unit of metal as the fixed costs are spread over more units.

In other words, attributable production to Silver Wheaton before the end of the decade could very well be 80,000-100,000 oz. Au per annum and as much as 110k-130k+ oz. next decade. If expansions are undertaken and completed by specified dates, Silver Wheaton will pay Vale (in cash and/or common stock) pre-negotiated amounts depending on the size of the expansion. While this will cost more, it also provides a nice incentive to Vale to undertake expansions in annual production sooner rather than later.

In late 2012, Franco-Nevada and the company Inmet agreed to a $1-billion precious metal stream financing for the Cobre-Panama Project. This 86% stream applied to both gold and silver. In 2013, Inmet was acquired by mining giant First Quantum Minerals, and the 86% streaming interest remained intact. Even though First Quantum changed the mine plan and deferred production roughly 16 months, production will be 17% higher. As you can see in the graphic below, the 86% stream will equate to roughly 90,000 ounces of gold and 1,500,000 ounces of silver for the first 13 years and then decrease over the next 18 years because gold and silver grades will decline.

After the first 31 years, the stream will decrease from 86% to 63.4% and 63.1% for gold and silver, respectively. Therefore Franco-Nevada generates cash flow from this investment by the spread between the low fixed on-going cost per ounce of gold and silver and the spot price of silver.

Streams have likely gained so much popularity because they allow royalty/streaming companies to grow much faster than they could by acquiring all the other types of royalties.

Advantages of this Model

- **Diversification** – Each company has numerous producing streams and/or royalties, thereby diversifying a large amount of the risk inherent in mining to countless assets. At the very minimum, the risks associated with these companies are far less than the average operator and, in most cases, the largest operators in the world. The smallest of the four companies still has 12 assets in operation and another 21 assets at various stages of development and exploration.

    - **Sandstorm Gold**: 12 assets in operation and another 21 at various stages of development. Revenue derivation: 80% from streams and 20% from royalties.
    - **Royal Gold**: 38 assets in operation and another 20 at various stages of development. Revenue derivation: 60% from streams and 40% from royalties (increasing to 75%/25% in 2015).
    - **Silver Wheaton**: 19 assets in operation and another 5 in advanced-stage development. Revenue derivation: 100% from streams.
    - **Franco-Nevada**: 183 assets in operation, 28 advanced-stage, and 137 more in exploration. Revenue derivation: 60% from streams and 40% from royalties (increasing to 75%/25%) by 2018.
- **Proven Operators** – Both Silver Wheaton and Franco-Nevada have cornerstone assets that are operated by proven operators with some of the largest mining companies in the world, including but not limited to Vale, Lundin, First Quantum, Barrick Gold, Newmont Mining, Goldcorp, Glencore-Xstrata, El-Dorado, Primero (backstopped by Goldcorp), Pan-American Silver, Hudbay Minerals, Kinross, KGHM, New Gold, Osisko, Coeur Mining, Anglo-Gold Ashanti, Teck Resources, Cenovus Energy, Canadian Natural Resources, and others. Sandstorm Gold focuses on junior producers, which is basically a niche within a niche. While this involves more risk, it is a much easier way to create significant value for shareholders. Royal Gold has a few of its cornerstone assets operated by proven low cost operators but is not nearly as robust as Silver Wheaton or Franco-Nevada at this time.
- **Tax Benefits** – The three Canadian companies (Sandstorm, Silver Wheaton, and Franco-Nevada) hold part or all of their streams in a subsidiary, which, according to Canadian law, are not subject to tax, as the operator pays the tax in its own country. Obviously, if a streaming agreement is held in Canada then Canada tax is paid. All other royalties are taxed at the statutory rate.
- **Fixed Costs** – Royalty companies have a fixed cost known at the time of the agreement. Typically there is an inflation adjustment, which increases the purchase price per unit 1% annually. In other words, there is a cost line, instead of a cost curve.

- **No On-going Capital Expenditures** – Royalty companies are able to participate in mining without incurring the hefty capital expenditures that are inherent to this industry. There are no sustaining capital requirements except for those that are made to acquire growth via the acquisition of a new royalty or stream. The ability to participate in a very capital intensive industry without any sustaining capital costs is a huge benefit, especially for shareholders.
- **Significant exploration and production upside** – While this has occurred several times in all of these companies, we will use one of Sandstorm's first streams to show just how impactful this can be.

A look back on how Sandstorm's First Stream progressed:

1) In 2009, Sandstorm made an upfront payment of $17,800,000 and roughly $3,500,000 worth of common stock to Luna Gold in exchange for a 17% gold stream at its flagship Aurizona Mine. Sandstorm would pay Luna an on-going price per ounce of gold of $400. Initially Aurizona was projected to produce 60,000 oz. of gold for 10 years. Then in 2011, Luna increased its gold resource by 250%, increasing the mine life to 30 years; and two more increases in its resource estimate currently totaling 4,670,000 ounces. Production of 50-60,000 oz. Au per annum would increase the mine life beyond seventy years. Annual gold production was then increased to 65-75,000 oz. per annum and again to between 80-95,000 oz.

2) The resource estimate (which will be updated once again in Q1 2015) relative to annual production was so large, Luna then decided to initiate the first phase of its three-phase expansion plan, which will increase production to 125-135,000 oz. annually (providing Sandstorm with nearly 21-23,000 oz. of gold per annum). This, however, has been delayed to depressed metal prices with a likely scenario being the Phase I expansion reaches completion mid-2015 but will not be optimized until 1H 2016 as its needs to buy more capital equipment. In other words, 2015 production will likely increase to no more than 105-110k oz. Au and 110-120,000 oz. Au in 2016. This is all dependent on the gold price because if the price rebounds in short order, this could all be completed Q3 2015.

3) Luna's medium-term goal is to undertake and complete its Phase II expansion. A feasibility study will be released Q4 2014-Q1 2015, which will definitely show taking on the Phase II expansion increases the projects Net present value (using a $1,200-$1,250 gold price deck). It is projected that once Phase II is complete, Aurizona will produce anywhere from 200,000-300,000 oz. per annum, or 42,500 oz. attributable to Sandstorm. It then plans to conduct a feasibility study for development of an underground mine, on top of the current open pit operation.

4) While it is very early, the company is forecasting additional production of 40,000-80,000 oz. per annum. In short, once the third phase is complete, Aurizona will produce anywhere from 260,000 to 380,000 oz. taking the mid-point (320,000

oz.), attributable production to Sandstorm will reach 54,000 oz. per annum. In other words, although nothing is guaranteed in the mining industry, there is a very reasonable possibility that this stream will generate more than $1 billion in revenue.

- **High Barriers to Entry** – It is unlikely any more companies will be able to compete with these four royalty companies for the foreseeable future, given that each company has already deployed significant capital and is already generating such robust cash flow. We think any company that may be able to compete would likely get bought out rather quickly.
- **Optionality** – All four royalty companies have significant optionality in their portfolios. This can take many forms but one example is a right of first refusal on a mine that gets exercised. Another is Franco-Nevada's right to purchases a 22% stream for $300m on Taseko's New Prosperity Project. This was acquired several years ago, however, Franco-Nevada arranged it so it could make sure all the permits were received before remitting any funds. So far, it has been unable to get all the permits necessary to begin construction, so if this should happen at any time in the future, Franco-Nevada still retains the right to acquire the 22% gold stream on the same terms.

Silver Wheaton and Franco-Nevada are considered the two strongest royalty companies due to management expertise, quality of assets in their portfolios, diversified asset bases, strong operators on the properties, and exceptional cornerstone assets.

We prefer Silver Wheaton, as we believe silver will outperform gold. But over the last several years, the company has acquired five gold assets and a sixth asset that can be converted into a stream if Silver Wheaton takes a liking to the feasibility study, giving it both silver exposure but with material gold exposure as well.

Despite being much smaller than the two other primary gold royalty companies, Sandstorm Gold will likely outperform them because it is a successful streaming company. At the time of this writing, Sandstorm Gold currently has embedded growth in the short, medium, and long-term. It is also actively looking for additional streaming projects, as it is a very well capitalized company relative to its market cap. Roughly 15-20% of its market cap is in net cash and roughly 20%-25%, when you include cash, investment, and assets in the process of being divested. It also has a fully undrawn $100m credit facility. This is not to say Sandstorm necessarily provides the best risk-adjusted rate of return.

The following is a brief overview of each of the four royalty companies' cornerstone asset base and the attributable production from each. Silver Wheaton's cornerstone asset portfolio shown below has four, arguably five, absolutely enormous streams, all of which have proven operators, with nice geographical diversity. San Dimas and Peñasquito are in Mexico, both having a significant upside potential in mine life and attributable production. These two as well as another two producing streams and 3-4 development projects will fuel growth out to 2018-2019. Salobo has a massive resource base, which in all likelihood will allow it to operate anywhere for 40-50+ years. Pascua-Lama could fuel longer-term growth in the company, and until then, Silver Wheaton is receiving 2.4m-2.5m oz. from three of Barrick's smaller mines. Lastly, Sudbury will increase near-term growth as the Totten Mine will reach production in 2015.

Silver Wheaton: Cornerstone Assets

Metal	Stream	2015 Prod	2017 Prod	2019 Prod
Penasquito [Ag]	25%	6.6-6.7m	7.3m	7.8m
San Dimas [Ag]	First 6m +50% After	6.45m	6.9m	7m
Salobo [AgEq]	25%	3.3m	3.8m	4.1m
Constancia [AgEq]	100%	3.0m	4.5m	4.5m
Sudbury [AgEq]	70%	2.5m	3m	3m
Rosemont [AgEq]	100%	-	2.4m	3.6m
Yauliyacu [Ag]	100%	2.9m	3.3m	3.4m
777 [AgEq]	50%/100%	5.2m	3.1m	2.8m
Optionality				
*Pascua-Lama [Ag]				8.75m

The chart of growth assets lists just the primary growth assets, but with others included in the total. For example, this total also includes Peñasquito finally reaching capacity, as it has found an additional water source, which has been plaguing it ever since first production. Silver Wheaton has a very solid diversified asset base and geographical exposure that includes Canada, Mexico, Sweden, Portugal, Nevada, Arizona, Chile, Brazil, Argentina, Guyana, and Peru. Its current embedded growth includes increased attributable production from Peñasquito and San Dimas as previously discussed. Salobo and Sudbury are also in the same boat, in that both are currently producing but will see increased production in the years ahead. Constancia and Rosemont are primary copper mines that Silver Wheaton owns both a silver and gold stream on. The former will reach commercial production in 2015, with the latter being forecast for 2017. Together these will create an additional 5.3m oz. Ag and 50k oz. Au production growth when operating at initial design capacity. Furthermore, Silver Wheaton has a 25% silver stream on the massive Pascua-Lama Mine and the right to acquire a 12.50% stream on the primary portion of one of the largest underdeveloped silver deposits in the world, Navidad, for $32.50m.

Franco-Nevada: Cornerstone Assets

Metal	Stream	2015 Prod	2017 Prod	2019 Prod
Candelaria [AuEq]	68%	67k	74k	82k
Cobre-Panama [AuEq]	86%	-	-	120k
Weyburn [AuEq]	11.71% NRI	26k	36k	40k
Goldstrike	4% NSR+6% NPI	34k	43k	43k
MWS	25%	24k	24k	24k
Sudbury [AuEq]	50%	31k	31k	31k
Palmarejo	50%	47k	50k	50k
Sabodala	6%	22.5k	22.5k	26.5k
Detour Lake	2% NSR	11.8k	12.7k	13.6k
Tasiast	2% NSR	5.2k	10.8k	16.6k
Subika	2% NSR	7.8k	11.2k	15.3k
Stillwater	5% NSR	17.5k	19k	18k
Optionality				
*Prosperity	22%	-	-	65k

Franco-Nevada, like Silver Wheaton, has high quality partners and geographical diversification. Some of its operating partners include Barrick, Coeur d'Alene, Newmont, Cenovus Energy, First Quantum, KGHM, Gold One, Newmont, Stillwater, and Kinross. Geographically, operations take place in Canada, Nevada, Panama, Utah, Ghana, South Africa, Mexico, and Chile. Furthermore, Franco-Nevada has an absolutely enormous portfolio of royalties and streams, which will support longer-term growth. Lastly, Franco-Nevada offers exposure to energy (oil and gas) currently accounting for roughly 20%-22% of total revenue. It also has a very large pipeline for oil and gas royalties, so expect these energy holdings to account for an increasing amount of revenue, assuming a fixed gold price.

Royal Gold: Cornerstone Assets

Metal	Royalty/Stream	2015 Prod	2017 Prod	2019 Prod
Mt. Milligan (Au)	52.25%	138k	142k	142k
Penasquito AuEq	2% NSR	27k	32k	33k
Voisey's Bay AuEq	2% NSR	24k	24k	25k
Andacollo (Au)	75%	37k	42k	42k
Ilovitza (Au)	25%/12.50%	-	-	23.75k
Phoenix Gold	6.305/3.15%		6.5k	10.5k
Optionality				
Pascua-Lama (Au)	5.23% NSR			42K

Royal Gold is currently undergoing a spectacular growth spurt, with Mt. Milligan alone increasing attributable production 100%. Once Mt. Milligan is operating at capacity, the only material growth driver is Pascua-Lama. It has a rather large 5.23% NSR on Pascua-Lama, which translates into roughly 35k-40k gold-equivalent ounces. This company has $1B in available capacity to acquire new royalties/streams.

Sandstorm Gold: Cornerstone Assets

Metal	Royalty/Stream	2015 Prod	2017 Prod	2019 Prod
Aurizona (Au)	17.00%	15k	23k	35k
Santa Elena (Au)	20%	7k	8k	7k
Black Fox (Au)	8%	8.4k	10.5k	10.5k
Bachelor Lake (Au)	20%	11k	13.5k	15.5k
Karma	Fixed Stream	1k	5k	5k
Oyu Tolgoi AuEq	6.76%/5.14%/0.5%	Production to begin 2022-2025, upwards of 35-45k

Sandstorm Gold has significant upside, however, its growth profile comes with more risk than the others. Aurizona just completed its Phase I Expansion, increasing attributable production from 15.6K to 23K oz. gold. It plans to engage in two further expansions in the future, Phase II as discussed above and Phase III in the future. A stream that will be more or less the same size as Aurizona (after Phase II Expansion) is Oyu Tolgoi. While the stream size looks small, Oyu Tolgoi is a copper mega mine, with significant copper, gold, and silver production. This stream will begin to deliver by roughly 2019-2022. It is located in Mongolia, so it is inherently riskier, however, it will account for 40%-50% of GDP by next decade.

We made the case for adding one or more royalty companies as a staple in a precious metal portfolio. Although royalty companies undoubtedly provide the best risk-adjusted rate of return, you won't see the returns captured in riskier exploration mining companies.

There are essentially five types of mining companies, all of which have a different risk-reward profile.

1. Royalty Company
2. Senior Producer – Defined as a primary silver producer that currently yields a minimum of 10m oz. silver (not silver equivalent). For gold miners, this is defined as a producer that yields 800k-1m oz. Au. Of course, different people have different definitions of the breakdown between classes of mining companies, but the general point remains the same: a senior producer has multiple operations in more than one geopolitically-safe mining jurisdiction.
3. Mid-Tier Producer – This is defined, for a primary silver producer, as an operation that produces 4m to 9.9m oz. The definition of a mid-tier gold producer is output of roughly 250,000 oz.-999,000 oz. gold per annum. Mid-tier producers typically have either one large silver or gold mine or two to three mid-size operating mines.
4. Junior Producers – This defines a primary silver producer as an operator producing up to 4m oz., and, for a junior gold producer, up to 250,000 oz.
5. Exploration/Development – Small micro-cap companies for the most part, with a success rate of roughly 1 in 4,000. The most over-hyped part of the mining industry, vital to its success but overplayed by both newsletter writers and, in our view, the industry as a whole. This is the area that the public in general

equates with mining, with many having "heard" a get-rich story from someone's brother-in-law's sister's second cousin.

Passive investors who want exposure to mining equities can invest in one or more of the following mining ETFs: GDX, SGDM, SIL, and SILJ.

Sprott Gold Miners ETF (SGDM) is a new ETF managed by Sprott Inc. Founded by precious metals expert Eric Sprott, this company is filled with dedicated and some of the most knowledgeable and successful people in the industry. Over the long- term , SGDM will likely outperform the others, in our view, because there is one big advantage of this ETF—it is managed by arguably the best team, relatively speaking. When other ETFs re-weight their holdings, oftentimes there are numerous low-quality producers that hamper performance. But SGDM currently holds all four royalty companies, accounting for over 27% of its total holdings.

The Market Vectors Gold Miners ETF (GDX) has holdings composed primarily of top-tier and mid-tier gold producers and silver producers with a much heavier weighting in gold miners.

The Global X Silver Miners Fund (SIL) debuted in April 2010. This fund owns a basket (currently) of 27 silver miners with a wide geographical dispersion.

PureFunds ISE Junior Silver ETF (SILJ) was launched in late 2012 as the first silver junior miner ETF and is a combination of junior producers and development-stage silver miners. There are also some mutual funds managed by Sprott Inc.,Toqueville Asset Management, and US Global Investors.

A Passing Look at ETPs (Exchange-Traded Products)

The exchange-traded note (ETN), a relative to the exchange-traded fund, is mentioned here in passing to discuss two examples that may have possible merit. ETNs are debt obligations similar in some ways to corporate bonds.

iShares Silver Trust (SLV): The Trust seeks to reflect, generally, the performance of the **price** of silver and to reflect such performance before payment of the Trust's expenses and liabilities. The Trust is not actively managed. It does not engage in any activities designed to obtain a profit from, or to ameliorate losses caused by, changes in the price of silver.

A disadvantage of SLV is that this is purely a paper play on the price and we do not consider it to be an actual precious metals holding. Although technically this is true of everything, outside of holding the metal itself, there are some that will let investors take delivery and others that we think have a better audit trail. Again, we advocate physical ownership first, and if need be, investment into the Sprott Silver Trust, which does allow for delivery.

CEF—an Outlier in an "ETF-like" Space: For those who want to have a "paper-metal" long-term hold vehicle, consider the Central Fund of Canada (CEF), established in1983—a full 21 years before the first gold bullion ETF was launched (Nov. 2004). It was thus the first gold (and silver) exchange-traded product. Founded in 1961, it was later reconfigured so that investors could trade it like a stock, and was listed first on the TSX (1966), then later on the AMEX (1986), with the ticker symbol CEF.

Inverse ETFs—a "Surgical" Trading Tool? An *inverse* ETF is a specialized investment vehicle that moves in the opposite direction of the security or index it is designed to track. In all other respects, it performs in an identical fashion to that of any other ETF. A variety of financial instruments, such as futures and options, can be housed within them, enabling the discriminating investor to perform a variety of trading strategies. For the truly courageous, "ultra" inverse funds utilizing 2 to 3 times leverage are available. They can be used to rebalance a portfolio and also help control/contain the risk faced by even the most skilled investors, market timing.

ETFs/ETNs Backed By Physical Gold and Silver: Sprott Physical Silver Trust (NYSE Arca:PSLV) Exchange Trust/ETF is a closed end fund. During its relatively short life (introduced in 2010), it has traded at a premium ranging from 7%-23% of NAV. It will be interesting to see how the premium fluctuates, perhaps along the lines of what has taken place over the years with the CEF, as metals move into the later stages of their secular bull cycle.

The Sprott Physical Gold Trust (PHYS), launched in early 2010, is a physically-backed gold ETF. As stated: *PHYS will store the underlying gold bullion at the Royal Canadian Mint, a Canadian Crown corporation that acts as an agent of the Canadian Government whose obligations generally constitute unconditional obligations of the Canadian Government. With the launch of PHYS, investors now have the ability to invest in gold bullion stored in a number of physical locations, including the U.S., Canada, UK, and Switzerland.*

"The Fab Four" Leveraged ETPs: In the interest of simplicity, ease of use, utility, and past experience, we focus primarily on the following four leveraged ETPs—DGP, AGQ, USLV, and NUGT.

1. **DGP: Power Shares DB Gold Double Long ETN** – INVESCO PowerShares states: "All of the PowerShares DB Gold ETNs are based on a total return version of the Deutsche Bank Liquid Commodity Index—Optimum Yield Gold™, which is intended to track the long or short performance of a single unfunded gold futures contract." Daily volume runs a fairly robust 100k-200k shares/day, but can spike to over one-half million.
2. **AGQ: ProShares Ultra Silver (2x Long Silver)** – Definition/Goals: "ProShares Ultra Silver seeks daily investment results, before fees and expenses, that correspond to two times (2x) the daily performance of silver bullion as measured by the U.S. Dollar fixing price for delivery in London." Note that performance can be an approximation of the movement in underlying silver prices. *This Ultra ProShares ETF seeks a return that is 2x the return of an index or other benchmark (target)* **for a single day**, *as measured from one NAV calculation to the next. Due to the compounding of daily returns,*

3. **USLV: ProShares Ultra Silver (3x Long Silver)** – Definition: *The VelocityShares 3x Long Silver ETNs linked to the S&P GSCI® Silver Index ER (the "ETNs") are senior, unsecured obligations of Credit Suisse AG ("Credit Suisse") acting through its Nassau branch. The ETNs seek to provide long exposure to three times (3x) the daily performance of the S&P GSCI® Silver Index ER (the "Index") plus a daily accrual equal to the return that could be earned on a notional capital reinvestment at the three-month U.S. Treasury rate as reported on Bloomberg under ticker USB3MTA, less the daily investor fee.*
4. **NUGT: Direxion Daily Gold Miners Bull 3x Shares ETF...and DUST** – Definition: *The Daily Gold Miners Bull 3x shares seek daily investment results, before fees and expenses, of 300% of the price performance of the NYSE Arca GoldMiners Index ("Gold Miners Index"). There is no guarantee the fund will meet its stated investment objective.*

<u>Options</u>

An option is a contract that gives the buyer the right to buy (call) or sell (put) and underlying asset or instrument at a specified price (strike) on or before a specified date. The expiration date typically occurs the third Friday of the month; however, more recently, some options contracts can expire the first, second, or third Friday of the month.

An equity option contract gives the buyer the right to exercise a contract equivalent to 100 shares. Options belong to a class of financial instruments called derivatives, as they derive their value from an underlying asset class. There are two main types of options contracts, from which an investor can take either side—the buyer (long position) or the seller (short position or "writing a contract").

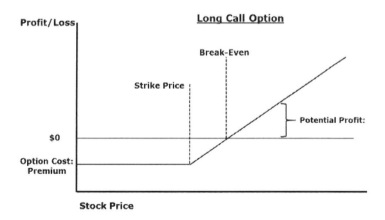

Long Call: The right to buy the underlying assets at a specified price ("strike" price) on or before a given date. Going long a call option has a maximum loss of the cost of the contract and unlimited maximum gain. The above graph is a depiction of the

payoff diagram for going long a call option. These are a great way to develop various strategies, including the following:
- Buying a call and/or put
- Writing a call and put
- Going long and/or short common stock/ETF
- Long and/or short a futures contract
- Buying a call and/or put on futures

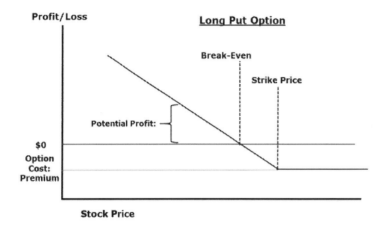

Long Put: The right to sell an underlying asset at a specified price ("strike" price) on or before a given date. Going long a put option has a maximum loss of the cost of the contract and a maximum gain of the contract price: Price of the contract – (maximum decrease in the underlying asset so that it is equal to $0 and $0.01 (in the case of equities and commodities, the latter is theoretical as no commodity will come close to $0.01) x option leverage).

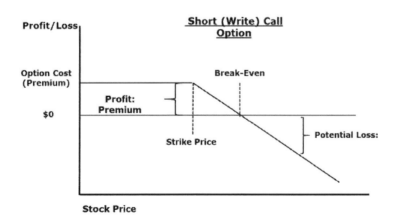

Short Call or "Writing a Call": Selling the right to buy an underlying asset at a certain strike price until a specified date. Writing a call has an infinite maximum loss and a maximum gain of the premium or price at which you sell the contract.

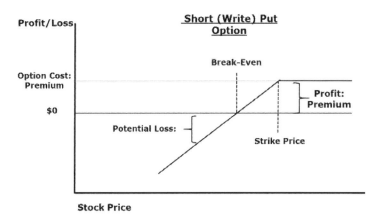

Short Put or "Writing a Put": Selling the right to sell an underlying asset as a certain strike price until a specified date. Writing a put has a maximum gain of the premium at which the writer sells the contract. The maximum loss is the price at which the contract is sold – (maximum decrease in the underlying asset so that it is equal to $0 and $0.01 (in the case of equities and commodities, the latter is theoretical as no commodity will come close to $0.01) x option leverage).

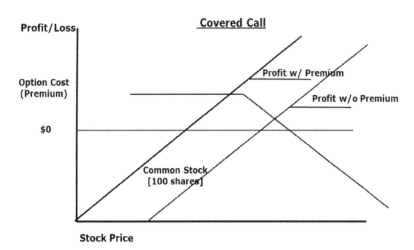

A covered call and variants of this are a popular strategy, both in the equity and futures market. The above graph shows a very basic covered call. The following example is a basic covered call: An investor owns 100 shares of Company A's common stock that is trading at Price X. A call is written with a strike price of X + 7 for $2.10, or $210. The expiration date is 6 months out.

- If the common stocks falls or increases $7 or less, the investor generates a realized profit of the full $210 on the call option, which expired worthless. And the change (increase or decrease) in the common stock x $100.
- If the stock price increases by $8.10, the investor generates the profit on the common stock [$8.10 x 100 shares = $810] and [($8.10 - $7 = $1.10), $2.10-$1.10 = $1.00 or $100] on the call option. Writing the call option still generated a profit because it was above the strike price but not above the strike price + the option premium.
- If the stock price increases $9.10, the investor generates a profit of $910 [100 shares x $9.10] on the common stock and [$0] on the call option. The common stock increased exactly the same amount of the option premium [$2.10] past the increase in the stock price to reach the strike price [$7.00].
- The stock price increases by $15. The investor generates a profit on the common stock of [100 x $15 = $1,500] but generated a loss on the call option [increase in the stock price beyond the strike price + cost/premium of the option = $15 - $7 - $2.10 = $5.90 = $5.90 x 100 = $590]. The net profit on this trade is $1,500 - $590 = $910.
- If the stock price increased beyond the strike price + option premium, the investor's account will be debited by that amount.

There are numerous variants of this, such as writing call options on a portion of the quantity of stock or commodities that are generally used by investors who are bullish on the stock or commodity in the long-term but want to generate profit in the short-term.

This strategy is very powerful for gold (silver) stocks as it can generate 15%-17% per annum, writing calls on stock in top companies owned outright. Of course, yield varies, but due to the nature of the volatility of this class of stocks it is worth considering as a way that investors can earn income from their "gold."

For example, if an investor wants to own 1,000 shares of Company A, they could write three calls, which expire one, two, three, or six months later at very high strike prices relative to that of the underlying asset. We could elaborate endlessly on strategies, but a book regarding options strategies should be read if interested. The payoff diagrams for futures options are exactly the same as those on equity options, just as the payoff diagram on futures is exactly like that of a stock if the leverage on a futures contracts is thought of as one share per unit. We say this because one only needs to think critically in order to come up with strategies, just by using the payoff diagrams.

Futures Contracts

A futures contract is the obligation to buy or sell a specified quantity of units (equities and commodities on primary markets) at a specified price on a predetermined date. In silver, one normal-sized contract is for 5,000 ounces of silver. A mini contract for silver exists and is for 1,000 ounces of silver.

Investors are highly cautioned that futures trading is NOT recommended. It is an area where few are successful. For every winning contract there is a corresponding losing contract. It has been reported that about 90% of the public that enters into the futures markets lose their money.

If an investor still wants extreme leverage with much less risk he should look into future options. Future options are a way to obtain significant leverage while also knowing the potential loss is equivalent to the cost of the contract. Silver future option calls are available on two contracts—the standard and mini. However, the 1,000-oz. future options are new but now trade on both the NYSE Liffe and CME, and these are extremely illiquid (the mini future options, not contracts themselves).

There are some advantages of buying future option calls instead of replicating the same exposure through a silver ETF or leveraged silver ETF. The first is time until expiration, which future option calls in silver going out up to four to five years, but those are very illiquid. While still illiquid, future options going out up to 3.5 years will usually get filled within a few days, and those expiring in 2.5-2.75 years typically get filled the same day.

If the exact same leverage is obtained using leveraged ETF leaps, it is much more expensive in almost all cases. Leveraged ETFs that own futures contracts (e.g., AGQ, which owns contracts in the first twelve sequential expirations), should significant contango develop, will be reflected in the futures contracts only, and only slightly in AGQ.

Obtaining leverage to gold using futures contracts is another strategy for obtaining leverage to silver if an investor thinks there will be a contraction in the gold-to-silver ratio. Typically, when both metals are in a bull market, the gold-to-silver ratio decreases, from which one can exploit the contraction by varying degrees, while limiting your downside (if both metals go down). This is possible to do because gold futures contracts are sized normal (100 oz.), mini (33 oz.), and micro (10 oz.). If an individual really wants to learn all the strategies that can be employed, it is best to buy a separate book focusing on just that. Once you become knowledgeable in this area, you can come up with your own strategies using payoff diagrams such as those depicted above.

The pricing of futures contracts pricing can reveal a coming rise in the price of a commodity. This is the case when backwardation occurs in the market, meaning the spot price of silver, for example, is higher than the price in the future. In other words, investors are willing to pay a higher price for silver now than in the future. This can be looked upon as having a negative discount rate, instead of a positive discount rate or cost of carry. In a typical market, contango is normal, or taking delivery in the future trades for a premium over the spot price in both the commodity and equity market (equity options cost more the further out a call option expires). Backwardation is not abnormal for many cases, such as in agricultural commodities, due to seasonal factors and producers hedging the price.

It isn't normal in silver or gold, and if meaningful, suggests a shortage of the metal. If the backwardation is meaningful, prices almost always rise in the near future. In order to judge whether it is meaningful, it is worth looking at the convenience yield. This is an adjustment to the cost of carry in the non-arbitrage pricing formula for forward prices in the market. While avoiding going on for several pages, we will give a brief overview of the formula. Generally speaking, backwardation is meaningful if the convenience yield is in excess of 10% going out as many as three months. Of course, many differ in this regard, but nonetheless, the higher the better. In the following example, the nearest month contract and a contract expiring between two and three months are used.

- F – Price of a commodity in the future, in this case, the futures contract going out six months
- S – Spot price
- T – Time (years) until expiration. For example, if expiring in six months, T would be 0.5.
- r = Interest rate on a T-bill going out T. In this case it would be the six-month rate on a Treasury bill.
- C = Convenience yield
- C = r - 1/T x Ln(F/S)

1 month T-Bill	0.38%
3 month T- Bill	0.52%
Spot Price	$17.80
Fwd Month Contract (Fwd)	$17.23
FWD +1 Contract	$17.31
FWD +2 Contract	$17.34
FWD +3 Contract	$17.42
FWD +6 Contract	$17.63

Fwd Contract (< 30 days)
C = r - 1/T x Ln(F/S)
C = .38% - 12 x Ln($17.23/$17.80)
C = .38% - 12 x -3.255%
C = .38% - 12 x -3.255%
C = .38% -12 x -39.06%
C = 39.44%

FWD +2 (3 months until expiration)
C = r - 4 x Ln($17.34/$17.80)
C = r - 4 x Ln($17.34/$17.80)
C = .52% - 4 x -2.618%
C = .52% + 10.472%
C = 10.992%

While there is no exact way to time or know when the market it becoming tight, this is to is an art, not science. Generally the nearest month should have a CY of at least >25%, a 2 or 3 month contract >=15% and if possible 4-6 month >=8%. This of course can change each and every time so it is more of a tool to get a feeling of the market tightness.

The following are the inputs for the example above:

- T = .0833 and .25
- S = $17.80
- F = $17.23 and $17.34
- The yield on a one month T-bill is 0.38% and .52% on a three-month T-bill.

The convenience yield is inversely related to inventory levels. Now this is a meaningful case and a convenience yield of this magnitude is not needed; rather, in our opinion, anything equal or greater than 6%+ (depending on the "risk-free" rate) makes things interesting. In this example, both the nearest month and that expiring two to three months later indicate a convenience yield of 39.44% and 10.992%, meaning taking a long position will likely pay off in the future.

Warrants

A warrant is the right to buy a stock at a fixed price until expiration. Warrants are similar to options in that warrants are the right to buy common stock at a specified price and date or earlier. Unlike options, warrants can have much longer expiration dates. The maximum length long-dated options have to expire is roughly 2.1-2.2 years, however when dealing with primary silver and gold mining companies, long-term equity anticipation securities (leaps) are available in a very few instances.

It should be pointed out that many financings—where a company initially goes to the public markets—are offers (stock/equity) in the company, usually during the initial stages, where warrants are used to sweeten the deal. Many warrants have three to six plus years until expiration, considerably lengthier than the longest time until expiration of leaps.

The majority of warrants are sold (purchased) on a 1:1 basis, which means if you purchase one warrant you have the right to purchase one share of stock unless otherwise stated. There are, however, a fair amount of instances of differing ratios, so it is important to keep this in mind when determining a fair price to pay for a warrant, in addition to calculating the leverage warrants have at various prices.

It is easiest to convert the cost, strike price, etc., where one warrant is equal to one share. Warrant pricing can be determined using the Black-Scholes options pricing model. In order to determine a fair price to pay for any warrant, the degree of leverage needs to be taken into account. However, the degree of leverage, as you will see, is dependent on the investor's appraisal of fair value of the stock.

Many times, when dealing with near, at, or in the money warrants, the time premium, if any, can be "eye-balled" to determine whether it's a fair price or the time premium calculated using a spreadsheet. We will use the following stock price, warrant price, strike price, time until expiration, and, because the leverage of a warrant changes at different prices, a personal appraisal of the company.

Stock Price	$8.00
Warrant Price	$1.10
Strike Price	$10.00
Time (Years) Until Expiration	3
Personal Appraisal of Company	$14.40

To determine the leverage of a warrant, we will first calculate the return on investment of common stock; however, this is necessary to do at prices both below and above our valuation of fair value. In order to show the range of potential leverage, we're using two prices both below and above our estimation of fair value. The two graphics below are the calculations of the return on investment for both common stock and the warrants at various prices:

Stock Price at Expiry	$11.50	$13.00	$14.40	$16.00	$17.50
Minimum Value of Stock	$8.00	$8.00	$8.00	$8.00	$8.00
Profit on Stock	$3.50	$5.00	$6.40	$8.00	$9.50
ROI Calculation	($3.50/$8)	($5/$8)	($6.40/$8)	($8/$8)	($9.50/$8)
Common Stock ROI	44%	63%	80%	100%	119%
CS Price at Expiry	$11.50	$13.00	$14.40	$16.00	$17.50
Minimum Value of Warrant	$1.50	$3.00	$4.40	$6.00	$7.50
Profit on Warrant	0.40	$1.90	$3.30	$4.90	$6.40
Profit on Warrant Calculation	($1.50-$1.10)	($3-$1.10)	($4.40-$1.10)	($6-$1.10)	($7.50-$1.10)
ROI Calculation	($0.40/$1.10)	($1.90/$1.10)	($3.30/$1.10)	($4.90/$1.10)	($6.40/$1.10)
Warrant ROI	36%	173%	300%	445%	582%

The minimum value of a warrant is calculated by taking the projected stock price and subtracting the strike price on the warrant.

Stock Price at Expiry	11.50	$13.00	14.40	$16	$17.50
Common Stock ROI	0.44	0.63	0.80	1.00	1.19
Warrant ROI	0.36	1.73	3.00	4.45	5.82
Leverage Calculation	(0.36/0.44)	(1.73/0.63)	($3.00/$0.80)	($4.45/$1.00)	($5.82/$1.19)
Leverage	0.83	2.76	3.75	4.45	4.90

If the stock is exactly $14.40 (our appraisal of the company), the warrants would generate 3.75x or 275% more than that returned by the common stock. The addition of warrants allows for significantly more investment strategies one can undertake, especially those companies which trade on a U.S. exchange, because then common stock, options, and warrants create various arbitrage and risk-mitigating strategies.

The qualitative is quite easy and can be simply said as follows: Look for warrants on high quality companies. The quantitative aspect first has to do with finding warrants with a long time until expiration as well as strong leverage to the underlying stock and how to identify mispriced warrants or those with very little to no implied time value.

Debt Instruments

Convertible Debenture/Debt. In the mining industry, convertible debt is essentially a call option on common stock of that company. Typically, a convertible bond, convertible note, and a convertible debenture pay interest but instead of repatriating the principal to holders of this debt, it can be converted into the common stock, calculated by taking the principal and dividing it by the predetermined conversion price.

If it is below the conversion price, the debt holder then receives the principal repayment. So this type of debt has characteristics of both debt and equity. This also allows for convertible arbitrage, which is done by having a long position in convertible debt and a proportionate short position in common stock.

For the most part, companies that engage in this type of financing have or would have a low credit rating and therefore the yield on this debt is similar to that of junk bonds. This makes it worth arbitraging for some, usually fund or money managers familiar with the mining sector.

There have been several innovations regarding the features of convertible bonds—the standard convertible and the mandatory convertible being the most common. The latter forces the holder of the bond to convert into shares, having two conversion prices. This entails both that the holder would receive the equivalent back in shares and that the holder cannot make a profit greater than the principal. There are a plethora of additional features that convertible debt may possess, including:

- Time discrepancy between the conversion date and the maturity date
- The conversion is fixed by number of shares per note

- The issuer may retain the ability to call each bond in early
- If the stock trades *x* number of days over *y* prices
- No conditions needed
- Price Resets – If the common stock increases beyond a predetermined specified price the conversion price would reset higher
- Countless other contingencies

Silver- or Gold-Linked Notes. There are a few unique debt instruments, including silver and gold-linked notes. These also have a variety of different structures and include a bond with typical periodic interest payments, and at maturity, the principal payment is based on a predetermined quantity of silver or gold ounces, multiplied by the spot price. The principal payment could be determined by the nominal value ($1,000) plus the percentage increase, if any, beyond a predetermined price multiplied by the principal. The principal payment can also be paid in a fashion similar to the previous two examples, but in specified percentages over multiple years.

Preferred Stock. Preferred stock is another type of hybrid security, possessing characteristics of both equity and debt. Preferred stock, in the event of a company going bankrupt, is senior to common stock and subordinate to secured debt, so upon liquidation, it is behind debt holders but in front of common stockholders. Like most financial instruments, there are different structures possessing a combination of various characteristics. Almost all preferred stock pays a dividend, regardless of whether a company pays out any dividends to shareholders of common shares. This type of stock is sometimes issued for various strategic reasons.

For example, some companies issue preferred stock to prevent hostile takeovers, such as issuing preferred stock with a "poison pill" (forced-exchange or conversion features). For a mining company such as a junior producer that has a lot of potential and/or is on its way to becoming a mid-tier producer, it may be a great choice if it is convertible preferred stock, which is converted into a predetermined quantity of shares. If the stock price of a given company moves to high levels on a relative basis, it can then realize the share appreciation instead of just the dividend it receives. To clarify, preferred stock does not enjoy upward movements in the stock price, as it is a debt instrument in that regard.

Chapter 11 : Mining Stock Appraisal

Many investors think the quantitative part of analyzing a company is of the utmost importance and that the ability to do this is the way to generate above-average returns. Instead, the most difficult aspect of identifying a relatively unknown yet high quality company that will generate those above-average returns is having an eye for quality. It is not that complicated: identify businesses you understand, verify that the management team is focused on maximizing shareholder value and then buy it correctly!

For example, let us examine Silver Wheaton (symbol SLW), which had its first cash flow stream, a 100% silver stream on Goldcorp's San Dimas Project. It is for a term of 25 years (ending 2029), where Primero received an upfront payment of $46m in cash and 540m shares in SLW, which at the time was called Chap Mercantile. Each ounce of silver was to be purchased at $3.90/oz., with a maximum inflation adjustment of 1% per annum. Once it began trading, the shares outstanding were consolidated on a 5-to-1 basis.

In all, Silver Wheaton paid $190m for the San Dimas stream in 2004. That year, the price of silver averaged $6.67 per ounce. In other words, at that time, some silver investors viewed this deal as mediocre. However, Silver Wheaton understood their long-term business plan and the upside for the price of silver.

In mid-2010, Primero Mining acquired San Dimas (then called "Luisman") from Goldcorp, the owner/operator at the time; however, because Goldcorp is a senior primary gold producer, San Dimas was a non-core asset and therefore Goldcorp had no financial incentive to optimize this operation, instead focusing on its larger company-building assets. But as a result of that acquisition, there were a number of amendments benefiting Silver Wheaton: the term of 25 years was abolished, increasing to life of the mine. For the first four years upon closing, Primero was required to deliver the 3.5 million ounces produced to Silver Wheaton and 50% of that produced beyond 3.5 million. Furthermore, Goldcorp was to deliver 1.5 million ounces. Once the fifth year begins after the date of the amendment, Primero is required to deliver the first 6.0 million ounces plus 50% thereafter.

Since Silver Wheaton acquired the San Dimas stream, it has generated cash flows in excess of $800m. At the time of this acquisition, the life of mine was 14 years, and 10 years later, it has not only replaced all the reserves that were delivered to Silver Wheaton—which would yield four years remaining until depletion—but also added to them, as the life of mine currently supports a 16-year mine life.

Beyond that, Primero has done a significant amount of exploration on the property, from which it is rather easy to say a significant amount of mine will be added.

In 2013, Primero undertook the first expansion at San Dimas, completing it by early 2014. In 2015, silver deliverable to Silver Wheaton will be 6.3m-6.5m ounces. Primero is undertaking a second expansion, further increasing production by an additional 20%. Once this is complete, silver deliverable to Silver Wheaton will increase to roughly 7m oz. per annum.

We will go through some qualitative tests to appraise the value of a given company. Keep in mind this is an illustration and will vary, depending on the risk appetite each individual possesses. We'll follow the qualitative tests with the quantitative tests. For the latter, we will use Fortuna Silver Mines, Inc. ("FSM") as an example, but note that valuation is <u>an art</u>, not a science and therefore will use arbitrary numbers for the appraisal process. Since there is some subjectivity to this method, let us also state that one's methodology improves over time as his/her "art" develops and evolves. We will go through a few illustrations, using different metrics in addition to mentioning others. In the case of Fortuna Silver, we will use one of the most widely used appraisal metrics—Net Asset Value—and relative valuation.

Qualatative Analysis

The graphic below represents absolute necessities when evaluating a mining stock. It must pass the Management-Assets-Geopolitics ("MAG") test. We cannot stress enough the importance of people or management when investing in mining companies, as they can provide both abnormal returns on high quality assets and very robust returns on mediocre assets.

You can have the best assets in the industry but without the right people, shareholder value will never reach its potential and, in many cases, could be destroyed. Once a company passes the management and assets part of the test, the next crucial part of mitigating risk is assessing the geopolitical environment. This not only includes staying away from countries that could nationalize mines but also not going to countries where permitting is difficult. For example, North America is considered solid, geopolitically. Yet the investor must search further and examine which states in the U.S. are mining friendly and which ones are not. Obviously this can and does change over time. Currently, the best state to perform mining in is Nevada.

The safest mining jurisdictions today are Mexico, Canada, Nevada, Australia, Chile, Peru, and parts of West Africa such as Ghana. This data is obtained from the Fraser Institute, which provides country risk assessment, and we agree with their evaluation most of the time. Even knowing what risks are anticipated ahead of time, things will and do change. Mexico has at times been considered to be a rather poor place, then at other times a spectacular place, and now with the new mining tax (2014), a less desirable place than a few years ago. Therefore, it pays to diversify into different "safe" regions.

The MAG Test

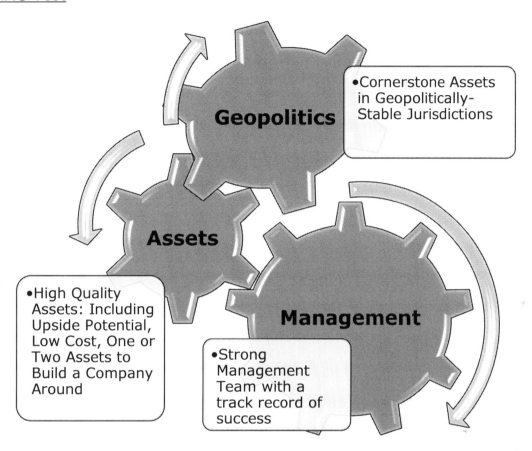

When it comes to assessing the management team, looking at past results is the premier method for determining capabilities. In other words, if the COO previously held the same position or was in charge of operations at a specific mining operation in the past, it is worth going back and looking at his/her execution. Go to that company's Web site and view old press releases, starting with the construction of the mine and going through the optimization. The same would go for a COO in charge of a company that had multiple mines, and the same general idea can be applied for the CEO and CFO as well. The look into management goes well beyond the executive positions, and you should carefully research the geologists and the people who comprise the board of directors.

If the management team is found to be of high caliber, an analysis of the company's operating, development, and exploration assets should then be evaluated. If possible, all aspects of each mine, the reserve and resource base, cost structure (extraction, labor, processing, sustaining capital, etc.), and upside potential need to be considered. The upside potential cannot be determined at the outset as grades could become better or worse at times. However, in some situations where a mine is going to be put into production and the project has much unexplored property then the possibility exists for increasing the mine life.

The next graphic is financially oriented. It is important that a company have a strong financial position for several reasons.

In this instance, let's say Mining Company A has a large net cash balance above that needed for organic growth. (Organic growth is where a company has enough profit to take a development asset through the construction process to reach production without needing outside funding. This is rare in the mining industry, but possible.) However, this company has a chance to make an accretive acquisition, increasing shareholder value. While this is a secondary consideration, it nonetheless provides us an example of how to establish a proper risk-reward profile.

Financial Position Requirements:

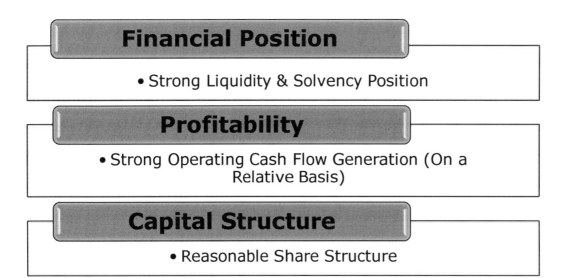

Current Ratio & Acid Test

The current ratio illustrates how many times current assets cover current liabilities. This is used to determine how liquid a company is to cover its current liabilities (12 months or less). It is considered liquid if this ratio is greater than 2x. It is prudent to look at the acid test as well.

The acid test is needed to determine how liquid a company is, just using cash and marketable securities/short-term investments. In the mining industry, accounts receivables and inventories are considered as good as cash equivalents, so the current ratio should suffice. Nonetheless, a good rule of thumb is for a mining company to have this ratio greater than 1x. It is calculated as (cash and equivalents + short-term investments) / current liabilities.

Interest Coverage

Interest coverage is a ratio that illustrates how many times over earnings before interest and taxes can cover the interest on long-term debt, if any. Typically, depletion, depreciation, and amortization would be added back to earnings before tax, as a non-cash charge. However, when dealing with any capital intensive industry there is a certain amount of capital investment required to keep current operations going, therefore earnings before interest and taxes (EBIT) / interest expense is more accurate instead of EBITDA/Interest Expense.

A strong interest coverage ratio usually indicates that a company has a strong liquidity and solvency position, but further analysis is necessary. A strong current ratio is 10x or greater. If a company has a very large cash position, this ratio is less important.

Non-cash working capital should also be positive, calculated as (inventories + accounts receivables + other current assets) – (accounts payable + notes payable + short-term debt + current maturing portion of long-term debt + accrued expenses and liabilities + other current liabilities).

There are several solvency ratios that should be looked at including but not subject to. These are exactly as they sound and are both measures of solvency

Debt/Equity

This is measured by taking current debt (due within one year) plus long term debt divided by the market value of equity, not the book value.

Total Assets/Total Liabilities

	Notes	March 31, 2014	December 31, 2013
ASSETS			
CURRENT ASSETS			
Cash and cash equivalents		$ **41,192**	$ 31,704
Short term investments		**20,924**	17,411
Accounts receivable and other assets	3	**15,341**	17,040
Prepaid expenses		**1,656**	1,578
Due from related parties	7 c)	**37**	-
Inventories	4	**14,358**	15,488
Total current assets		**93,508**	83,221
NON-CURRENT ASSETS			
Deposits on long term assets	3	**2,709**	1,882
Deferred income tax assets		**189**	151
Mineral properties, plant and equipment	5	**221,943**	216,961
Total assets		$ **318,349**	$ 302,215
LIABILITIES AND EQUITY			
CURRENT LIABILITIES			
Trade and other payables	6	$ **21,457**	$ 15,897
Due to related parties	7 c)	**29**	20
Provisions	9	**429**	622
Income tax payable		**1,016**	50
Current portion of other liabilities	8	**146**	227
Total current liabilities		**23,077**	16,816
NON-CURRENT LIABILITIES			
Other liabilities	8	**4,076**	2,343
Provisions	9	**11,263**	10,112
Deferred income tax liabilities		**27,266**	25,284
Total liabilities		**65,682**	54,555
EQUITY			
Share capital		**189,349**	189,092
Share option and warrant reserve		**15,708**	15,200
Retained earnings		**45,097**	40,244
Accumulated other comprehensive income		**2,513**	3,124
Total equity		**252,667**	247,660
Total liabilities and equity		$ **318,349**	$ 302,215

- Current Ratio – (current assets/current liabilities) = $93,508/$23,077 = 4.05x
- Acid Test – (cash and equivalents + short-term investments)/(total current liabilities) – ($41,192 + $20,924)/($23,077) = $62,116/$23,077 = 2.69x

- Non-Cash Working Capital – (accounts receivables + prepaid expenses + inventories + other) – (current liabilities) = ($15,341 + $1,656 + $14,358 + $37) – ($23,077) = $31,392
- Debt-to-Equity : No Long-Term Debt
- Total Assets/Total Liabilities = ($318,349/$65,682) = 4.85x
- Operating Cash Flow/Long-Term Debt = no long-term debt

Profitability – Determining profitability, as in every other industry, cannot be done solely by looking at the line item **Net Income**. This is not only because there may be one-time expenses and/or write-downs, but also because profitability in capital intensive industries needs to be adjusted for capital investment and non-cash charges.

There are two profitability measures which need to be examined—operating cash flow and free cash flow. Operating cash flow is defined as (net operating income + depletion, depreciation, and amortization – sustaining capital).

Net operating income is defined as (net income +/- one-time expenses + write-downs/impairment charge). As we will discuss later, this is needed to calculate the Net Asset Value of a mine.

The second measure of profitability is free cash flow, which is calculated as (net operating income + depletion, depreciation, and amortization – gross capital investment). The value of ANY asset is the present value of all future cash flows. Or to put it another way, the value of a company is the present value of all dividends. Dividends are few and not that significant in most situations presently, but once a mining company reaches the mature stage in its life cycle, dividends usually are paid in meaningful amounts.

	Notes	Three months ended March 31, 2014	2013
OPERATING ACTIVITIES			
Net income for the period	$	**4,853** $	6,665
Items not involving cash			
Depletion and depreciation		**6,045**	4,884
Changes in non-cash working capital items			
Accounts receivable and other assets		1,388	3,771
Prepaid expenses		(92)	59
Due from related parties		(37)	(8)
Inventories		877	246
Trade and other payables		5,317	1,342
Due to related parties		9	(28)
Provisions		(8)	(8)
Cash provided by operating activities before interest and income taxes		25,434	22,381
Income taxes paid		(1,126)	(893)
Interest expense paid		(2)	(7)
Interest income received		62	169
Net cash provided by operating activities		24,368	21,650
INVESTING ACTIVITIES			
Purchase of short term investments		(8,925)	-
Redemptions of short term investments		5,000	1,984
Expenditures on mineral properties, plant and equipment	14	(10,003)	(18,057)
Advances of deposits on long term assets		(2,869)	(1,985)
Receipts of deposits on long term assets		2,041	1,967
Proceeds on disposal of mineral properties, plant and equipment		17	-
Net cash used in investing activities		(14,739)	(16,091)

Operating Cash Flow – (net operating income + depletion, depreciation, and amortization – sustaining capital)

    $4,853 + $12 + $6,045 - $8,362 = $2,548 ($10,192 annualized)

Free Cash Flow – (net operating income + depletion, depreciation, and amortization – total capital investment)

    $4,853 + $12 + $6,045 - $10,003 = $907 ($3,628 annualized)

    Sustaining capital is awfully close to total capital expenditures, especially considering that the San Jose Mine has yet to reach full capacity. It is likely that operating cash flow was understated, but we cannot prove that as fact. Instead, this will be determined by any changes in future quarters.

    The following charts show the all-in costs for both mining operations as well as the company as a whole. Note that the adjustment below in depletion, depreciation, and amortization is different from that seen in the statement of cash flows. That is because that portion from the operating mines is the only amount that should be added back.

All-in-Costs *Caylloma*			All-in-Costs *San Jose*		
Caylloma	Total	Per/oz.	San Jose	Total	Per/oz.
Operating Cost	$3,835	$7.48	Operating Cost	$4,841	$5.06
G&A	$2,691	$5.25	G&A	$5,252	$5.49
Royalties	$220	$0.43	Royalties	-	-
Net Interest Exp	$70	$0.14	Net Interest Exp	$137	$0.14
Taxes	$1,427	$2.78	Taxes	$2,786	$2.91
Sustaining Capital	$1,780	$3.47	Sustaining Capital	$6,582	$6.88
Refining Cost	$637	$1.24	Refining Cost	$1,243	$1.30
Total Before Adj	**$10,024**	**$20.79**	**Total Before Adj**	**$19,597**	**$21.77**
Adjustment	($1,956)	($3.81)	Adjustment	($3,817)	($3.99)
Adjusted Total	**$18,728**	**$16.97**	**Adjusted Total**	**$36,621**	**$17.79**

Fortuna All-In-Costs			
Callyoma	33.88%	$16.97	$5.75
San Jose	66.12%	$17.53	$11.59
Fortuna Total			**$17.34**

Other expenses			
Selling, general and administrative expenses	7 a), 7 b)	7,943	5,616
Exploration and evaluation costs		-	148
(Gain) loss on disposal of mineral properties, plant and equipment		(12)	14
Operating income		**9,273**	**11,006**
Finance items			
Interest income		61	215
Interest expense		(268)	(200)
Net finance (expense) income		**(207)**	**15**
Income before tax		**9,066**	**11,021**
Income taxes		4,213	4,356
By-product credits		**(14,959)**	**(13,294)**
Refining charges		**1,880**	**1,757**

Before expanding the capital structure, having multiple operating assets greatly reduces operational risk, as countless operational issues could potentially arise at any mine. Having mining operations in multiple countries also makes a mining company more robust, assuming it is profitable.

Having low cost operations is necessary to survive the ups and down of any commodity based business, notably the bear markets that both silver and gold have been in since 2011. It is important that a mining company's operations are able to generate positive operating cash flow in ALL price environments. High grades and metallurgy increase the probability of a mining operation. Production growth is usually rewarded in the market. **Capital Structure: Share Structure**

Continuing with Mining Company A, it has met our first two criteria and now we examine organic growth versus an acquisition.

In both scenarios, both companies need to raise $200m in order to construct a mine and get it into production. Mining Company A decides to finance mine development through six different equity offerings, the last five of which come with one-fourth of 1 share purchase warrant attached, leaving the company with 253m shares outstanding until the warrants are exercised. Suppose after it reaches production, fair market value is $6.47 ($1.9b market cap) for the company, and its share price trades at $5.10 (fully diluted), meaning in the future it would reach $6.47, providing an investor with a 26.83% rate of return.

In Scenario B, management is aware of maximizing shareholder value on a per share basis. The reason Equity Offering #2 has a higher share price is that when streaming deals are announced, they usually cause the stock of the seller of the stream to increase. After it reaches production, fair market value is $1.75B (less than Scenario A due to the sale of the precious metal stream). From a shareholder's point of view, if he bought the stock at $7.25 per share, he would have generated a 99% rate of return.

To clarify further, we will look at it from another angle. Given the market capitalization, the stock of Mining Company A is trading at and supposing this increases $400m. So in Scenario A, the market cap is $1.9B, or $6.47 per share, a 26.83% increase in the stock price.

In Scenario B, the market cap is now $1.75B, or $14.43/share, a 99% increase. In scenarios A and B, if the shareholder owns 1,000 shares, he/she would make $1,370 = (1,000 x ($6.47 - $5.10) in Scenario A, and $3,300 = (1,000 x ($14.43 - $7.25) in Scenario B.

Scenario A	Offering Price	Shares Issued	Capital Raised	Warrants Issued
Equity Offering 1	$5.00	15,000,000	$75,000,000	0
Equity Offering 2	$3.50	25,000,000	$87,500,000	6,250,000
Equity Offering 3	$2.10	18,000,000	$37,800,000	4,500,000
Equity Offering 4	$1.35	35,000,000	$47,250,000	8,750,000
Equity Offering 5	$1.00	50,000,000	$50,000,000	12,500,000
Equity Offering 6	$0.70	35,000,000	$24,500,000	8,750,000
Total		178,000,000	$322,050,000	40,750,000
Shares Out/Fully Diluted Shares Out		253,000,000	$293,750,000	

Scenario B	Offering Price	Shares Issued	Capital Raised	Warrants Issued
Equity Offering 1	$5.00	15,000,000	$75,000,000	0
Sale of 10% Precious Metal Stream			$110,000,000	
Equity Offering 2	$4.50	25,000,000	$112,500,000	6250000
$25m Debt Facility - 5-year Term			$25,000,000	
Total		40,000,000	$322,500,000	$6,250,000
Fully Diluted Shares Outstanding		115,000,000	$121,250,000	

Quantitative Analysis

We will appraise Fortuna Silver in the example to follow. The most popular valuation models in this industry include (Net Asset Value), Discounted Cash Flow, and other analysis based on earnings. The inputs we will need are the discount rate, which is calculated simply by determining your personal required rate of return on an investment given your perception of risk and your appraisal of opportunity costs.

The next is the production growth rates of the company's assets going out as far as possible as well as the capital expenditures required to bring a mine into production (if a new operation is responsible for production growth of any degree).

Lastly, we need to calculate the cost of production or the cost of producing an ounce of the primary metal, in this case silver. Companies either report "cash costs" or AISC (all-in-sustaining costs), which have been generally widely accepted at this point in time. While the AISC measure is much more representative of reality, it is still incomplete! Therefore, we take the reader through the financial statements of this example case, but not all companies include all the required data for as complete an analysis as one might wish. Inputs needed for use in the valuation models:

- Silver or Gold Price Deck: This, along with the discount rate is extremely important and necessary to truly generate significant rates of return. For the purpose of this exercise, we will use $26 in 2015 into perpetuity.

- Discount Rate: In academia, what is taught is called the Capital Asset Pricing Model, which, as we will show, makes several illogical assumptions. The formula is as follows: R(f) +[Mrp(B)-R(f)].

- R(f) is the risk-free rate, or the interest earned on Treasuries. Typically, the 10-year Treasury yield is used; in this case we make it a round number, 3%. Next is (B), or Beta, and this makes the assumption that the volatility in a stock against that of the overall market index (typically the Russell 5,000, DJIA, or S&P 500) equates to how risky it is.

- Mining companies are volatile by nature; most analysts use 1.6, with 1 being the market index. M(rp) is the average market return, or the rate of return if you simply invested in a market index. In academia, this is taught to be between 7% and 9% or so, which is net of inflation or the real return. Putting this together, the discount rate would be 3% + [8% (1.9) – 3%] = 3% + [12.80% - 3%] = 3% + 9.80% = 12.80%. This represents the cost of equity, denoted as Ke.

- Let's suppose this particular company has a debt-to-equity ratio of 20%. If the company has publicly-traded debt, take the interest rate the company's bonds are yielding and if there are no bonds, simply divide the interest expense in either the latest 10-K financial statement (divide it by the amount of long-term debt outstanding) unless it is more than three months (one quarter) into current year, then take the most recent 10-Q financial statement and do the same math operation. Then multiply the result by 4 in order to annualize the interest, and for this purpose of this exercise, we will assume a 3.50% interest rate.

- Once this is complete and under the assumption the statutory tax rate is 30% (most mining companies are based in Canada, where the total tax rate, state + federal, etc., is closer to 30%), we will take the cost of equity Ke(80%) + Kd(3.50%)(1-T)(20%) = WACC (weighted average cost of capital) = 12.80%(80%) + 3.50%(70%)(20%) = 10.24% + 0.49% = 10.73%.

We use a much simpler formula, which is better than the CAPM. There is no such thing as a "risk-free rate" in the U.S. Being conservative, we could state the real rate of inflation is 5%, therefore a 3.00% yield is actually **(-2.00%).** It is best to use your subjective required rate of return, given your assessment of risk. We will go through the MAG test and the Checklist 1 and focus on whether it has multiple operations and, if so, in multiple countries.

As seen in the graphic below, Fortuna has over $62m in cash and cash equivalents and short-term investments ($41,192 + $20,924), with no long-term debt, so there's no need to look at its interest coverage. Fortuna has a current ratio of $93,508/$23,077 = $4.05. We will use 8.40% as our required rate of return, also said as the cost of capital.

Next, we have to calculate the all-in costs per oz. and as discussed earlier, while Fortuna reports its own AISC, it does not include all the costs of doing business. Fortuna produced 957,154 oz. of silver from its San Jose Mine in Mexico and 512,833 oz. of silver from its Caylloma Mine in Peru. We will start with the operating costs for each mine, which are the costs of extraction, processing, transport, and labor. We can find the operating costs for both mines in the two graphics below.

There are a few things we have to account for here. First, Fortuna plans to expand mill capacity at San Joe to 3,000 tpd, or 50%, which we assume will start in the summer of 2015 with a completion date one year after.

Fortuna discovered a new high-grade zone roughly 12-16 months ago, which has a significant amount of mineralization and so production will increase because of this anyway. 2014, 2015, and 2016 production were forecast to be 4m, 4.3m, and 4.5m oz. of silver production.

Now we take the expansion into account and make some minor assumptions that won't impact our valuation more than a few cents. Including the expansion, the second half of 2016 will be impacted as mill throughput will be higher for the second half of the year, but not the full 50% because it will take some time to both ensure mining capacity can feed the mill enough material and because initially the expanded mill will undergo the usual optimizations.

We forecast 2016 production to be 5.1m oz. followed by production of 6.4m-6.6m oz. in 2017 onward. This increased production will cause costs per ounce to fall, across the board, as everything will be spread across more silver being produced from the mines.

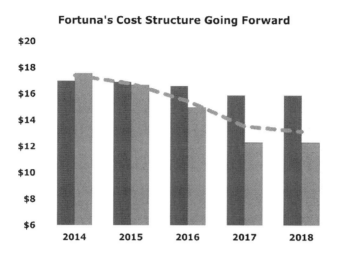

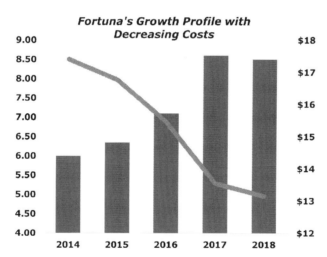

Net Asset Value Calculation

After we've tallied the all-in cost per ounce at each mine and adjusted the all-in costs for the San Jose Mine following the mine and milling expansion by 50%, we can now proceed to do the first and most popular valuation method in the mining industry, which is calculating the NAV and applying various multiples to this.

The fact that Fortuna produces a healthy amount of both silver and gold (used as a byproduct credit), has multiple operating assets in more than one stable mining jurisdiction (Mexico and Peru), is debt free, and has a growing cash position and production growth (to which the market usually gives a premium) suggests a NAV multiple up to 1.30x or thereabouts.

Remember that valuation is an art not a science and therefore caution is advised in doing your own analysis. Almost all companies provide a best-case scenario, and taking perhaps 80% to 90% of their projections (grade, mill rate, hours of operation, etc.) can go a long way for the prudent investor to place any analysis into the real world.

This is not to say that many of the situations don't turn out even better than projected, but that is not the way to think. Being conservative, at least at first, will be the most beneficial to the investor.

We have already discussed the silver price deck and cost of capital, so we have all the figures we need to determine the Net Asset Value of the company, but first we need to forecast the life of mine for both San Jose and Caylloma. Again, this requires a certain touch that one acquires after learning more about the industry. Below, Caylloma's silver resource is displayed and broken down by type.

Proven & Probable Reserves – Resources known to be economically feasible for extraction. These are often referred to as simply "reserves" or "2P reserves."

Measured Resources – Indicated resources that have undergone enough further sampling that a "competent person" (defined by the norms of the relevant mining code; usually a geologist) has declared them to be an acceptable estimate, at a high degree of confidence, as to the grade, tonnage, shape, densities, physical characteristics, and mineral content of the mineral occurrence.

Indicated Resources – Economic mineral occurrences that have been sampled (from locations such as outcrops, trenches, pits, and drill holes) to a point where an estimate has been made, at a reasonable level of confidence, of their contained metal, grade, tonnage, shape, densities, and physical characteristics.

Inferred Mineral Resource – That part of a mineral resource for which tonnage, grade, and mineral content can be estimated with a low level of confidence. It is inferred from geological evidence and assumed but not verified geological/or grade continuity. It is based on information gathered through appropriate techniques from location such as outcrops, trenches, pits, workings, and drill holes that may be of limited or uncertain quality and reliability.

Caylloma has a history of replacing reserves, but to be conservative we will apply a 65% multiple to inferred resources as well as an 85% multiple to measured and indicated resources. We came up with adjusted reserves of 33.265m oz. and because the mine produces 2m oz. of silver a year, the life of mine for the purpose of this exercise is 33.265/2.0 = 16.63 years, but we will round down to 16. It will therefore produce 2m oz. from 2015 to 2030.

Determining the mine life requires some assumptions, most notably, how much of M&I and inferred resources will be converted into reserves. The most conservative approach is to only use proven and probable reserves to determine the mine life of a particular asset.

The San Jose Mine is a different story for several reasons. First of all, it's a new mine in that it has only been in production for two or three years. Fortuna is just now emerging as a mining company that generates material operating cash flow, meaning over the course of when Fortuna was just drilling on the property to find an ore-body and determine the economics of the deposit.

Fortuna at the time was only trying to drill out enough reserves to dictate a life of mine long enough for the cash flow generated by operating the mine for so many years to dictate a positive net present value.

Next, based on a look at recent resource updates and drill holes, it is clear that the recent significant increase in inferred resources is only the start. Why inferred? It is a cost savings to the company to first classify them as inferred resources. These can be converted to 2P reserves later, as required by the company.

San Jose

2P Reserves	22,800,000	X	100%	22,800,000
M&I	2,000,000	X	100%	2,000,000
Inferred	35,100,000	X	80%	28,080,000
	Total Adjusted Reserves			**52,880,000**

Remember we are assuming Fortuna begins its expansion plan in the summer of 2015, with completion to be achieved in the summer of 2016. From there it will spend the second half of 2016 ramping up capacity so that by the time 2017 starts, Fortuna will be producing 6.4m oz. of silver annually. This dictates a mine life of nine years. Whether or not this happens is irrelevant for our purpose.

Caylloma

2P Reserves	13,500,000	X	100%	13,500,000
M&I	4,900,000	X	80%	3,920,000
Inferred	24,000,000	X	50%	12,000,000
	Total Adjusted Reserves			**29,420,000**

The next two charts depict the NAV calculation breakdowns of the San Jose Mine and the Caylloma Mine, and the third chart is of the company as a whole, including net cash.

Year	Production	Revenue	Costs	OCF/Profit	Discount Factor	Present Value
2015	4,300,000	$107,500,000	($72,240,000)	$35,260,000	1.088	$32,408,088
2016	5,000,000	$125,000,000	($75,000,000)	$50,000,000	1.184	$42,238,862
2017	6,400,000	$160,000,000	($87,040,000)	$72,960,000	1.288	$56,649,768
2018	6,400,000	$160,000,000	($87,040,000)	$72,960,000	1.401	$52,067,802
2019	6,400,000	$160,000,000	($87,040,000)	$72,960,000	1.525	$47,856,436
2020	6,400,000	$160,000,000	($87,040,000)	$72,960,000	1.659	$43,985,694
2021	6,400,000	$160,000,000	($87,040,000)	$72,960,000	1.805	$40,428,028
2022	6,400,000	$160,000,000	($87,040,000)	$72,960,000	1.964	$37,158,114

Year	Production	Revenue	Costs	OCF/Profit	Discount Factor	Present Value
2015	2,000,000	$50,000,000	($33,800,000)	$16,200,000	1.088	$14,889,706
2016	2,000,000	$50,000,000	($33,400,000)	$16,600,000	1.184	$14,023,302
2017	2,000,000	$50,000,000	($32,400,000)	$17,600,000	1.288	$13,665,514
2018	2,000,000	$50,000,000	($32,400,000)	$17,600,000	1.401	$12,560,215
2019	2,000,000	$50,000,000	($32,400,000)	$17,600,000	1.525	$11,544,316
2020	2,000,000	$50,000,000	($32,400,000)	$17,600,000	1.659	$10,610,584
2021	2,000,000	$50,000,000	($32,400,000)	$17,600,000	1.805	$9,752,375
2022	2,000,000	$50,000,000	($32,400,000)	$17,600,000	1.964	$8,963,580
2023	2,000,000	$50,000,000	($32,400,000)	$17,600,000	2.136	$8,238,585
2024	2,000,000	$50,000,000	($32,400,000)	$17,600,000	2.324	$7,572,229
2025	2,000,000	$50,000,000	($32,400,000)	$17,600,000	2.529	$6,959,769
2026	2,000,000	$50,000,000	($32,400,000)	$17,600,000	2.751	$6,396,846
2027	2,000,000	$50,000,000	($32,400,000)	$17,600,000	2.993	$5,879,454
2028	2,000,000	$50,000,000	($32,400,000)	$17,600,000	3.257	$5,403,910

Asset	Total	NAV/Share
Caylloma	$136,460,386	$1.08
San Jose	$352,792,793	$2.80
Net Cash	$62,101,000	$0.49
Total	**$551,354,179**	**$4.38**
Shares Out		126,000,000
Shares F/D		133,200,000

Net Asset Value multiples are not only a great valuation tool, but also a great tool when deciding to buy a stock. For example, if you find a company you've been wanting to buy and it starts trading at .30x NAV, you will most likely be able to generate a 200% rate of return and the company would still be trading just under NAV. This valuation was easily obtainable in mid-2013.

Sensitivity Analysis: Change In Silver Price [Horizontal] & Chance in NAV Multiples [Vertical]

$4.38	$20	$22	$24	$26	$28	$30	$32	$34	$36	$38	$40
0.60	$1.67	$2.13	$2.59	$3.05	$3.51	$3.97	$4.43	$4.89	$5.35	$5.81	$6.27
0.70	$1.87	$2.41	$2.94	$3.48	$4.02	$4.55	$5.09	$5.63	$6.16	$6.70	$7.24
0.80	$2.07	$2.68	$3.29	$3.91	$4.52	$5.13	$5.75	$6.36	$6.97	$7.59	$8.20
0.90	$2.26	$2.95	$3.64	$4.33	$5.02	$5.71	$6.40	$7.09	$7.78	$8.47	$9.17
1.00	$2.46	$3.23	$3.99	$4.76	$5.53	$6.29	$7.06	$7.83	$8.59	$9.36	$10.13
1.10	$2.65	$3.50	$4.34	$5.19	$6.03	$6.87	$7.72	$8.56	$9.40	$10.25	$11.09
1.20	$2.85	$3.77	$4.69	$5.61	$6.53	$7.45	$8.37	$9.29	$10.21	$11.14	$12.06
1.30	$3.05	$4.04	$5.04	$6.04	$7.04	$8.03	$9.03	$10.03	$11.03	$12.02	$13.02
1.40	$3.24	$4.32	$5.39	$6.47	$7.54	$8.61	$9.69	$10.76	$11.84	$12.91	$13.98
1.50	$3.44	$4.59	$5.74	$6.89	$8.04	$9.19	$10.34	$11.49	$12.65	$13.80	$14.95
1.60	$3.64	$4.86	$6.09	$7.32	$8.55	$9.77	$11.00	$12.23	$13.46	$14.68	$15.91

In our example, Fortuna Silver was trading at $5.51, which is richly valued given the current silver price and relative to almost all other high quality silver producers. At $5.51, it is trading using a $26 price deck and a net asset value multiple of 1.20x, which is in line for the size, diversity, and cash flow of the company. We will do a discounted cash flow (DCF) model to gain more insight into the company. The following is a very basic DCF model, which is also a popular valuation approach.

Relative Valuation – Used When Determining Which of Two Similar Companies Is the Better Value

This is done by comparing multiples such as price/operating cash flow, price/free cash flow multiples, or these divided by projected three to five years' growth. Others include price/revenue multiples. The latter may be useful when comparing low cost mining companies and average- to higher cost companies. This is because higher cost mining companies have greater leverage to the underlying metal. If you have two companies, one with low growth but also low cost ($16/oz.) silver and another with a lot of growth but higher cost ($21/oz.) silver, should the price of silver appreciate to $30 or $40/oz., the higher cost company will see its margins improve a great deal more than the low cost mining company.

Discounted Cash Flow: Assumptions - $25 Silver & 8.80% Cost of Capital

Year	2015	2016	2017	Terminal
Caylloma	2,000,000	2,000,000	2,000,000	
San Jose	4,300,000	5,200,000	6,400,000	
Revenue	157,500,000	180,000,000	210,000,000	$231,000,000
Basic Cash Costs	$4.75	$4.42	$4.19	
COGP	($30,462,500)	($32,474,000)	($35,996,000)	($35,996,000)
G&A	($31,963,000)	($32,889,927)	($33,807,556)	($33,807,556)
EBITDA	95,074,500	114,636,073	140,196,444	161,196,444
Mexican Royalty Tax	($4,944,379)	($6,163,231)	($7,828,930)	($9,001,624.41)
EBITDA	$90,130,121.11	$108,472,842	$132,367,514	$145,604,265
DD&A	($27,657,892)	($32,188,465)	($41,075,721)	($45,183,293)
EBIT	$62,472,229	$76,284,377	$91,291,793	$100,420,972
Net Interest Expense	($190,000)	($40,000)	($185,000)	($185,000)
Earnings Before Tax	$62,282,229	$76,244,377	$91,106,793	$100,235,972
Taxes	($17,127,613)	($22,873,313)	($27,332,038)	($30,070,792)
Net Operating Profit	$45,154,616	$53,371,064	$63,774,755	$70,165,180
New Capital Investment	($33,500,000)	($32,736,000)	($14,195,332)	($14,195,332)
Sustaining Capital	($34,717,291)	($36,001,831)	($37,931,000)	($37,931,000)
Add Non-Cash Charges	$27,657,892	$32,188,465	$41,075,721	$45,183,293
Discount Rate	1.09	1.18	1.29	1.29
Operating Cash Flow	$35,013,986	$41,865,215	$51,959,605	$525,443,814
Free Cash Flow	$4,223,545	$14,210,587	$40,937,645	$398,448,144
Cash BoY	$82,000,000	$86,223,545	$100,434,132	
Cash EoY	$86,223,545	$100,434,132	$141,371,777	
Value of Equity	$519,819,921			
VPS	4.13			

Now that we've briefly covered basic mining valuation approaches (more can be found by our subscribers as we are currently working on several videos going through these), we should also use a couple other metrics. This is because you want to appraise a company as many ways as possible, remove the outliers and either take the lowest or take and average.

We will just use two more, that which was made popular by Ben Graham and another by Joel Greenblatt.

Once the qualitative aspect checks out, Graham took the trailing twelve month earnings per share, (which will want to switch with operating cash flow given the industry) multiplied by 7 plus 1.65x projected 5-7 year growth rate.

$0.28 x (7 + (1.70 x 6.50%)) = $0.28 x (7+ 11.05) = $0.28 x 18.05 = **$5.05/share**

The latter is best used for relative valuation. First you simply find EBIT (Earnings before interest and taxes) then divide it by Enterprise Value.

$62.47m/Enterprise Value. For Enterprise value we will assume the current stock price is $3.80 and net cash is $30m. This equates to $448.28m. The final step is as follows: $62.47/$448.28 = 13.93% earnings yield. This can be looked at quality of earnings.

Next we want to see how efficient the capital invested into a company really is. Fortuna's ROC is very robust. $62.47m/$221.943m = 28.14% Return on Invested Capital.

Lastly once this is done for a group of say 5 mining companies, select the best one or two which rank the highest on average between the two categories.

Chapter 12: Beyond Silver

Before moving beyond the silver market, it is perhaps best to inform the reader that there is a very high probability that the best lies ahead for silver investors. First, the fundamentals for investing in the precious metals have never been stronger in all of recorded history because the distortions in the money and financial markets have NEVER been this great or widespread.

Secondly, almost all markets go through three distinct up phases during a major secular bull market, punctuated by two bear market contra moves that shake off many of the former believers. It is very likely this book is being published just at the end of the second bear move within the overall bull market.

Finally, the authors have time and time again stressed that in the last silver bull market roughly ninety percent of the move came in the last ten percent of the time. This is an almost unbelievable fact! If we count the prior bull market, when silver was removed from the coinage at the monetary value of $1.29 per troy ounce in 1964, to the end of the bull market in January 1980, we are looking at 16 years.

Had a novice or even a savvy speculator (investor) waited until January of 1979 to purchase silver at a whopping $6.00, pretty much the all-time high for the last bull market up until that point in time, Many would have thought such an investment to be purely nuts. However, what took place over the next 12 months took silver up over 800%. In other words, silver rose around more than 400% after 15 years, but in the final year it went higher by twice that amount! More PROFIT was made in silver during the last panic/manic phase by a factor of 2 than by those patient investors who had held silver for 15 long years.

Will this happen again? Certainly, no one knows for sure, but we do know that all major bull markets exhibit a euphoric high where the price continues to go higher and higher as more people come into the market. Silver investors have already caught a glimpse of this during the 2011 run up to almost $50.

Will it be different this time? In many ways it will be doubtful that much will change when viewed from the perspective of human emotion/behavior. What will have changed this time is the fact that the market has much more potential to move far higher because it is a global market this time, the Internet makes price data available in seconds, and to repeat, the amount of physical silver available is actually less than was available during the last bull market.

As bold as this statement may seem, it is possible that buying silver in sizes such as 20-30 million ounces at a time, which has been done in the past, may not take place in future due to tightness in the market. Why? Silver investors know that when the monetary demand is soaring, the industrial demand remains constant and the silver market will be forced higher. However, as the panic buying develops, many silver users will get caught up in the silver squeeze and buy silver to hold, putting further upward price pressure on the market.

Planning to take profits of course is extremely important and we will be following the markets closely and plan to sell into strength and letting our members know. However, it is possible that gold, and silver to a much lesser extent (if at all), could be remonetized. This means there would not necessarily be a "taking profit" situation but rather a transition period where perhaps China or the BRICS use gold as a backing or partial backing to a currency.

It is almost certain that the precious metals will get overvalued when measured in real terms, not necessarily in paper terms. This means it is difficult to forecast what "price" gold or silver will sell for in U.S. dollar terms for example, but if we measure how much gold or silver is required to purchase a home or the Dow Jones for example, we will have a means with which to measure if the metals are getting into an area that warrants profit taking.

Thus, many frustrated silver investors have a great deal to look forward to, yet the main idea will be: don't stay too late and don't get too greedy. Selling into strength will be the goal here, when there are many market participants wanting very expensive silver.

Some readers have followed our work on the Web site www.Silver-Investor.com and are familiar with silver's role as money—this is in addition to the earlier chapters in this book. However, what has not been discussed previously is the Why precious metals? This requires a somewhat complex answer but can be a question that the reader can ponder as well. First, many monetary historians have emphasized that "anything" can be money, and indeed point out that at certain times salt, animal hides, cows, and several other "items" or even tally sticks have served the purpose of "money."

We have no argument there, but it is important to note that natural money evolved into gold and silver time and time again and this is a direct result of the population agreeing in large part on what was the most useful form of money.

But the bigger part of the question has been why even gold and silver? For this writer, it seems to boil down to trust or honesty! There is no real trust issue with a certain weight of 0.999 fine gold or silver. It is a universal measure of value. The value can vary and it certainly has over time in real terms. Nonetheless, the market has determined that these two precious metals not only form most of the basis of trade throughout history, they are also readily saved. In fact they have been saved for generations. This is not true of paper currencies, which can be saved for relatively briefer periods of time, but at some point the trust in them wanes and a run to gold begins.

It has been pointed out that there have been several instances of banking problems under a "gold standard," as if gold were the problem. Again, the problem is honesty! It does not matter what the system at the time chooses or is forced to use as "money"; it boils down to trust and honesty. With man in the equation there is no such guarantee that some will not try to cheat at some level. This is unfortunate and clearly indicates that people, not a specific metal, are the problem.

It has been important to this writer to not only think outside the box and think critically but to question nearly everything. At times even the monetary system itself has been questioned. Not how it is comprised but what the world would look like if there were no money. In other words, if honesty prevailed in all human endeavors and the basic needs of every human on the planet were met. . . .

This thought process is just formulating so it is requested that the reader explore this area on their own, but ideally some of the ideas of Jacques Fresco on the Venus Project gave pause to the question: just how civilized is the planet when humankind is in a constant state of war? There is so much of a division in the world as to the resources available and the management and distribution of those resources.

The Venus Project proposes a plan for social change, one that works toward a peaceful and sustainable global civilization. Its main objective is where they state human rights are NOT paper proclamations but a way of life. The Venus Project questions the basic assumptions we have as a society. They ask such meaningful questions as, *what it means to be human*, *what it means to be a member of a "civilization,"* and *what choices we can make today to ensure a prosperous future for all the world's people*.

Their stated objective is, "Directing our technology and resources toward the positive, for the maximum benefit of people and planet, and seeking out new ways of thinking and living that emphasize and celebrate the vast potential of the human spirit."

They state, and we agree, that we cannot eliminate these problems within the framework of the present political and banking establishment. "The Venus Project calls for a straightforward approach to the redesign of a culture, in which the age-old inadequacies of war, poverty, hunger, debt, environmental degradation and unnecessary human suffering are viewed not only as avoidable, but totally unacceptable."

We realize to make the transition from our present culture, which is politically incompetent, scarcity-oriented, and obsolete, to this new, more humane society will require a quantum leap in both thought and action.

The Venus Project has an interesting view on the monetary system: "As long as a social system uses money or barter, people and nations will seek to maintain the economic competitive edge or, if they cannot do so by means of commerce they will by military intervention. We still utilize these same outmoded methods.

"Our current monetary system is not capable of providing a high standard of living for everyone, nor can it ensure the protection of the environment, because the major motive is profit. Strategies such as downsizing and toxic dumping increase the profit margin. With the advent of automation, cybernation, artificial intelligence, and outsourcing, there will be an ever-increasing replacement of people by machines. As a result, fewer people will be able to purchase goods and services even though our capability to produce an abundance will continue to exist."

Certainly, it may be important to interject here that we do not necessarily agree with everything stated by the Venus Project, nor have we studied it thoroughly, but let us assert that their point is well taken when they add,

Today money is used to regulate the economy not for the benefit of the general populace, but for those who control the financial wealth of nations.

Far from having the answers or agreeing with all that Jacques Fresco proposes, it is a fascinating thought experiment because he is such a deep thinker and asks the types of questions that put many current world views into question.

One idea that is seldom discussed is the fact that regardless of the political power structure in place, socialism, fascism, communism, capitalism, or any other, the one cold, hard truth is that they all depend on a monetary system. Obviously we favor an honest monetary system that best suits all people everywhere, and so far history has determined the precious metals to be the most trusted form but hardly perfect. Further, over time even these money metal systems get corrupted and the population suffers the consequences.

Early in my education the idea that money was power was proposed. After some worldly experience it seems this statement is valid. Many people can be "bought" and in this author's opinion the political class is the most easily bought. Truly, any form of government will not function when moneyed interests are pulling the strings from behind the scenes.

We have discussed at length many reasons the current system is very likely to go through major changes in the next few years. The system as it exists is breaking down globally, yet there are factions that are breaking away from the Anglo-American alliance that has held global power for so long. The BRICS (Brazil, Russia, India, China, and South Africa) have moved away from the U.S. dollar on several fronts and this trend continues.

The speculation on what the future holds runs the gamut, yet it is clear that most settlement is done electronically and society at large is moving toward a cashless system where every purchase can be recorded. Is this simply another way for the political class to monitor their "citizens"?

Wishing this chapter to stress solutions, there are some other areas we have explored, and one that we have connected with is the Thrive team, which produced the movie *THRIVE: What On Earth Will It Take*, which is available on the Internet to anyone connected to the World Wide Web. The Thrive team has examined almost every aspect of the human condition, and their look at the banking system and the problems we face due to this structure is very similar to ours. For the record, we may not agree with every aspect of the Thrive team, but to our current thinking they cover such a wide array that many of the issues they address we have not explored enough to even form an opinion.

This provocative documentary film is the result of decades of research by Foster Gamble and his wife, Kimberly Carter Gamble. Foster set out to answer some fundamental questions about the striking imbalances he witnessed all around him. After great effort and years of research it was decided to produce a movie (*Thrive*) that would address the vast number of systemic issues that are literally ruining billions of lives, and Foster's film also goes into practical and profound solution strategies. Since the film's release, thousands of people have been forming self-created solution groups, inspired by the informed solutions presented in *Thrive*. From their Web site:

THRIVE is an unconventional documentary that lifts the veil on what's REALLY going on in our world by following the money upstream—uncovering the global consolidation of power in nearly every aspect of our lives. Weaving together breakthroughs in science, consciousness and activism, THRIVE offers real solutions, empowering us with unprecedented and bold strategies for reclaiming our lives and our future.

Another fascinating area is the open source revolution. Robert David Steele, who trained more than 66 countries in open source methods calls for re-invention of intelligence to re-engineer Planet Earth. Steele has over 18 years' experience in the U.S. intelligence community followed by 20 years in intelligence training. Yes, he even spent time with the CIA, but today that agency may fear him. In 1992, despite opposition from the CIA, he organized a conference on open source intelligence where policy decisions were derived from open PUBLIC sources available to ALL, not through secret activities.

The CIA put up blocks to his doing another conference, so he quit and founded Open Source Solutions Network Inc., and later a non-profit Earth Intelligence Network, which runs the Public Intelligence Blog. Anyone committed to finding solutions, or perhaps even looking for their life's passion, must read his book, *The Open-Source Everything Manifesto: Transparency, Truth, and Trust.*

Steele's systems approach reveals the corruption, inefficiency, and unaccountability of the current system and its political and financial masters with increasing inequalities and environmental crises. Yet he also offers a comprehensive vision of hope that activists are taking to heart and are implementing today.

We have spent a great deal of time discussing capitalism and the benefits of this system if adhered to strictly. In human affairs, the theory and the practice always vary and today capitalism has morphed into a destructive system much closer to socialism, where almost everything has become "commoditized," including water. Even people are now defined as "human resources," as if the person is merely there to serve some purpose defined for them by someone or something at a higher level.

The founding idea that all men are created equal was so powerful that it stirred the hearts and souls of people everywhere. Yet it took a great deal of effort and time before this ideal was really available to all, and many today would argue that the words ring as untrue. Not to argue this, let us examine that the words were intended to mean all were equal under the law, and the law could not, would not, and should never favor anyone for any reason. Justice for all was the ideal. How far from that intention we have strayed? Many today consider a fascist state to be the most accurate definition of the current living conditions for many who were at one time living in the "free" world.

As difficult as it has been to wake people up to the idea that in a corrupt monetary system precious metals offer a way to personally escape the system at least at some level. a far greater task has been to move into the idea that freedom is the most important value of all, and it is being usurped by a ruling class supported by enforcers.

Is human behavior subject to the same laws as any other natural phenomenon? Our customs, behaviors, and values are largely byproducts of the culture one is subject to from birth. Most sociologists would argue that humans are not born with greed, prejudice, bigotry, patriotism, and hatred, but that these are all learned behavior patterns.

Today, we face huge questions and the global population is growing restless. "Change" is in the air as people are literally taking to the streets in protest. In other domains, the use of technology is bringing about a global-based payment system—bitcoin and the follow on cyber currencies.

If we choose to conform to the limitations of our present banking-controlled economy then it is likely that we will continue to live with its inevitable results: war, poverty, hunger, deprivation, crime, ignorance, stress, fear, and inequity. On the other hand, if we embrace concepts with a different consciousness than what put us into this position, then certainly we suggest humanity will evolve out of its present state into a more promising future.

RESOURCES

Twitter @silverguru22
Email support@silver-investor.com
Books-Get the Skinny on Silver Investing
    Silver Manifesto

Research/ Education
The Mises Institute: Mises.org
The Four Horsemen film: fourhorsemenfilm.com
Hidden Secrets of Money: hiddensecretsofmoney.com
Thrive
Koos Jansen: Bullionstar.com and InGoldWeTrust.com
Americas Great Awakening: AmericasGreatAwakening.com
John Williams: Shadowstats.com
Kitco.com
Mining.com
Steve Rocco: SrsRoccoReport.com
The Silver Institute: Silverinstitute.org
CPM Group: cpmgroup.com
Gold Anti-Trust Action Committee: GATA.org
Society for Mining, Metallurgy and Exploration: Smenet.org
USA Watchdog.com

Recommended Reading:
Economics:
Human Action – Mises
Money, Credit & Economic Cycles – de Soto
What has the Government Done to Our Money? – Rothbard
The Road to Serfdom – Hayek
The Mystery of Banking – Rothbard
The Case Against the Fed – Rothbard
End the Fed – Rothbard
Deflation and Liberty – Hulsmann
Law, Legislation and Liberty
The Law – Bastiast
Capitalism: The Unknown Ideal
The Black Swan: The Impact of the Highly Improbable
Individualism and Economic Order

Investing:
Financial Statement Analysis: Ben Graham
Security Analysis: Graham
Financial Statement Analysis and Security Valuation: Penman
The Dark-side of Valuation: Damodoran
The Intelligent Investor: Graham
The Most Important Thing
Common Stocks and Uncommon Profits
The Dao of Capital
Bull: A History of the Boom and Bust 1982-2004
Evaluating Mineral Projects: Applications and Misconceptions: Torries

Websites of Interest
CommodityOnline
HardAssetsInvestor
Safe Haven
Zero Hedge
Jesse's Cafe American
Gold and Silver Daily
Financial War Reports
The Gold and Oil Guy
Financial War Reports
Gold ETF Investor
Gold Miner Pulse
Junior Mining Network
Mining Stock Report
Mining.com
The Gold Report
321Gold
Gold Stock Bull
International Business Times
Gold Money
Run to Gold
Gold Editor
Dont-tread-on.me
TF Metals Report
24 Hour Gold
Mineweb

It is impossible to list all of the websites we visit and in this age of "over-information" some of these will no doubt change or perhaps disappear in the future. This list will be maintained on TheSilverManifesto.com website.